LABOUR INPUT AND THE THEORY OF THE LABOUR MARKET

LABOUR INPUT
AND THE THEORY
OF THE
LABOUR MARKET

G. E. Krimpas

A HALSTED PRESS BOOK

John Wiley & Sons
New York

First published in 1975 by
Gerald Duckworth & Co. Ltd.,
The Old Piano Factory,
43 Gloucester Crescent, London NW1

Library of Congress Cataloging in Publication Data

Krimpas, G.E.
  Labour input and the theory of the labour market.
  "A Halsted Press book."
  Bibliography: p.
  1. Labor economics. 2. Job evaluation
3. Labor supply. 1. Title.

HD4901.K69 1975   331.1   75-15836
ISBN 0-470-50796-9

Published in the United States
by Halsted Press, A Division of
John Wiley & Sons
New York

Typeset by
Specialised Offset Services Ltd., Liverpool
and printed by
Unwin Brothers Limited, Old Woking

Contents

'The wages of labour vary according to the small or great trust which must be reposed in the workmen.' Adam Smith

'Lorsqui'il faut de la capacité et de la confiance, on paie encore le travail plus cher.' Cantillon

'It is a familiar rule in all business that every man should be paid in proportion to the trust reposed on him and the power which he enjoys.' David Hume

Preface

This book is constructed around an empirical relationship about relative work and relative pay which it attempts to interpret in terms of concepts and propositions of economic theory. Such an interpretation is necessary because the conceptual variables which enter the relationship, as well as the method of their empirical measurement and the hypothesis of causal relation between them were not originally derived from economics, theoretical or applied. The principal concepts involved are called *time-span of discretion* (TSD), *felt-fair pay* (FFP) and *capacity* (C). They are an original discovery, in a field where theory is scarce, of Elliott Jaques and the team of researchers who subsequently formed the Glacier Institute of Management. These three concepts are the principal elements of a theory of evolution of organisational institutions. It is inside these institutions that the reality of work and pay is mainly found in industrial society.

The concepts of work and pay formulated by Jaques are of psychoanalytic origin and, on the face of it, are entirely independent of any economic process. The first question therefore likely to arise in the economist's mind is, What, then, is Jaques' theory about? After some attempts to answer this question in a way useful to economists I have come to the conclusion that there is virtually no payoff in merely transliterating Jaques' theory, which was worked out inside another discipline (even if it has partly invented the discipline), into 'economese'. The exercise is bound to be both tedious and irritating for the reader, who can in any case acquaint himself directly with the forceful presentation of the first-hand version. Moreover, simple transliteration appears of dubious value when the object of the exercise is to explain rather than just to present what Jaques' social-analytic theory may mean when treated as economics.

In line with this view, the work of Jacques and his colleagues is only drawn upon, not presented or explained in its own terms. Explanation is confined to making precisely explicit what is drawn upon, while showing that the elements so withdrawn have a different role inside the original structure. This is a point which needs stressing in that my own explanation of the empirical relationship which represents the empirical data collected for this study not only differs from Jaques' in terms of toolkit (*cum* terminology), but also, perhaps more essentially, differs in terms of the level of aggregation of 'societal' variables — 'men' versus 'classes' of men — which are respectively postulated as the operative variables. This and other methodological points occupy a large part of the argument.

My own work in this field started with straightforward measurement in terms of Jaques' empirical procedures.[1] It was part of a research project based at Brunel which was designed as a three-year job overall, the objectives being (a) to produce a sample of observations of the main variables, TSD and FFP, (b) to test for the significance of the association between them and, therefore, (c) to test the truth of the principal hypothesis proposed by Jaques in his work.

The field-work phase took over a year and a half. Some difficulties were administrative, viz. to convince industrial establishments that there was some profit in serving as guinea pigs for academic research. There were other, more important, methodological difficulties which will be indicated below.

The second phase of the project involved statistical analysis of the principal data obtained, the purpose being to 'explain away' the apparent relation between them as the result of artefact.[2] The problems here were two-fold: on the

1. Part of the work was shared with J.S. Evans in the first year and, for shorter periods, with other colleagues and students from Brunel.

2. In retrospect this analysis of the data ought to have been conducted by a professional statistician. In the event it was conducted without one and I am grateful to Tom Wisniewski, and later also to Jim Thomas, who tutored me on the essentials of the job and checked that I was asking statistically sensible questions and interpretating the answers according to the rules.

The mechanics of the work also turned out more difficult than anticipated. Since the computer didn't speak to strangers there was some (mutual?) frustration, while the eminence of the Brunel Computer Science Department was not an undisguised blessing. In the end Margaret Hawkins and her assistants proved the validity of the law of the division of labour.

one hand, economic theory was no help in asking questions of the data or even in suggesting the relevant range of variation of the 'causally' related variables. So the difficulty was to decide on relevant tests to which the hypothesis should be submitted without knowing at the time what would turn out to be relevant when theoretical justification for the relationship could be derived from economic theory.

On the other hand, to go beyond the stage already achieved by Jaques, it was necessary to sub-divide the hypothesis into separate propositions and set different subsets of the data against separate hypotheses, in some kind of dialogue of one to the other. So far as this goes, I take it to be the standard procedure.

In the present instance, however, there was an additional peculiarity which had to be taken into account. For Jaques' work is not only 'evolutionary', having developed from the germ of one idea towards many, mutually interdependent directions. *It also deals simultaneously with many levels of abstraction*, from the most 'unmediated' percept right up to the most 'ideal' concept. This totality, so to say, of the work is, in my view, one of its major strengths. It is also the main reason for the charm, but also, simultaneously, for the misgivings which it engenders, often to the same person. It is not the case, as critics have said, that although Jaques writes about 'facts', there just aren't any. The work is impregnated with empirical content at all levels, both as 'assumptions' and even more as 'predictions'. Nor, somewhat ironically, is it the case, as Jaques himself has claimed, that his work is 'facts' and nothing else. While appreciating his concern to defend himself against the charge of 'idle speculative theorising', it seems to me that he has in his way contributed to some kind of no-man's land, splitting off his own contribution from the well-delineated orthodox disciplines of economics, sociology and psychology, which contain departments concerned with 'labour'.

So I have had to make up my mind how to chop up the totality of Jaques' work into hypotheses and line these up against the facts, without in the process killing off the unity which makes them interesting. But while doing this 'testing' exercise one is continuously led to ask, what sort of *economic* theory of the labour market is compatible, related to, or perhaps suggested by, the social-analytic theory of work and pay relativities?

My participation in the research project officially finished with the formal presentation of the statistical analysis. An expanded version of that report was presented at the Royal Economic Society Conference on Pay Structure which was held at Durham in September 1972. That meeting presented a first opportunity to discuss some of the questions which require economic theoretical hypotheses to be resolved and to provide some suggestions along the lines of this book.

The book is divided in two parts, the first dealing mainly with theory while the second is largely a report of the empirical evidence. Part I has four chapters. The first is an attempt to define labour input in terms of economic decisions characterising a process of resource allocation. The concept of labour input, as defined here, is measurable in calendar-time units. In effect what is done is to transpose Jaques' TSD concept into a world of resources, decisions about maximisation-minimisation and scarcity. This static formalisation does not involve any contradiction with Jaques' formulation of the concept. As a by-product, there may be an interesting implication from this formalisation of the TSD concept for the theory of centralisation and decentralisation in economic organisations as developed by economists.

Chapter Two describes the problems involved in the field work. This is necessary because the method of measurement cannot be properly understood apart from the detail required in its practice. Although this discussion may appear as somewhat tedious, it is, in my view, essential as a prerequisite for judging the appropriateness and worth of the analysis of the data that were generated in this way.[3] It is only when one gets to the level of concrete detail required in the practice of the analytical technique which generates the data that it becomes clear how remarkably sharp the TSD measure

3. I believe that time-span analysis will never be convincing to the non-practitioner (the burghers of Padua allegedly remained incredulous of Galileo's telescope, yet refrained from sticking their eye to the eye-piece, at any rate as the story is told by Brecht); nevertheless, a blow-by-blow account of how it works in practice may be an encouragement to others.

In arranging my part of the field work with the firms that offered to co-operate, I committed myself to a full write-up which was presented to the firms. The reports contain detailed descriptions of more than fifty time-span analyses, from the role of dustman to that of managing director. These reports form the basis of Part II of this book.

is in terms of operational rigour, a characteristic which of course cannot be deduced from its logical consistency. It is also seen in this chapter that the empirical procedure finally arrived at for measuring Jaques' TSD variable is analogous to the formalisation described in the first chapter.

Chapter Three is a report of alternative tests aimed at showing that the hypothesis of the existence of a relationship is untenable. Despite serious misgivings about the appropriateness of 'positivist' methodology in the field of the social sciences I have gone the whole hog with it in this instance. This was mainly on the grounds that the logic of the theory has already been persuasively argued by Jaques, so that further analysis should rather take the line of maximum hostility to his way of thinking. This is of course what the methodology of 'progress by refutation' is perfectly designed to do. As it turns out, Jaques' hypothesis about the existence of a relationship between the proposed measure of work and relative pay is *not* refuted by 'the facts', at least insofar as I can do the job. But it is not confirmed by the facts either, if we want to play the game according to the rules. Ultimately we are let down by positivism to our own devices, which is to say our beliefs. We may not succeed in disproving a proposition, but we needn't believe in it either. To the extent that belief has to do with degree of plausibility, however, I would expect that, as a result of these tests, Jaques' theory would be more plausible. The question then is: Plausible enough for what? How does it work, what does it mean? The analysis of Chapter Three, which of course for the statistician is elementary, is neither easy nor satisfactory for the economist, whose perennial questions are not only about what 'is' but more about the 'how' and often also about the 'so what'.

Part of the answer may lie with the mechanics of the story. Chapter Four accordingly starts by discussing the 'how' of a labour market whose quantity variable is Jaques' TSD. This market determines differential pay through a process of search, by both supply and demand forces or agents, continuous disequilibrium in the small being the consequence of overall economic evolution. It is suggested that the micro short period phenomena of this labour market can be legitimately considered as partial phenomena, the feedback from the labour market to the macro-economic forces which determine growth and distribution being very indirect or muted. Micro labour market phenomena may, on the other hand, enter more directly into partial aspects of the growth and distribution story, particularly by inducing or constraining firms' policies towards expansion, product mix and pricing. An important, if somewhat implicit, role in the explanation of the labour market phenomena is given to the industrial composition of employment, which is in turn taken as determined by the macro phenomena of growth and distribution in the context of a competitive economy — not meaning by this any kind of 'perfect' competition, and specifically without recourse to the orthodox general equilibrium concept of equilibrium.

Another part of the answer, that concerning the 'so what' question, may be more philosophical: What really *is* the time-span of discretion? I try to sketch an answer in the last sections of Chapter Four. Here I make use of (as well as face up to) the peculiarity of the empirical relationship, which shows up as a kink. The presence of the kink suggests the hypothesis of a 'dual' labour market (an idea somewhat analogous but in important ways different from hypotheses using the same term in recent work on the pay structure).[4]

The chief distinguishing characteristic of this dual labour market is that labour power is, mainly, a *substitute* for machinery below a certain level of the variable labour input, proxied by TSD, while it is, mainly, a *complement* for machinery above that level. This economic hypothesis is then related to a more general view of the process of production involving labour power and leads to the identification of two classes of labour power which are significantly different 'commodities', if not even *opposed* to each other — insofar as one of them can appropriate some of the functions of 'capital', namely the power to have a prior claim on income, whereas the other cannot. This interpretation of the social basis on which the functioning of the labour market is constructed has, however, no place for a concept of 'human capital' which, in analogy to 'physical capital', may be treated as a 'factor of production', etc.

It turns out that, in arguing the implications of the dual

4. e.g. Bosanquet and Doeringer (1973).

labour market hypothesis, the logical (and legal) status of the empirical set-up required to do work analysis is crucial. For a 'true' time-span emerges in the process of transforming the relational situation from a descriptive-analytical to a policy-analytical situation or, if one prefers, from positive to normative. *Labour input, which is demanded, supplied and 'measured', always in an organisation context, is designated as a 'complement' or 'substitute' in the process of capital accumulation, precisely as labour power is appropriated and integrated into the life of the organisation.* Treating labour input as TSD therefore enables us to see income distribution directly as a consequence of the process of production, independently of exchange or 'market' phenomena, i.e. through prices, profit margins and the state of demand, etc.

The aggregative arguments at the end of Part I cast something of a shadow over the relatively harmonious universe of the micro phenomena discussed previously. There are obviously clear limitations to the view that labour economics starts, and again finishes, with the overall per-sistent regularities of the pay structure. In the light of the less tranquil experience of recent years it will not be altogether surprising if such consistencies begin to waver, as has already happened with most of the macro-economic great ratios and stylised facts.

I only intend to draw tentative conclusions on the 'so what' aspect of all this, and I hope that this is not obscured by the apparent dogmatism of style. Yet it seems to me that a fair amount of good is likely to emerge if economists occasionally ask those unfashionable 'essentialist' questions, about what is. I am aware that when calling labour power 'labour input' and then using 'TSD' as the proxy, I am just giving things names. Capital, after all, is not what capital is called but its name. So labour too is its name — say, 'disutility'.

One must nevertheless ask: Whose labour? For labour, or rather labour power, is not a primary input, on a par with 'land'. Men, like capital, are reproducible, only twiceover: once, when they are born; and a second time, when they enter the labour market. Twice they are born as clay, never as putty. The life horizon of this clay, unlike that of clay-machinery, is exogenously given; and there is not, for men, a scrapping rule, whereby an obsolete man can give way, via the surplus which his labour power has created, to free capital which can then be re-invested to produce another labour unit. How, then, do men adapt to a changing world but by changing their *own* value?

If we want to go behind the laws of motion, so to speak, to the laws of value of society which underlie them, if we wish to measure the worth to a historical society of labour time, not for the production of surplus but for the reproduction of labour, then we must ask what labour is. The answer cannot be given exclusively by individual psychology, much though psychology may have to do with it: it must also have to do with how, where labour power is a commodity, the social system operates to determine the level of social subsistence, not only for some abstract average but for all the individual working members of society. This level of subsistence must be accepted by all, for that is a condition for the operation of the system as a whole.

The empirical findings reported in Part II may suggest some of the ways in which men accept their 'fair place' in society. The self-consciousness that can be seen when taking part in the dialogue with men — who realise and take part in their own 'measurement', together with some kind of relief for knowing the logic of what they already knew in their social existence — may perhaps be experienced by reading the raw material which is the background for the formal analysis.

The four chapters of Part II are respectively reports on work analysis and measurement in four organisations which offered their cooperation for the field work phase of the study. It will be clear to the reader why one should be grateful for being allowed to tap their real versus hypothetical experience on the manner of work in industrial society. For obvious reasons, the anonymity of persons and organisations must be respected. Even if others did not raise this point, having once done the job of work analysis I would now make it a rule for myself whenever the purpose is academic as distinct from managerial.

Chapter Five reports on the pilot project whose results were omitted from the analysis of the data. The purpose of this report is to show by contrast the validity of the method used for the derivation of the data analysed here. Chapters Six and

Seven are reports on the two largest samples of work roles I obtained. Their interest lies in the analysis of complete pyramids of roles from top to bottom, the first in production the second in service employments. Chapter Eight is a report on an extant role of planning of ancillary roles which did not yet exist. This work was done subsequent to the analysis of the data and benefited from less stringent conditions which enable one to see further into the loose and open-ended mechanisms of the labour market.

I must again stress that the explanation suggested for the phenomena of relative work and pay is more than formally tentative, since the requisite range of validity is large as well as complex. I have just tried to be clear about which bit applies to what. Having neither taught nor been taught labour economics (in that order, as is often the case), my knowledge of the literature is perhaps all too restricted even for purposes of this exercise. The justification for embarking on it lies in my guess that unless an economist brings these valuable and suggestive social-analytic concepts inside standardised territory, it is unlikely that anyone else will do so, and that would be a pity. So, as it happened that I worked in this field, it should be I who should undertake to build the bridge.

It will be clear that I am heavily indebted to Elliott Jaques, since his work was my point of departure. I am grateful not least for his immense patience over the long process of my making up my mind and for his warm sympathy with my attempts to be as critical as I could of his own work in which, to put it mildly, he is strongly committed. Outside the direct sphere of Jaques' work, I derived benefit from that of Lydall, Phelps-Brown, Routh, Crossley and Marglin. My colleague Keith Norris made numerous comments. Dr Routh in particular strengthened my confidence that the hypotheses I have advanced should be spelt out in detail. John Vaizey always gave practical help and made it a pleasure to be in an overworked department. I thank them both. Above all I must express my gratitude to Professor Joan Robinson, whose extensive comments on the theoretical part of the argument taught me not just what, but also how, I ought to be thinking. The usual disclaimer must, however, apply most forcefully in this case. I must also thank Christine Stephens who typed and retyped many versions of the manuscript with infinite fortitude and good humour.

Brunel University, 1974   G.E.K.

PART I

Theory and Measurement

CHAPTER ONE

Defining a Unit of Social Work

1. Neo-classical eclecticism

To justify a new approach to the concept of labour input and its place in the economic analysis of the labour market, we start by looking at the methods at present used in the literature. In formal terms the theory of the labour market is the sum total of propositions about work and pay which can be found in all permutations of elementary types of models, which can be distinguished between them by various types of abstraction, e.g. micro-macro, static-dynamic, short-long period, partial-general, etc. Applied problems, behavioural hypotheses, causal propositions, etc., are then logically justified inside some selection deriving from such basic sub-models. In Marshall, for example, we find the subject of labour treated three times over: first qualitatively as an input in the productive process, later as a cost, and finally as a participant in the distribution of the national dividend. Marshall's is probably the only case of an economist who treated the phenomena of labour under virtually all model types, usually by shading his discussion as if through a trajectory between ideal types.[1] However, Marshall's doctrine has been preserved by the neo-classical logicians in a selective way. The propositions that were kept are particularly those which are amenable for presentation as states of equilibrium. Gone are almost all but the pure propositions and virtually all the shades.

Now the concept of equilibrium used in the analysis of the labour market has been essentially adopted from Walras, not

---

1. It is almost tempting to ignore the sequel of theoretical analysis of labour since, in a very fundamental sense, 'everything' is in Marshall. It is equally tempting to serve up Marshall's analysis for fresh consideration, to see whether many will realise how much there is in it to be re-learned which has since been forgotten.

from Marshall. This concept has been subjected to exhaustive analysis in recent years, culminating in the perhaps definitive treatment of Arrow and Hahn (1971), and in the process its limitations have been shown as effectively crippling.[2] The prospective, or potential, new notion of equilibrium recently suggested by Hahn[3] may indeed turn out to be suitable for a theory of the labour market. Such a notion of equilibrium involving the stability of expectations is not incompatible with the analysis in Chapter Four below. In the present toolkit of the labour market theorist, however, supply and demand have meaning only in the strict context of the Walrasian concept of equilibrium, the notion of equilibrium being necessary in particular for the pricing of labour services in the context of profit maximisation.

It is however difficult to see how labour market theory can proceed as if nothing had happened to alter the whole direction of economics as a result of the 'second' Keynesian revolution. It should in fact be unnecessary, after all that has been written by the post-Keynesian school, to rehearse the clash of views between the neo-classical and the Keynesian basic hypotheses about the essential, monetary, nature of the economy. In summary, what has emerged is that the neo-classical notion of equilibrium rules out any theory of investment in a context of historical time and therefore uncertainty. The neo-classical theory of the rate of profit for the economy is logically inconsistent even in the context of logical comparisons. Profit maximisation and factor pricing at the micro level are tautologous propositions, true by definition at equilibrium and meaningless apart from it. There is nothing in equilibrium analysis which is applicable to a world of historical time.

No doubt, as Joan Robinson remarked in another context,[4] there is some commonsense in the slogan of 'supply and demand', at least in the sense that Marshall used the words, as the interraction of supply price and demand price in the historical short period. These terms we shall also use

---

2. N. Kaldor, 'The Irrelevance of Equilibrium Economics', *Economic Journal* (1972), but also R.F. Hahn, *An Inaugural Lecture*, Cambridge 1973.

3. R.F. Hahn, *An Inaugural Lecture*, but see also A. Asimakopulos on the meaning given to equilibrium by Keynes in 'Keynes, Patinkin, Historical Time and Equilibrium Analysis', *Canadian Journal of Economics* (1973).

4. 'The Production Function and The Theory of Capital'.

later. But their use involves more than a change of terminology from the conventional analysis. To justify the approach to the notion of labour input and its implications for the economic analysis of the labour market, it is necessary to survey some propositions in labour economics from the standpoint of the post-Keynesian revolution.[5] In essence I take this to mean that there is no room for comparative-static analysis of events that can occur only in historical time. Statics is simply a device to permit economists to draw supply and demand diagrams: it may only be used to define the equilibrium characteristics of the variables.

Let us, to fix ideas, begin by asking: What is the place of the labour market in a post-Keynesian macro-economic model? Its place is simply that 'location' in the economy from which the money wage is read off. The labour market determines neither the real wage, nor employment, nor the distribution of output between wage and non-wage incomes. This is because the money wage, although endogenous, is an independent variable in the short period. The economy operates in real historical time, and there is a differential lag structure in the response of different variables because they are asymmetrically, or 'causally', related. There can be no supply of labour apart from a given price, because *labour is not the prime mover of the system.* Its supply in the short period accordingly is governed by demand, while price is determined by autonomous expenditure, particularly by the investment expenditure of corporations and secondarily by the consumption expenditure of wealth-holders which is independent of current income. The nature of the economy, in a world of uncertainty, is such that investment expenditure is necessarily the prime mover; decisions about investment cannot be taken as the result of the outcome of investment expenditures but must precede this outcome; investment must be 'given' for the short period. The labour market is the tail-end, not the prime mover, of the system, because under capitalism autonomous expenditure is beyond the reach of those who supply labour. The demand for labour

5. A summing up of the debate concerning the implications of Keynesian economics for capital theory can be found in the concluding note by Joan Robinson, 'The Unimportance of Reswitching', *Quarterly Journal of Economics* (1973).

depends on its real cost, not on the money or the real wage. Within the customary experienced, or expected, limits of the demand for labour, the supply is elastic, because labourers have no alternative in the short period to obtaining income by wage employment at the given wage. We cannot therefore draw a short-period supply-and-demand diagram without taking the price level as given, while the price level in turn depends on expenditure.

It is because *historical* time matters in the Keynesian view of how the economy works that there is no room either for statics, except for logical comparisons, or for equilibrium, except as a state of rest, but not necessarily on anybody's supply or demand schedules. *'Statics' and 'equilibrium' are part of the technical toolkit, not part of the theory.* The question then arises: Is the Keynesian *methodological* revolution irrelevant when we go from the macro to the micro level?

It seems to me that the attempt to ignore it in labour economics has led to inconsistency. Professor Crossley has recently provided an excellent review[6] of the literature, which gives considerable evidence of eclecticism as between logically inconsistent 'model types'. It is interesting to note that there is no longer any serious attempt to treat the labour market as a significant locus from which to explain the macro-economic distribution of income.[7] The general view now is that the macro-economics, at any rate, is determined

6. R. Crossley, 'The Present Pay Structure: Theory and Evidence', Paper presented to The Royal Economic Society Conference on The Pay Structure, Durham 1972.

7. Lest there be misunderstanding, my claim above, that the labour market is a passive component of the macro-economic Keynesian model, is not meant to imply that, in some sense, the labour market is 'weak', or that it doesn't matter. For one, by making the labour market autonomous in the determination of the money wage, the model makes this market anything but powerless. If the money wage enters into the determination of current profits, as it does, it may well influence future investment expenditure and therefore also the future share of wages. In the extreme case the labour market is even more important; it may not even determine the money wage itself but simply dispute whatever wage offers it receives from the production sector, thus making the *ex post* money wage dependent on struggle about the determination of the real wage or employment within the short period. In this case, of course — Joan Robinson's 'inflation barrier' — the model lacks sufficient relations to determine the outcome, which is simply the theoretical counterpart of a world of social instability in which the rules of the game are challenged.

by a Keynesian mechanism: there is yet room for various neo-classical 'syntheses' as soon as the problems are further down on the aggregation ladder. The ecclecticism in the selection of model types required for these syntheses can perhaps best be seen by looking at three specific areas where hypotheses from many hats are drawn to explain the peculiarities of the real world. These are: first, the short-period inelasticity of labour supply to the industry; secondly, the nature (or place in the market structure) of firms as determining the short-period demand for labour; and, thirdly, the nature of the information mechanisms operating in the labour market.

A.   Let us assume that labour, or at least skilled labour, is like clay-capital goods, in the sense that it cannot enter alternative employments. Accordingly the short-period res-ponse of labour to rising money wages and/or enhanced job opportunities is sluggish. Similarly the resistance of labour to wage reductions and/or reduced employment offers is a cushion against violent fluctuations in these two variables. The labour market is a stabiliser. It is now hoped to show that these propositions are 'empirically' true: correct use of terminology would however be to say 'descriptively' true.[8] Associations may, in other words, turn the right way round but the theoretical model which underlies them may still be logically invalid.

To see that the model is logically inconsistent we must dispute its implicit assumptions. The model is based on a partial view of the labour market, it assumes that it is determined but not determining. This assumption must be disputed not only on the grounds of the magnitude of the market involved but because the analysis is supposed to cover *a period of historical time*. In the short period, we are told, labour cannot be expected to move in response to the inducements available. But we expect it to move in the 'long period'. If, however, we mean a long period of historical time, things happen in the meantime. If there is sustained as well as exogenous demand for labour, then we can logically

---

8. There is in fact serious doubt that they are true in any sense, see O.E.C.D., *Wages and Labour Mobility*, 1966, and Crossley, op. cit.

predict that labour will move, roughly as in 'vintage' capital models. But this 'if' is not a deduction from the logical 'long period', while 'sustained' and 'exogenous' are incompatible concepts for the historical long period. What we can say is that, if labour expects demand at higher pay to be sustained, then the long-period elasticity may be greater than the short-period one. But if labour doesn't expect this to be the case, then it may be that the short-period elasticity is greater than the long-period one. The descriptive validity of the proposition associating labour movement toward higher paid jobs cannot therefore be a test of a theory where both elasticities 'exist' at the same moment.

Salter, from whose *Productivity and Technical Change* (1960) this and other hypotheses about the 'long-period' redeployment of labour stem, was careful to say that his empirical findings are only compatible with a neo-classical process, so that there was, in his view, a logical break between the theoretical and the empirical parts of his book. Nor does he take a partial view of the labour market. On the contrary, the implicit prime mover, effective demand and through it the injection of technical change, was an active agent in promoting the qualitative redeployment of labour as well as the qualitative change of all inputs and outputs in the transformation of the economy. It merely happened that, for the period investigated through cross-sectional analysis, earnings per unit of labour were unrelated to the growth of output, productivity, employment and prices, so that he could say that the supply of labour to industry appeared as independent of the level of wages offered.

Now it may well be that a historical long-period cross-sectional analysis reveals that *ex post* wage differentials are independent of the *ex post* values of other variables. But from this one cannot deduce anything about the process involved; and, particularly, one cannot argue that wages attracted labour where it was most 'needed' and, having done so, then 'settled' to long-period inter-industry equilibrium. For that is precisely the part of the story which is missing from the cross-sectional analysis. The cross-sectional test cannot in other words distinguish between a relative wage-labour mobility hypothesis and a job-opportunities hypothesis, or, indeed, any other non-*ad hoc* hypothesis, since it abstracts from the effects of decision-taking in historical time.[9]

B.   The second area in which logical eclecticism can be seen is in the determination of wages as a factor price, that is to say in the theory of the firm. According to the orthodox theory, if the firm is a short-period profit maximiser, then all factor prices are equal to the respective marginal products, while in the long period, when all firms operate at zero normal profits, the same wage will be paid to each class of labour. In practice, however, it turns out that there are systematic differences of pay by firm which persist over a historical long period. How can the orthodox theory accommodate itself to this fact?

A commonsense hypothesis could be that there is differential impact of investment in saving labour *and* increasing pay for some kinds of firms. In fact, it is the size of firms rather than the volume of profits that qualifies as the best quantitative explanation,[10] and this is compatible with the above commonsense assumption. But the neo-classical story is not compatible with anything. Differences in firms' size are inexplicable even in their existence, much less in their explanatory power.

To avoid the need of *ad hoc* explanations, it seems that the notion of short-period profit maximisation must go, because it ties the theory of the firm to the equilibrium factor prices of marginal productivity theory. It is not possible in the orthodox theory to divorce costs and prices from revenues because the short period is conceived as always capable of yielding an 'internal' equilibrium. But if we split pricing decisions from the short-period maximisation of profits ('long-period' profit maximisation being a logically empty statement), then there is no sense in using the term equilibrium at all. We can only say that firms have a strategy

9. It is interesting to record that a recent study, by Don Wharton at Brunel, showed that the Salter coefficients change sign for the more recent period, albeit just below the level of statistical significance. This result could be interpreted theoretically as a short-period negative supply elasticity such that (relative) reduction of employment co-varies with an increase of (relative) earnings. In other words, those industries that shed labour are those where productivity, output and earnings go up and so, to cap it all, does the (relative) price.

10. Crossley, op. cit.

concerning labour which is compatible with their overall strategy of growth, profits, prices, product differentiation, etc. And labour also has a strategy, with respect to pay, training, mobility, security, etc.

C. In the debate concerning the reappraisal of the economics of Keynes, considerable importance has been given to information and its costs. In particular the aim of showing that Keynes can be interpreted as a general equilibrium theorist has led people[11] to suggest a neo-classical mechanism operating in historical time whereby the labour market loses its pre-Keynesian equilibrating role. Information 'market' imperfections have also been invoked to explain otherwise inexplicable differentials and immobilities — as well as the converse phenomenon of large gross turnover of persons in similar occupations with the same pay through different firms. Informational characteristics of the labour market have, finally, been coupled with the aspect of fixity of human skills. Fixed, durable but non-transferable human capital[12] endows some if not all labour with reserve powers to search. Unions are not so much necessary to give to workers a power symmetric to that of firms as they are useful as information-processing mechanisms and dampers to short-period shocks.

The objection of course is not to the realism of the view that information is important and not a free good, but that the concept of *uncertainty*, which is the counterpart of the assumptions concerning information, makes the notion of equilibrium untenable. For equilibrium is possible only in a constrained situation where maximising behaviour is possible. Where there is uncertainty the horizon is necessarily open-ended and decisions are constrained equally by expectations and by past givens. It follows that expectations must be brought in at the start of the analysis because they cannot be added 'later'; and, once brought in, there is no room for the neo-classical equilibrium propositions. In an analysis of the labour market involving time, we must, therefore, abandon the neo-classical notion of equilibrium. The nature of causal

11. Particularly Clower and Leijonhufvud.
12. Which, incidentally, depreciates the 'wrong way round'; see the Appendix to Chapter Four on 'The Returns to Management Education'.

analysis leaves no room for maximisation, so that the margins and their relation to factor prices also disappear.

To conclude this discussion of problems which appear in the literature: the vanishing concept of equilibrium is a big loss for the neo-classical story. For whereas the supply price of labour could be taken as psychologically determined, at least the demand price was linked to solid, measurable, stuff like product prices and costs. But without the notion of equilibrium, the y-axis of the supply and demand diagram has no link with the x-axis other than psychology for both supply and demand relations in which it figures as the independent variable. The supply and demand construct is meaningless away from the point of equilibrium: it merely says that there must be curves going through that point. Relative pay neither is explained nor explains anything. Without the neo-classical story, on the other hand, labour economics is left in a very poor theoretical state.

Apart, however, from the general point of the relation between orthodox theory and labour market phenomena, on which there is considerable if not overwhelming dissatisfaction,[13] there is another point on which there has been remarkably little discussion.[14] This point arises peculiarly in the labour market context as the problem of measurement of the variable 'quantity of labour' which appears on the x-axis of the supply-and-demand diagram. It is this problem, of the definition of a measurable as well as relevant concept of labour input, which is the present point of departure for the analysis of the labour market.

2. Net advantages

It is interesting that the Marshallian partial equilibrium analytical device has not only survived in altogether alien places[15] but was also transformed into a postulate; that

13. Crossley, op. cit.

14. I am only aware of papers by Reder, Oi and Weiss (see the references) which have anything at all concrete to suggest on the qualitative component of labour input. There is nothing in the literature, so far as I am aware, on the economic definition of labour input. Job evaluation practice and economic theory have never really met.

15. E.G. Dennison, *Why Growth Rates Differ?*, Washington D.C., 1967.

demand and supply schedules must always exist independently of each other; and that there can be no feedback between
them — when this was no more than a necessary condition
for the definition of the 'simple' market. We will remove this
assumption in Chapter Four. For the moment we confine the
discussion to the quantity axis of the supply-and-demand
diagram as if the two sides can be taken as independent.

When we look from the demand side, the building block of
marginal productivity theory preserves the essentials of the
Marshallian simple market. If price is given as a horizontal
straight line, then equilibrium quantity demanded is determined by the intersection of price with the downward
sloping demand curve. But this simplicity is not present when
we look from the supply side. Labour input offered, in
whatever units it ought to be or could be measured, is not
dependent only on price. The quantity axis of the diagram
measures a composite which, together with price, constitutes
net advantage. There is thus an asymmetry: the firm demands
labour input in return for a wage, while the individual
supplies a 'state' of his life and gets another 'state' of life, of
which one component is the money wage.

Now this characterisation is of course formally erroneous.
The quantity axis must be the same whether interpreted in
supplied or demanded *units*. It is the shape and position of
the supply curve which is dependent upon everything in net
advantage other than the wage. What the diagram shows is
the partial dependence of quantity supplied on the wage
which intersects with the total dependence of quantity
demanded on the wage. It is not necessary that a solvable
system should have as many unknowns in every equation as
there are equations.

In what sense, however, is this system solvable when there
are essentially three unknowns but only two equations? In
what sense can we talk of the price elasticity of supply
except by suspending disbelief for long enough to utter
'ceteris paribus'? For we know that the supply and demand
for labour is not the same thing as the supply and demand
for, say, carrots. In the case of labour, the quantity axis *does*
mean something different when looked at from the supply
versus the demand angle. The simple labour market diagram
leaves too much outside. And we should feel this particularly,

since we know that the variable left in — the wage — does not explain labour mobility: surely the one thing that the supply-demand story cannot afford not to explain. To go further into the costs of *ceteris paribus*, consider that, when labour input is defined as manhours, which are considered a disutility while utility is the mix of income and leisure (with trade-offs between all three variables), it turns out that the wage is both a poor and a weak explanatory variable of manhours supplied.[16] The only empirical work which to my knowledge predicts sensible behaviour of the labour supply is the explanation of variation in the participation rate as a function of the pressure of aggregate demand, where the variable 'vacancies' is brought in to replace the otherwise empty box of *ceteris paribus*.[17] But 'vacancies' is hardly a satisfactory characterisation of labour input.

Let us accordingly attempt to define labour input so that nothing is left out under *ceteris paribus*. We first introduce a definition of labour input and then proceed to some evidence that it has inherent meaning.

In the days where labour meant mainly pushing, shoving, digging and carting about, it was natural to think of labour input in terms of hours of work. Effort similarly meant more or less what it said. The supply of effort could without difficulty be identified with disutility, while the demand for effort was the demand for labourpower in a sense not dissimilar to horsepower. Labour was a substitute for all sorts of animal power as well as for some kinds of inanimate power (e.g. oars *versus* wind). If the classical economists viewed labour as a complementary rather than as a substitute factor, it is because they had in mind its complementary relation to land; if the wage-fund doctrine was the original theory of factor prices, it was because labour only differed from land in that it had to be maintained during the period of production. Conversely, if there was no theory of employment it was because of Malthusian demographic theory and Say's Law, and if there was no theory of relative wages it was because all that was considered labour could be reduced to comparable manpower units.

16. H. Brems, *Quantitative Economic Theory: A Synthetic Approach*, New York 1967.
17. L.C. Hunter, D. Robertson, *The Economics of Labour*, London 1969.

Now it is precisely the notion of labour input as essentially manpower, hence measurable in units of hours of work, that is too far from the facts of life to be of use today, and it is not surprising that the measured pay-hours relation is insignificant. The fundamental fact of the modern labour market is that *human services largely consist of decisions.* Accordingly, if we seek a modern equivalent to the classical man-power-effort concept we must look to some construction which enables us to define and measure *the size of decisions.* We should not, of course, expect that such a measure of work will be as simple as that of manhours worked. Common language and sense accept that work is a multi-dimensional activity, so that a relevant concept of the size of work will only have a measurable counterpart by means of a theory showing how to aggregate the quasi-infinite real world dimensions into some manageable whole.

It is helpful in approaching the definition of labour input in terms of the size of decisions to start by asking what the output may consist of. The general view is that while input is clear and distinct, output, the individual worker's contribution, disappears in the totality of the firm's final product, at least in a complex industrial economy. Here we argue the exact opposite.[18] This is because under modern industrial organisation it is necessary, not just possible, to define output for the individual worker in the institutional framework of managerial structure. In industrial reality, we can think of the individual worker's output not as the number of nuts and bolts that he contributes to the construction of 'widgets', but simply as *what he is accountable for.* The characteristic of the industrial system which is pertinent in our context is that *the decision-making apparatus is organised hierarchically,* in the sense that for any one employee there is a manager, that is to say a control system (a) to specify the job, (b) to modify the job, (c) to review and evaluate the job, and (d) to select and de-select the occupant.[19] *Required output for any individual job is*

18. The true phenomenon of fusion only appears in research work, where the specific parentage of components of the final product get inextricably mixed up because the final product is an idea.

19. Jaques' theory of work organisation insists that what I call a 'manager' must in fact be a single individual with necessary authority, because decisions (a)-(d) do not consist of independent elementary components but must be a totality

the totality of responsibilities imposed by the management system. The output one is accountable for is simply what is defined by the management system, and it is, therefore, the same thing as the input which one supplies.

What does this input and output consist of? A job may be defined, or specified, in terms of separate dimensions. One dimension, for example, could be that this book must not exceed fifty thousand words; another could be that there must be at least one reference footnote per thousand words; another that sentences should have no more than thirty and no less than ten words. A dimension in this sense is the elementary managerial unit of job specification.

Note however that such job dimensions are not elementary in any objective sense. For example, the London Transport bus driver is accountable for (a) the speed limit (by national legislation), (b) his route, (c) the maximal acceleration and deceleration speeds at stops, etc., etc.; but he is not told the precise speed and acceleration for every yard in his route and what to do in every possible contingency. In other words, he is not programmed, either because it is not technically possible or because it is too expensive. It is for this reason that the output is that of a human operator who can exercise discretion. His job specification contains *specified* discretion. The elementary constraints on the job are elementary because the decision-making managerial apparatus defines them as such.

But there is more to the point. To continue with our example, the bus driver is not told how many pounds per square inch to apply to the brake. If told that, he is not told how much neuro-muscular energy to employ so that the right quantity of pressure will result. If he could be told that, he is not told how much volition to exert, what wilful decisions to take so that the rest follows. And so on. *What can be prescribed is finite. In principle, therefore, no human job can be specified absolutely.* There is an objectively unspecifiable part of a job which remains there until the job is pro-

---

which can only be achieved if they are joined as one single person's decision. In other words, decisions can only be aggregated or disaggregated with respect to decision-takers. Although I agree with this, as will be seen below, at the same time I don't wish to discuss the management aspects of the matter, so I prefer the formulation as stated more generally in the text, because it is sufficient for present purposes.

grammed, in which case the previously unspecifiable component is simply transferred to the accountability of the programmed job's designer.

Accordingly it is not only the number of dimensions defining a job or their concrete characterisation that are a matter for subjective managerial decision. It is also a necessary as well as subjective decision *not* to specify a job beyond a certain point. Instead of complete specification, human work is controlled by the *practice* of management in a specific sense which we now introduce in a formal manner.

A dimension can be formalised as consisting of three components. The first can be formalised as a boundary condition, as in the examples above. This is the prescribed content of the dimension. The second can be formalised as qualitative, as well as quantitative, tolerance limits around the boundary condition. This is the discretionary content of the dimension. The third can be formalised as an envelope around both prescribed and discretionary content. It refers to *the time in which marginally substandard discretion* (i.e. observations within the tolerance limits) *can be detected by the practice of management: this is the time-span of discretion.*

These three components have a dual existence: as themselves and as part of a whole. The first refers to a quantitative specification in appropriate units, such as ten thousand words plus or minus one percent. The second refers to the qualitative judgment of management which cannot be specified other than by subjective terms such as 'good enough' or 'not good enough'. The third refers to calendar time.

But the implementation of the first two components takes time. They become finished output only when that output is delivered for adjudication to management, which is the time when the third component comes into play. The third component therefore dominates in the sense that it gives meaning to the other two: neither quantity or quality is finished output; neither exists, until management has accepted it as such. It is this characteristic of work which gives rise to the idea that the dimension of a job can be sufficiently specified in time units.[20]

20. The terminology 'time-span of discretion', which Jaques introduced for this concept, may have the wrong connotations for economists trained to think in

Two examples may clarify the argument.

The first is a low-skilled woman's role in a food-producing factory. Confectionery bars are coming out of a cooling plant for wrapping. The woman is at the receiving end with the job of rejecting damaged pieces. The dimensions of the work are therefore two: reject damaged pieces; don't reject good pieces. Damaged pieces are defined as those which are perceivably, given the speed of the line, chipped. This is the first, technical, component of the two dimensions. Her discretion in both dimensions is to decide whether any one piece is sufficiently chipped. The third component is the time in which she would be detected exercising sub-standard discretion.

Now if she fails in the first dimension and does not reject damaged pieces, she will be detected within at the most five minutes by the section leader further down the assembly line. If she fails in the second dimension and rejects intact pieces she will be detected by the forewoman who periodically checks the contents of the rejects basket, at intervals of approximately twenty minutes.[21]

The second example is the job of a managing director of a shipping firm. One among many aspects of his work concerns the buying and selling of ships on owners' behalf. One dimension of the job is buying. Specified components of this dimension are the available budget, the maximum running costs, the size and type of vessel within some limits (e.g. tankers of between 35 and 55 thousand tons), some minimum net return on own funds, etc. Unspecified components of this dimension are all factors which can be subsumed under the umbrella of the 'entrepreneurial' decision. Examples of such components are the timing of the purchase with respect to the shipping cycle, the risk of technological obsolescence, unforeseen increases in costs, the re-opening of the Suez canal, etc. Such items cannot

terms of the Marshallian time periods. I would prefer to use the term 'delegated time-horizon of decision-making responsibility'. Provided, however, that we know what we mean, the terms obviously don't matter.

21. My definition of dimension is more elementary than Jaques' definition of task, as will be seen below. The above job consists of a single task in that there is no discretion over priority in time between the two alternative dimensions, because they co-exist, appear and reappear, concurrently. What I here call a 'dimension' other people might prefer to call 'degrees of freedom'.

obviously be specified, otherwise the services of an entre-
preneur would not be required. Finally, the time component
of this dimension is the 'normal' economic lifetime of a vessel
which is of the order of 18 years. The three components are
the same for the converse, selling, dimension. Thus over a
period of up to 18 years this decision-taker has discretion to
buy or sell a ship subject to the specified constraints.[22]

To return to our formal approach, a dimension is the
elementary decision unit which is defined for a specific work
role by management. It is defined by three sets of para-
meters: a set of measurable quantitative specifications, a set
of qualitative non-measurable specifications, and a time
variable. The time variable gives meaning to the *decisional
content* of the other two sets, because it is the delegated
time-horizon of responsibility for performance in the other
two sets. It envelopes the other two sets; and, under certain
conditions which we will examine below, it may stand as a
proxy for the 'size' of the dimension as a whole. Translating
this definition into an example: *you* have authority over *my*
work in the firm, and *you* delegate to *me* the work of writing
this book, on this subject, up to such and such a size, with so
many references etc.; *you* decide that *I* must deliver it to *you*
in one year's time, and then *you* and *I* will know whether it is
'good enough' or not, because *you* will *decide* on this and tell
me so. Over that year *I* am providing labour input; by the end
of the year at the latest *I* will provide *you* with labour
output. The decision content of the role is defined by the
practice of the management system.

The argument so far aimed to suggest the idea that the
time component of a dimension is a *plausible* parameter to
specify the size of the dimension. We now look at the same
component as a *necessary* parameter. What is the meaning of
open-ended, or 'infinite', delegated horizons for an individual
employee of a modern corporation? If I don't have to deliver
output by a certain calendar date, then I don't have to deliver
it at all. In this case the specification of the job's dimensions
is nullified by the implicit delegation of another dimension
which gives me the effective option of not implementing the
original one. At any one time I don't have to follow the

---

22. These two examples come from the 125 work roles analysed during the
field-work phase of the study.

specified constraints because 'I am not on that job yet', while the unspecified constraints cannot come into play until I have delivered my output for qualitative appraisal. But I don't have to deliver any output at any time, so that I can always postpone starting or delivering to tomorrow. In other words, I am given a non-job. In this sense the time limit on completion makes a job of the other components of a dimension; it is a necessary component for the job dimension to exist.

Now we come to the crux of the matter: to show that the time component is also *sufficient* to determine a job dimension, it must be shown that it is in some sense an accurate proxy for the 'size' of decisions. The 'size' of a job sounds like a dauntingly elusive concept to pin down in formal terms. Yet in everyday life we do evaluate the size of jobs all the time. A heuristic example from university teaching might help to show the line of thought. Under-graduates are given frequent, say fortnightly, tutorials, so that they are not left 'on their own' for too long. These tutorials usually become less frequent as the years progress. Under the old American grade point system there were weekly 'quizzes' for Freshmen and Sophomores, monthly one-hour 'exams' for Sophomores and Juniors, one paper at mid-term and one three-hour 'exam' at the end of term for Seniors. We now expect Part II students to be able to cope with their last year's work as one whole; this becomes two years for M.Sc. exams, and we give three years to the Ph.D. student. In planning these requirements, the length of time allotted is not independent of the amount and complexity of work that must be digested and integrated. But the amount of prescribed work, on its own, is not a sufficient guide to the time required. It cannot be properly quantified, because the units are sufficiently different: how many theorems to how many novels per annum? The discretionary components cannot be quantified at all, because being qualitative they have no units. Hence our evaluation of the size of a job inevitably leads to, as well as follows, the time component which is 'normally' considered pertinent to that sort of job. Thus a Ph.D. is a three-year job, whereas a first-year tutorial paper is a one-week job.

Is our view of a three-year job, however, an accurate

representation of what we want to mean by the size of a job? What is there, for example, to prevent the university authorities from defining a Ph.D. as a four-year job? We would obviously lose the objective of measuring the true content of work if the time-size of jobs were merely a whim or a random administrative convenience. It is not that, because it cannot be afforded that it should be so. This is seen most clearly in the standard employment situation, where people are paid to deliver *economic* output. If we take as the range of application for these concepts the industrial economy, where there are costs and payoffs because of scarcity, it is easy to see that *time is a scarce resource which must be economised.* Insofar as there exist pressures to economise, whether from some form or other of competition or by administrative forces and processes, there will be pressure to reduce the delegated time horizon so as to minimise, and if possible reduce to nothing, the 'slack' on the decision-making input of human resources. Since the pressures in university education cannot be as sharply defined, because the nature of the desired output is harder to pin down, it is not surprising that the educational system is designed to tolerate a considerable amount of slack. This must be so as long as the pursuit of originality or creativity is among the system's objectives. If this objective were dropped, then leisure-type sleeping-*cum*-thinking would not be good enough, whereas under present objectives such activities are indistinguishable from reading, writing, etc. But this free component of university education shows up by contrast the costly environment of the industrial economy. The pressures to economise resources in a costly environment therefore constrain the time component of a dimension to be an accurate measure of its size.[2 3]

We proceed with our discussion with the help of a diagram. A dimension, the elementary unit of delegated decision-making choice, figures as a set in n-space. Suppose it is 3-space.

23. The above approach to the definition of the time-span of discretion is not different in substance from Jaques' own. The latter, however, is rather more difficult to follow, as it is developed over a much broader canvas. See particularly his *Measurement of Responsibility* and *Equitable Pay.*

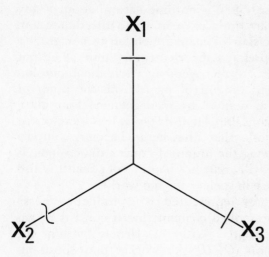

Figure 1.

x_1 may stand for prescribed content with quantitatively definable limits (e.g. a report of no less than ten thousand words etc.); x_2 may stand for discretionary content which does not have cardinal but ordinal units, e.g. good enough or better; x_3 is the maximum time prescribed for completion and delivery of the output, e.g. 3 months.

As it is, this set cannot be characterised any further because its qualitative components can only be ordered. But it can be transformed into a unique bounded and compact, and hence convex, set which is cardinally measureable. This is because x_1 and x_2 have no meaning apart from x_3. The implementation of x_1 can only be verified by x_3, while x_2 can only exist by x_3. The n-set thus collapses onto the time axis and therefore acquires time units of measurement. But time is compact, while the time limit is an upper bound. The dimension of delegated decision-making responsibility is therefore represented by a convex set which is cardinally measureable in time-terms. Our labour input theory building block is thus a convex set — a useful building block by all accounts.[24]

We next define a *task* as the union of dimensions such that there is no possibility of choosing among them through time. The task, as it were, is the natural aggregation of elementary

24. The idea to represent decisions on n-space and then map this onto 1-space, which also ensures the convexity property, is not alien to Jaques' concept. The further suggestion that this representation ties in with organisation theory must owe something to Koopmans's presentation of general equilibrium competitive theory in *Three Essays on the State of Economic Science* (1957).

dimensions. Of course, there is nothing natural about it any more than there is anything elementary to the dimension. Both represent a decision of management so to construct a job. But the task represents the elementary unit of output from the point of view of management, while the dimension represents the elementary unit of input from the point of view of the worker as defined by management: I am given choices along dimensions, but I deliver tasks. It is therefore at the point of the task that the input becomes output. Formally the task, being the union of convex dimensions, is also a convex set. We will argue in Chapter Four that it is also social value — the place in society for the worker.

The task can be now represented as a production possibility space. Every prescribed element that it consists of has some discretion associated with it. Hence, within the delegated time horizon (O, H) the worker must push his possibility curve outwards, because in this way he achieves greater quality and quantity. Accordingly, economising by the worker appears in this construct as movement away from

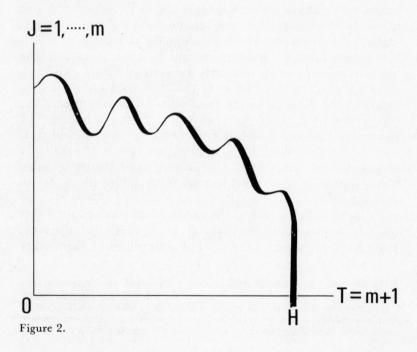

Figure 2.

the origin. *H* is the binding constraint because it contains all the qualities of the whole (*m*+1) tuple. One can therefore measure the set by collapsing it onto the *OT* axis. Whether seen from the point of view of the worker or from that of the organisation, the task as an equilibrium construct implies maximising-minimising behaviour. The organisation economises by pushing *H* down; the worker economises by pushing *H* up. At equilibrium the task is performed at *H*.

Jobs may consist of one or many tasks. The latter is the case if some dimension can be implemented with discretionary priority against others through time. The additional dimension, to exercise discretionary freedom of priority, is of course also defined by management. This does not violate the convex character of a job, however, since a multi-task role can be represented as the union of the separate tasks. To see this, remember that the time dimension is the overall binding constraint and is hence antagonistic to the achievement of quality over the discretionary component of the job, i.e. all discretionary components of the other dimensions. When there are many tasks, there is the possibility of cross-subsidisation, in time terms, between tasks. When some tasks are longer, the borrowing is necessarily against them. The union of the individual task-sets is the maximum area over which time-borrowing can be carried out. But the union is of course the size in time terms of the largest, i.e. longest, task. Hence that is by itself sufficient to determine the size of the job.

This can be put on a diagram (see figure 3 overleaf). Writing each dimension as a separate ray from the origin we ask:
Given the firm's organisation, what is the interval between now and detection of sub-standard discretion along each dimension? This is the upper bound. We draw a circle from the origin to mark off that interval. And so on for every dimension. The union of these circles is the same as the longest dimension.[2][5]

The advantage of a convex elementary building block is that the union of such constructs remains convex. This means that the work of the individual decision-takers adds up to the

25. The union of sets is here defined as in Koopmans, op. cit.

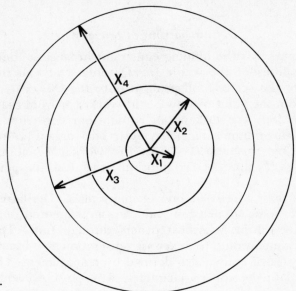

Figure 3.

work of the firm. Conversely, the work of the firm is disaggregated into the work of the individual employees. The management job of the firm is to divide up the total work into disjoint convex sets, one per decision-taker. If it can do that, then it can also decentralise the job of maximisation. By building the firm up from its elementary building blocks, we get a fresh insight into the problems of communication, control, etc. investigated by such economists as Simon, Marsh and T. Marschak.[26]

To sum up: The phenomenon we want to understand is the unit of social work, and the terms by which we describe it are task and time-span. 'Task' refers to a thing while 'time-span' refers to an attribute of that thing. When we describe a specific task by listing the elements it consists of, there is nothing wrong in leaving the time element as the last. But a description is not the same as the characterisation of the concept. The crux of the matter is that work is such by virtue of the responsibility quantum it contains. The dimension on which it can be observed is time, because time is the dimension along which responsibility is exercised. *Responsibility is no other than being on one's own.* The time-span aspect of work therefore exhausts all that there is to social

26. H. Simon, *Models of Man,* New York 1957, T. Marshak, *Econometrica* (1959).

work. There is no other element to a task which makes it more of a task, or more understandable, or more observable, or more measurable. A task *is* its time-span.

A theory of social work has two elements to define: the agent doing the work and the unit of work done. The agent here is the individual worker. He is free to choose on the object of his work within a set of constraints, whether imposed by himself or by the social setting. The constraints appear sharper if we restrict the field to employment work in organisations. An organisation may be defined as a set of roles organised hierarchically. Any one role may be defined as a set of tasks. A task is specified, i.e. described, by three sets of constraints, the prescribed content, the discretionary content and target completion time. The main methodological point is that it is *in principle* impossible to specify a task fully. A task needs a worker, it cannot exist as a form of social work without one. Anything which can be fully programmed or mechanised or automated would not need a human agent and would, economic conditions permitting, be so automated. If a job is automated, then it requires no human agent and it isn't a task. But if it isn't automated, then it does need an agent and it is his task. It is a task *because* it is somebody's task, because it is assigned to him and he is accountable for performing it.

To conclude this somewhat formal approach to the specifications of the work unit we must stress two important characteristics which make it drastically different from any other approach toward the measurement of labour input. The first of these is that work is defined for the individual worker, not for the bits and pieces produced, and for the organisation, not for the costs of production viewed as technical data. Of course the technological as well as the market environment of the firm (or, broadly, the 'institutions' of society) enter the determination of the size of the work unit,[27] but they do not impinge on its logical status. *The task is not a technical datum but a social relation.* Regardless of the institutions of the labour market, such as trades unions, etc., the relation which precedes production is an asymmetric one: between a single individual and a collective which we call 'the organisation'.

27. E.g. we don't get undergraduates writing three-year dissertations.

This leads to the second characteristic of the present definition of work, namely that the unit of work as such that *work does not constitute a disutility*. On the contrary, it will be argued that the efforts of people to get the right kind of work is precisely in the quest of 'utility', and that all this is logically independent of the question of pay.

It was of course natural, when work was understood to mean muscle power and long hours, that it should be considered as the disutility component of the labour supply function. That function represented, for each individual worker, trade-off points from the triplet of work, a disutility, leisure, a utility that required money for its satisfaction, and pay, a utility that could only be got by exchange with a disutility. As is evident, however, the present definition of work can well accommodate the statement that too little, as well as too much, work can be disutility, whereas within some limits work itself is a utility. Going back to our academic environment, it is plausible that an undergraduate who is given a postgraduate work assignment would consider this too much work and therefore a disutility. But it is even more plausible that the demotion of a postgraduate to weakly quizzes, a level of too little work, would be disutility without qualifications. Over-promotion and over-demotion can be seen in industry in a more glaring light, and entirely independently of the question of pay (see Part II). What matters for the present context is that the present unit of work does not preclude the forces of utility from playing a positive as well as an active part in the work situation.

These two important characteristics of labour input are taken up in detail in Chapter Four below. Before we see how a labour market may function with such a unit of work, we turn to the problems of measurement in Chapter Two and the analysis of the empirical evidence in Chapter Three.

Methodology and Method of Work Measurement

1. Introduction

The last chapter was confined to presenting a formal definition of work which has some desirable logical characteristics. But we are only interested in the logic insofar as it is relevant to understanding social reality. We must have a view of the relation between the logical construct and the manner in which reality can be interpreted through its use. A different approach to the definition of the unit of social work is accordingly undertaken in this chapter. In Chapter One we argued that of all the aspects of a task there is one, and only one, which has determining status, and that is target completion time. This is so because time is the residual dimension in the specification of task without which the others fall apart. It is the umbrella under which are covered all the non-specifiable elements of the task. We now add three other reasons which connect the logical with the empirical, and finally the theoretical, part of the study. First, the time-span of discretion is the one dimension that contains no element of previous knowledge. No element of training deals with a form of question which ought to read 'how long for what?' Secondly, it is the one dimension which is common to all tasks, a fact which enables us to reduce all work to a comparable measure. And, thirdly, it is also the element which empirically predicts what is subsequently considered as the supply price of labour. The time-span of discretion can therefore be considered as an economic variable, labour input.

The last point is related to the material mainly of Chapter Three. As a bridge between the logic of the concepts and the analysis of the specific empirical hypothesis, we discuss in this chapter the problems of task measurement in practice. It will be found that the formalisation, the methodological discussion and the use of the measuring technique are highly related between them. This discussion should also convince the reader that my acceptance of the present approach to the definition of work was not facile.

2. *Method of measurement*

I first sum up the lessons derived from the pilot run of the research project at Brunel. As a result of the pilot, the technique of the project was established in a way that permits a considerable extension of the area to be covered. Further, the technique employed is such as to permit any individual person to apply it, provided that he receives sanction to do so from the highest pertinent managerial executive. *A fortiori*, the technique is useable directly by management as part of its executive work.

Parallel to the question of technique, the pilot and subsequent work based on the amended technique has some interesting methodological implications. The design of the pilot project was aimed to reduce the possibilities of 'contamination' of the data through the process of observation. Observation, in this case in the form of interview, was aimed at two distinct types of measurement; one being the time-span of discretion, the other felt-fair pay.

A primary source of contamination that was felt to be absolutely inadmissable was from the one type of datum to the other. If there existed a definite relation between the two types of observation, which is precisely the proposition it was desired to test, then there ought to be every precaution against prejudging the issue through insight into one of the two types of data by pre-knowledge of the other. We should also be secure against the charge of having, consciously or unconsciously, 'forced' the data into producing the desired relation. We felt insecure originally about the degree of forcing implicit in the method of measurement by interview.

I still accept this source of contamination as valid and of possible mischief, although of trivial practical importance. The reason is my gradual detachment from the general plausibility of the time-span — felt-fair pay proposition as well as the emancipation from feelings of subjectivity in their measurement. In this, the most important cause has been the clarification of the logic of time-span measurement. Despite this, reasons of acceptability of the results by third parties were considered as compulsory constraints for keeping the two measurements distinct. Hence, when the project got properly underway, the interviewer who did the task analysis and recorded the time-span was in total ignorance of the felt-fair pay results. These were collected separately by another interviewer (using a set questionnaire) who recorded them in standard form and kept them separate until the write-up of the task analysis. This procedure, however, does not dispose of other sources of contamination from the so-called 'forcing' technique; but it definitely disposes of any possibility of helping the measurements along toward a pattern.

We shall have still more to say about the theory and the technique later on. Of greater importance, however, is what the pilot run revealed about the nature of time-span. In retrospect, the technique used for the pilot was ideal for obtaining *individual perceptions* of tasks, as distinctly and separately seen by the occupant of a role and his immediate manager, in separate communication with two interviewers who did not communicate results until their descriptions were written up. The technique was, therefore, the wrongest possible for measuring tasks which did not arise out of automous individual situations, such, for example, as leisure tasks. The tasks which it was aimed to measure derive specifically from a concrete executive framework, apart from which they have no meaning. But by treating them as we did, we reduced them to tasks which had effectively the status of being self-assigned and were therefore not logically distinct from leisure tasks.

The first point to strike our attention was that the employment of different interviewers for obtaining separate information from manager and subordinate meant throwing the burden of doubt arising from any discrepancies on the ability of the interviewer. For in the measurement of the time-span of any role there arose four possibilities: first, the perception by the occupant of a role in his own tasks could be inadequate; secondly, the perception by the manager of the role concerning the tasks given to the role-occupant could be inadequate; thirdly, the interviewer of the occupant could be inadequate; fourthly, the interviewer of the manager could be inadequate. If there were any difference in the task measurement obtained in the two interviews, a fact which would become apparent when the write-ups came up for comparison, it would not be possible, *in principle*, to determine which of the four causes was at work or how many of them. All the issues of 'data contamination' automatically arise and cannot be resolved unless one can pinpoint the source.

Let us for the moment leave aside the question of inadequate perception of tasks by occupant and manager to argue the effects of inadequacy of the interviewers doing their two separate measurements. This brings into focus the crucial role of the interviewer in work measurement through task analysis and his influence of 'forcing' the observations he records. Unless it can be shown either that the role of the interviewer is nil or that his influence is known, it will not be possible to establish a technique of objective validity either for analytical or for prescriptive purposes. Unless the interviewer is shown to be in some sense nothing other than a recording instrument, there is no sense in calling the results obtained by him 'data'. Discussion of this point must, therefore, be meticulous, even at the peril of being pedantic. We shall first look at the matter as it arises in practice.

Supposing that a research team is admitted into an organisation and goes about its way under conditions securing 'confidence'. It is stipulated by the team that they wish to interview people separately, that each interview is to be held in private with one member of the team, and that the results of the interview will not be passed back to any member of the firm. It is expected that under such conditions the persons interviewed will feel free to express their real thoughts and feelings, without fear of loss or expectation of gain as a result of what they say. These are the conditions secured for the Pilot-Project.[1] In order simply to dot the i's concerning the conditions of extreme confidence

1. If the reader should wonder why a firm will allow a research team to investigate its executive pattern and have people use working time to participate in such a project, the answer is that the firm as such gets no more out of the research project than might be got as windfall of insight by those individuals who submit to interview.

engineered for the pilot-project, the person was asked at the beginning of each interview whether he wished to have the interview at all and was told that, if his answer were 'no', even that would not be communicated outside.[2]

Having secured the pilot firm's co-operation under these exceptional conditions, a list of roles for interview was selected and appointments were made. The roles selected were a subset of the pyramid immediate under on the factory manager. There were two production superintendents and one quality control manager. Immediately below them there were a number of foremen and quality control superintendents. On the quality control side we went another step down to senior quality controllers, broadly of the same rank as the production foremen. We thus had in all 15 roles lined up for interview, of whom all but the factory manager at the top were eligible for time-span measurement.[3]

Now as to the pattern of the interviews. For the task analysis of any one role two and perhaps three interviews were necessary, one with the occupant of the role, one with his immediate manager, and, perhaps, if there was doubt about the immediate manager's requisite authority on the assignment of certain tasks, a third with the manager once removed. The burden imposed by this procedure on the firm, as well as on the research team, is apparent. The factory manager had to be interviewed as many times as he had immediate subordinates. In our case this meant three interviews, which tended to overshoot the two-hour mark in each case. Each person in intermediate positions also had the burden of many interviews: at least one on himself and as many more as he had immediate subordinates. For some superintendents this meant up to three interviews, again over the two-hour mark. The only persons who had to submit to a single interview were those at the 'bottom' of a hierarchical chain. But these people were only a third of the total and any addition to their number by the inclusion of collaterals would have automatically added interviews to the more

2. This ultimate attempt to secure confidence did not in the event materialise, since invariably no persons who had agreed to be interviewed shirked it in the end.

3. Task analysis requires two roles, those of manager and subordinate, to determine the subordinate's tasks in a pyramid. In a pyramid one therefore loses the tasks of the top role.

pressed people standing above them in the executive chain.

Apart from the time-consuming aspect of the burden implicit in the technique, there was also significant cost in terms of mental effort. It was found that managers needed a good hour before falling in with the framework of the interview, and they invariably found it a considerable mental strain. With but one exception, repeated interviews with the same manager needed the same preparatory hour before getting underway. It is hard to say whether it was accidental to the pilot firm or whether it is generally a feature of the technique, that the time and effort associated with interviews produced a sort of resentment, sometimes leading to the comment that far too much time was being used up without apparent benefit.[4]

The most important lesson concerned the effect of the technique. For the conditions of confidence were only too successful in isolating the individual interviewee from the executive context. The interview was distinctly seen as 'time off' from executive work, very much as if privately owned leisure-time were sacrificed in order to do an outsider a favour at the behest of the company, whose goodwill was somewhat at stake.

This should not be interpreted to mean that individuals interviewed were ungracious or that they were grudging about the misuse of their time. In fact nearly all of them were quite interested; sometimes they were even delighted to explain the working pattern of a role and, when describing their own role, might have been happy to go on forever. The interviewer, however, could not simply hold an interesting conversation about roles and personalities: he had to insist, sometimes at great length, about the rigorous formulation of his subject's experience into tasks. And here there were a number of traps. If the interviewee was the occupant of a role, he was more interested in describing his work than a manager usually was describing the work of his subordinate. But, generally, the occupant was less able to perceive his own

---

4. One specific difficulty for the pilot firm was that the time-span exercise came in the wake of a major exercise carried out by the firm, which had resulted in all managerial posts being defined 'by results', in other words expressed in terms of general responsibilities. This exercise was intellectually satisfying to management, so that further investigation was seen as approaching hair-splitting.

work, as distinct from the work of the executive cluster in which his role was fitted and, particularly, from the work of his manager. The term 'we' rather than 'I' before the verb 'to do' usually denoted this type of indeterminacy, which was often difficult to resolve.

This particular difficulty — let us call it 'non-identification with own-role responsibilities' — was minimal when the interview was with the manager rather than with the occupant of the role. It was usually possible for the manager to respond with a fair degree of ease about what he gave his subordinate to do, as distinct from what he himself had to do for his own manager. But this did not mean that he was in any better a position to define in specific task form what he held his subordinate accountable for, in the absence of independent knowledge by the interviewer of what the occupant of the role held himself to be accountable for. Further, the manager of the role was much less involved in describing his subordinate's tasks in the necessary detail. Hence, distance from the role and objectivity were here matched by less interest or knowledge for the description.

These difficulties lie behind the statement made above, that the burden of proving the 'truth' of an interview was inevitably thrown back on the interviewer. The outcome of the interviews could not be resolved except by cross-examination of the interviewers.

When two observations are made independently, there is obviously no reason why the measurements should be equal. In this case, however, the independence of observation was, so to speak, two-dimensional. Two independent measurements of the same phenomenon using the same instrument may naturally yield different results, and then the discrepancy may be variously accounted for by reference to either objective or subjective factors, viz. accidental external factors impinging on the measurement, or mistakes in the use of the measuring instrument. In our case, it was aimed to measure the same phenomenon, viz. the same underlying task and the same time-span. But the two independent measurements we were taking were also affected by our using effectively different instruments, the independent perceptions of two people: the manager of the role and the occupant. That the two distinct perceptions may also be of different status, we did not realise at the time. Hence a discrepancy in our measures did not necessarily arise either from the process of measurement or from the ability of the person taking the measurement. It may have arisen from the direct object of measurement, the independent perceptions of two people concerned with the phenomenon in different, in fact 'opposite' ways. And if these perceptions differ, then we can no longer hold that it is the same phenomenon that is being perceived and recorded. This third source of error makes it impossible to resolve a discrepancy in terms of distinct sources, which could be in principle removed. One is simply pushed to remove discrepancies on the grounds of plausibility or commonsense. At this point, however, the technique ceases to have objective validity.

In the facts of the case, we obtained during the pilot run considerable discrepancies both in time-span and felt-fair pay for the same role. It should be noted that the status of these discrepancies falls into different categories.

A discrepancy between felt-fair pay as given by the occupant and the manager is not of particular significance. The manager has only indirect personal stake in evaluating the 'true' worth of his subordinate's work; hence, his statement of it is, so to speak, 'costless'. By contrast, the occupant makes a statement of essential commitment as to his real personal worth on an objective scale, which places him in a specific position on the social ladder, both inside his place of work and in society generally. Having obtained answers to the felt-fair pay question from both sides of the coin on several occasions, there is no doubt as to which of the two answers is the more painful to commit oneself to.

On discrepancies concerning the time-span, however, the presumption of greater validity is reversed. Not only is it more difficult to obtain task information from the occupant. It is also impossible to dispel the feeling that the interviewer is being served up with a magnified role. Here it is the occupant of the role who is in a position to offer relatively 'costless' information, that is to say tasks which do not involve him in any work, either because they are not his or sometimes because they don't even exist at all.

This is not to say that people lie about their work, a proposition on which the evidence is nil. It is to say that two new sources of 'contamination' may be at work. First, in cases where the manager of the occupant's role is successful, perhaps by introducing a strong team spirit, the occupant is carried by the atmosphere of the work and is concerned about the whole as well as about the distinct part for which he is himself accountable. Secondly, perhaps in cases where the manager is not so successful, or where there is 'disequilibrium', for any cause whatever, between the person and the role that he is currently filling, wishes, desires, and plans about how the work ought to be, can be brought up from, so to speak, the sub-conscious, even without the slightest conscious ill-will, as a description of how the work actually is. Whenever in an interview the feeling or presumption was generated that the tasks described were due to some such form of fantasy, it proved impossible to shake the description without the danger of accusing a person's honesty or his ability to perceive his work accurately.

The impression should not be created that in the pilot run we obtained wildly contradictory evidence. The vast majority of the individual tasks and a clear majority of the time-spans of roles presented no discrepancies at all, as between the two interviewers or the two types of interview, with manager and occupant respectively. But a technique is always tested at the margin, and by that test our technique during the pilot run proved exceptionally revealing. The following discrepancies came to the fore:

Type I, where the descriptions of the tasks were not identical. This discrepancy has no effect on the time-span measure but should cause worry about the different perceptions of manager and occupant and/or about the ability of the interviewers. In general, interviews with the occupant produced a more detailed and, perhaps, more accurate description.

Type II, where the descriptions of the tasks were or were not identical but the time-spans were different. This discrepancy was much more infrequent than the first type but was clearly more disturbing. In general, time-spans produced by interview with the occupant were longer and usually coincided with more complicated descriptions of the tasks, or were descriptions of more complicated tasks, presumably for the reasons under the heading of fantasy discussed above.

Type III, where some tasks, often the longest, were given by only one side, usually the occupant, of the executive context. Added to the element of inadequate perception and fantasy, we have here the element of incompleteness. This element was particularly frequent in the case of the manager, whose commitment to the purpose of the interview can be presumed less than the occupant's.

The discrepancies of Types II and III led to careful examination of the implications of the technique used on the pilot run. On the one hand, such implications were purely practical: how to organise the interviews, how much time should be required, whether to go according to a definite pattern through an executive hierarchy, whether first to explain the meaning of task, whether to suggest the meaning of time-span by explaining its postulated relation to felt-fair pay; last but not least, how to train the interviewer so that he could tell whether he was producing tasks and whether he had exhausted them. A not unimportant, although different, practical implication concerned the possibility of implementing the research project: a very time-consuming and trying exercise was requested from firms which were admittedly offered very little in return. The possibility that any research project can succeed in such circumstances is certainly not great.

There are also methodological implications of greater importance. Whenever a discrepancy of Types II or III occured, there was no difficulty in finding plausible reasons for it. An acceptable and convincing source of 'disequilibrium' could usually be found on the side of the occupant, such that it could explain away those of his perceptions which clashed with those of his manager. This was made possible by the mass of ancillary information which was obtained during the interviews. It was also possible to trace implausible statements made by the manager to other sources of 'disequilibrium', usually concerned with short tenure of the role of manager and consequent incompleteness of information, or transition to a new executive structure. Plausible as such explanations may be, they did not resolve the two essential points which led us back to theory:

First, how can the interviewer be certain that he is actually getting out tasks; in other words, how can the burden of what actually constitutes a task be not on the interviewer but on something entirely objective?

And secondly, how can it be ascertained that the distinct perceptions of manager and occupant both refer to the same tasks; in other words, how can the basic phenomenon under consideration be known to be the same when it is perceived by two observers who have different, in fact opposite, status with respect to that phenomenon?

These questions lead to the cornerstone of the theory, namely the concept of task, its logical status and, therefore, the conditions for its observation. It is these considerations which eventually led to the formalisation presented in the previous chapter.

It is noticeable that the technique of time-span measurement is strong enough not to depend on the person using it, even under the unfavourable conditions of the confidential relation. Nevertheless, the job of the analysis is to reveal a situation which exists, not to adjudicate on what the situation might have been or should be which, under the present system, is the job of management. Reporting back upwards is essential to explain a job specification, in task form, which is the actual, explicit or implicit, decision of management. Reporting back downwards is also essential, to ensure that the extant situation is both fully perceived and taken seriously by management. The people most securely fit to do time-span measurement are therefore the firm's own managers, for whom some kind of task specification is in any case an inevitable part of the job of role specification.[5]

In conclusion, then, the conditions under which task

5. In the firm in which the management was particularly interested in following up the detailed work on job analysis, the technique was more or less automatically picked up, to the point where job-specification sheets were compiled in task form, that is to say with the time-span of each task made explicit. It is notable that this interest developed exclusively for purposes of job specification and not in any relation to pay, since the time-span felt-fair pay relation had only been discussed with higher management in very general terms, while, at the time of the work analysis, the interviews on felt-fair pay and the rest of the questionnaire had not yet been administered.

analysis can be carried out and time-spans of roles recorded are: (a) higher management must decide to instruct role occupants and managers to participate in the analysis, and (b) higher management must accept that all analyses will be reported back, upwards and downwards, in the management hierarchy involved, which implies that the results of the exercise will be public, at least within the firm.

3. The field work

These lessons from the pilot exercise were put to use as follows: first, the results of the 16 pilot interviews were written off to experience and not utilised in quantitative analysis because they were obtained under confidential conditions.

Secondly, a new sample was derived through 'consultancy-type' interviews with 10 different firms. All interviews were reported back to higher management and therefore have the status of management decisions.[6]

Thirdly, the firms selected for interview were obtained from the immense list with which Brunel University has been in contact with throughout the operation of the sand-wich-course programme. 64 firms were selected from the list (on the not unreasonable, as well as non-random, basis of familiarity with their names). These were sent a letter explaining the nature of the project and the demands of time made of them: 60 firms replied. Of these, 10 were definitely

6. One should not put too much emphasis on this decisional character of the recorded time-span measurement, since it is quite possible that they were decisions, so to speak, arrived at lightly. Such costless decisions by a firm may substitute management bias for interviewer bias. But even that should be enough for present purposes. The management's concept of reality in their own firm is likely to be both sharper and more committed than the casual research worker's, who is naturally more concerned about the fate of his project than on how a firm actually behaves.

Nevertheless, a costly decision by the firm, on job specification (which is precisely what a task-cum-time-span analysis is), that is to say a decision involving also the question of pay, will not be taken lightly. The perfect conditions for time-span measurement are therefore those of full consultancy, whereby a firm submits to the exercise in order to determine its management structure and its payment policy. It is in this sense that the people best fitted to do time-span measurement are the firm's own managers. In issuing a task instruction they cannot but see that it is related to what they are prepared to pay for the implementation of the task.

not interested, 10 were not uninterested but could not agree to the exercise (usually because they were involved in some other time-consuming job-evaluation project), 10 were interested in principle but were not prepared to proceed immediately, and 30 were interested to discuss with us to obtain more information and arrange for us to proceed. In the event, we had time to work in only 10 firms, which happened to be the first in the sequence of arrangements. Their characteristics were as follows:

Firm 1: This is the whole executive structure of the training department, constituting the bulk of the personnel department, of a nationalised industry in Scotland. There were 16 interviews ranging from 1 month to 1.5 years in terms of time-span and from £1,170 to £2,900 in terms of felt-fair pay.

Firm 2: This is the major part of the research department of another nationalised industry in London. There were 22 interviews with time-spans ranging from 3.5 days to 1 year and 9 months and felt-fair pay ranging from £1,150 to £3,750.

Firm 3: This is the basic research department of yet another nationalised industry located in the area of Oxford. There were 16 interviews with time-spans ranging from 1 day to 3 years and felt-fair pay ranging from £900 to £4,850.

Firm 4: This is the top management of a small firm in the wood-manufacturing sector in the Nottingham area. There were 5 interviews with time-spans ranging from 3 months to 1 year and felt-fair pay ranging from £1,500 to £2,500.

Firm 5: This is again the top management of another small firm in the building sector in the London area. There were 4 interviews with time-spans ranging from 2 days to 6 months and felt-fair pay ranging from £1,000 to £1,850.

Firm 6: This was the whole of one department producing a specific product from start to finish in a large food-manufacturing firm in the London area. There were 46 interviews with time-spans ranging from 20 minutes to 1 year and 3 months and felt-fair pay ranging from £780 to £2,500.

Firm 7: This is the top management of a small firm in the textile distribution sector in the London area. There were 4 interviews with time-spans ranging from 2.5 days to 6 months and felt-fair pay ranging from £702 to £1,900.

Firm 8: This was part of the management structure of a local authority in the London area. There were 5 interviews with time-spans ranging from 1.5 months to 14.5 months and felt-fair pay ranging from £1,200 to £2,600.

Firm 9: This was a small part of the high management structure of a large modern electronics firm in the London area. There were 4 interviews with time-spans ranging from 3.5 months to 3 years and 3 months and felt-fair pay ranging from £2,850 to £4,000.

Firm 10: This was the single role of the managing director of a shipping firm in the City of London. Time-span was 18 years and felt-fair pay was £25,000 per annnm.

This collection of firms has the following desirable characteristics:

1. Different sizes of firms and different sizes of sample from each firm which do not depend on the size of the firm.

2. Different sectors of industry: three manufacturing firms, three utilities, three firms in the services, one in local government.

3. Different regions of the country: the South-East area, Scotland and the Midlands.

4. Different types of employment: jobs range from practically unskilled manual, both light and heavy, to semi-skilled, skilled, professional and post-doctoral research.

5. Different underlying technologies: by any criterion the firms cover the whole range of technology, from the most primitive to the frontiers of science.

6. Different levels of employment: the jobs range, in terms of responsibility, from wrapping food parcels to running vast organisations.

7. Both men's and women's roles: 22% (35) of the roles were designed for and occupied by women.

Some of these characteristics have been postulated to be determinants of relative pay. Although it would be possible to analyse the separate effects of all these factors on felt-fair pay, the analysis of the data ignore all except one (women's *versus* men's pay) in order to examine the explanatory power of time-span when taken by itself.[7] With respect to the difference between men's and women's pay, it was accepted that there is systematic bias against women's pay on the grounds usually offered, e.g. education, opportunity, intermittent withdrawal from the labour market, etc. We proceeded to correct for such bias on the assumption proposed by Jaques that up to £575 per annum, women's pay should be marked up by 33%, between £575 and £1,500 per annum it should be marked up by 10%, and between £1,500 and £3,000 it should be marked up by 5%.[8]

Time-spans were recorded in their natural units, as used by management, such as hours, days, weeks, months and years. For purposes of quantitative analysis they were converted to hours by transforming one day into 8 hours, one week into 5 days, one month into 4 weeks and one year into 12 months. The analysis therefore ignores the effect of irregular hours, overtime and length of holidays, etc., as well as the effects of employment stability, length of service and security of tenure. Felt-fair pay statements were converted into pounds per annum on the same basis as above. Thus corrected and converted, the raw data are presented in Appendix A to Chapter Three. There are 125 observations in all.

The data on time-span and felt-fair pay made available by Professor Jaques are somewhat different to those obtained for the Brunel project and require a different method of standardisation (Chapter Three, Appendix A, Firm 11). These data were a by-product of Jaques' social-analytic work at Glacier and were obtained through the method of 'confidential' interview. The data are rather less systematic

7. Apart from the fact that the time-span is very powerful in explaining the variation of felt-fair pay, it was thought that the assumptions underlying the multivariate regression model which would be used in the analysis of partial correlation, particularly with respect to random sampling, are not really met in the sample.

8. Partial justification for this procedure was given by the pay questionnaire, in which women were also asked to state a felt-fair pay figure for the same job, had it been designed for and occupied by men.

than those of the Brunel project in that they do not refer to any one department of the firm from top to bottom. These data cannot therefore be considered as a random sample of the total population in the firm or indeed of anything else.[9]

The important difference between the two sets of data derives from the fact that Jaques' research extended over a number of years. Thus the felt-fair pay figures are not directly comparable insofar as absolute payment figures have followed an upward trend through time. Data extending over such long time-periods can only be made comparable by the use of some assumption. Jaques assumes that desired (i.e. felt-to-be-fair) pay relatives remain invariant with respect to the wage and salary bill for the economy as a whole. Figures can therefore be adjusted by inflating upwards according to some comprehensive earnings index. This assumption was adhered to for the purposes of the comparison.[10] Felt-fair pay values in Jaques' sample were adjusted upwards, according to the Ministry of Labour Index of Earnings, to the summer of 1968, to which our own data refer.

With respect to the non-randomness of both samples — Jaques' as well as the one obtained for this study — there is a serious problem which transcends merely technical difficulties. It is in fact difficult upon reflection to attach any meaning to random sampling when one has no other than *a priori* knowledge of the properties of the time-span distribution with respect to other variables. Since what is at least partly in question is the existence of the variate called the time-span of discretion, the only way to apply quantitative methods is to obtain a large rather than a small number of observations, over as large as possible a range of the space on which the variate is defined, and use it as a predictor of another variate whose innate existence is not in question and which should, according to the theory, be related to it. As seen above, the new sample covers a very wide range, from the lowest paid to the highest paid jobs, with reasonable uniformity of coverage except for the very top of the range.

9. The Brunel project data are of course not a random sample either.

10. Other assumptions can of course be used to make 'dated' observations comparable. What should be clear is that each method of adjusting the data implies a different assumption about the underlying behaviour of the labour market.

Jaques' sample is more restricted in range but equally uniform as to coverage. It consists of 70 observations ranging from 6 hours to 2.5 years on time-span and from £920 to £6,500 on felt-fair pay. Both samples put together therefore provide 195 observations. The analysis of these data is presented in the next chapter.

CHAPTER THREE

Quantitative Analysis of the Empirical Data[1]

1. The total sample

The data were analysed by regression methods. Time-span was treated as the independent, and felt-fair pay as the dependent, variable. The range and distribution of time-span dictated the use of a logarithmic scale to spread the observations out evenly. Felt-fair pay was also plotted on a logarithmic scale since this did not distort the essential shape of the relationship.[2]

The scatter of all 11 firms put together is presented in Figure 1. Intuitively, the underlying relation is curvilinear overall with a kink at about the middle of the range.

Looking for a relationship over the whole scatter implicitly assumes that the observations come from the same population. On this assumption a variety of non-linear regressions were fitted and resulted in values of the coefficient of correlation uniformly over 0.85. As better and better fits did not appear to be a good line of attack, the data were subsequently analysed by means of linear regression and split up into various sub-sets on which standard tests were performed.

Writing x for log (base 10) of time-span in hours and y for log (base 10) of felt-fair pay in pounds per annum, we fitted the polynominal

$$y = a_n x^n + a_{n-1} x^{n-1} + \ldots + a_1 x^1 + a_0$$

1. I am grateful to Tom Wizniewski who was selflessly willing to act as my intermittent tutor in statistics and to Margaret Hawkins who helped over the dialogue with the computer.

2. Lest the double-logarithmic plotting resulted in artificial smoothing of the data, all regressions were also run in semi-logarithmic form. This made no difference whatsoever.

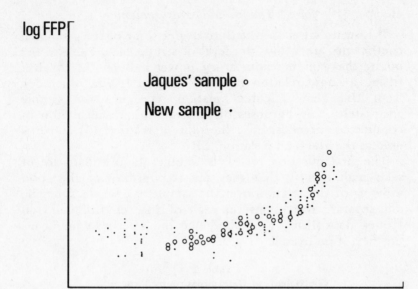

Figure 1. N = 195

for all powers up to fifth degree. These are presented below
for the 195 observations, with the standard errors of the
estimates and the t-values in parentheses under the estimated
coefficients:

Table 1
Regressions on Total Sample, N=195

(1) $y = 2.950 + \underset{(15.05)}{0.1257x}$ 　　　　　　　　　　　　　　　$r^2 = 0.54$

(2) $y = 3.084 - \underset{(9.28)}{0.1673x} + \underset{(17.00)}{0.08239^2}$ 　　　　　　　$r^2 = 0.8165$

(3) $y = 3.067 - \underset{(0.10)}{0.003311x} - \underset{(1.73)}{0.03677x^2} + \underset{(5.75)}{0.02128x^3}$ 　$r^2 = 0.8435$

(4) $y = 3.062 - \underset{(2.16)}{0.09375x} + \underset{(2.05)}{0.09728x^2} - \underset{(1.91)}{0.03511x^3} + \underset{(3.13)}{0.007234x^4}$

　　　　　　　　　　　　　　　　　　　　　　$r^2 = 0.8512$

(5) $y = 3.065 - \underset{(1.97)}{0.98838x} + \underset{(0.85)}{0.06659x^2} - \underset{(0.15)}{0.008593x^3} - \underset{(0.05)}{0.0008671x^4}$

　　　$+ \underset{(0.49)}{0.0008197x^5}$ 　　　　　　　　　　　　$r^2 = 0.8514$

It is seen that above the third degree some of the estimated coefficients are below the level of significance. More to the point, the gain in explanatory power in terms of r^2 after fitting a cubic relation falls off sharply. It was concluded from this that a cubic relation represents the sample adequately. For purposes of illustration and calculation of confidence intervals, etc., the plot of relation (3) above is used as the Standard Relation (SR).

The first question to ask is whether Jaques' data are of such high quality that they are responsible for the good showing of the relation over the sample as a whole. Carrying out separate regressions on each of the ten firms and on Jaques' data (firm 11) we find that the latter is by no means the 'best' firm overall.

Table 2
Coefficients of Determination by Firm (r^2)

Firms	N	Linear	Quadratic	Cubic	Quartic	Quintic
Firm 1	16	38.53	39.29	45.44	45.44	45.44
Firm 2	22	70.12	83.37	84.07	85.05	85.05
Firm 3	16	86.27	91.84	92.00	93.12	93.19
Firm 4	5	24.70	31.86	32.39	—	—
Firm 5	4	72.05	95.95	—	—	—
Firm 6	46	24.81	34.35	34.35	34.36	34.74
Firm 7	4	22.47	99.99	—	—	—
Firm 8	5	87.10	88.74	—	—	—
Firm 9	4	92.23	99.87	—	—	—
Firm 10	1	—	—	—	—	—
Firm 11 (Jaques)	70	78.17	87.47	93.17	95.24	95.24
Sub-total 1-10	125	50.82	79.25	82.22	82.93	83.10
Total 1-11	194	54	81.65	84.35	85.12	85.14

Five firms (3, 5, 7, 8, and 9) have higher r^2s than firm 11 when fitting a quadratic, and three of them (firms 3, 8, and 9) are also higher when fitting a linear relation. Firm 11 takes the lead when fitting a cubic relation and remains there subsequently, although by a very small margin over firm 3 and not far from firm 2, whose performance consistently improves for higher degrees of polynomial. The results for the firms which are represented by a small number of observations are obviously not significant beyond the quadratic, so that their good effect on the total is not seen when fitting higher degree curves.

It can further be seen from Table 2 that Jaques' sample does not significantly affect the total. The last three rows show Jaques' sample (firm 11), then the new sample (firms 1 to 10) and finally the total. The gain over the new sample attributable to adding Jaques' is then seen to be approximately two percentage points on the r^2. Accordingly, Jaques' data can well be used together with the new sample for purposes of analysing variation over the total range of data as well as by firm.

The same point can be made by looking at Figure 2, which shows the Standard Relation fitted over the whole range of data (N=195) as before. The curve denoted B represents a similar cubic fitted over the new sample alone (N=125). B is virtually indistinguishable from SR. The curve denoted A represents a similar cubic fitted over Jaques' sample and it is drawn over the narrower range of that sample.[3]

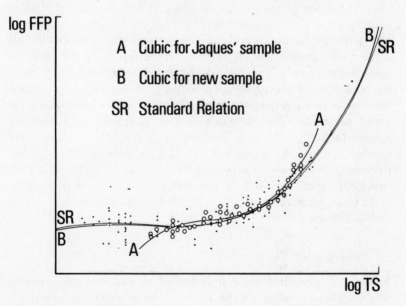

Figure 2. A=cubic for Jaques' sample, B=cubic for new sample, SR=Standard Relation.

3. It should also be noted that the cubic polynomials fitted over the range of the data are not monotonically increasing, whereas fourth- and fifth-degree polynomials are. Since, however, these relations are used merely to represent the samples for analytical purposes this is of no importance.

A strict comparison of Jaques' with the new sample cannot be made without using the F-test, to determine whether the two samples come from the same population. The same procedure must also be applied to indicate whether *any* two of the firms in the new sample come from the same population: in particular, whether specific attributes of the sample from each firm — such as size of sample, range of x and/or y, position of each sample in the overall range, as well as region and type of technology, etc. — can be said to differentiate the overall population of firms and roles into separate significant entities. Use of the F-test does not however seem appropriate for answering these questions. With respect to comparing Jaques' sample (N=70) with the new sample (N=125), it is clear that the large number of observations renders the test spuriously over-sensitive. With respect to comparing any two other firms, or particular characteristics of them, the number of observations dwindles too rapidly.

Further, it is not merely a question of size. Underlying all difficulties in the use of rigorous techniques is the lack of randomness in the process of obtaining observations. It may be possible for other studies to be so designed as to obtain observations in numbers which permit analysis of variance by strict methods. The methods in this chapter are both more elementary and more selective: they reflect the view that *confidence in the existence of the postulated relationship depends on a sequence of exploratory steps* rather than on one-shot pass or fail tests whose validity depends on statistical properties which it is hard to believe obtain in this field of study.[4]

2. Variation among firms

From this point of view it is useful to examine the reasons for variation among all the firms. Jaques' data stand out by their uniformly high tightness around all relations fitted. But some other firms display the same or even greater regularity. Firms 2, 3, 5, 8, and 9 (see Table 2) give high r^2s from linear

---

4. I am indebted to Tom Wizniewski for instructing me on the merits of the above argument.

fit onwards. This has nothing to do with the number of observations obtained in each firm: 'good' firms are to be found among those from which we obtained many and few observations: thus for firm 2 $N=22$, for firm 3, $N=16$, whereas firms 5, 8 and 9 have only four to five observations each; and the same is true of 'bad' firms: thus for firm 1, $N=16$, for firm 6, $N=46$, whereas firms 4 and 7 have only five and four observations respectively. Nor is it true that 'good' firms have drastically different pay and consultation systems, with the result, presumably, of a well-perceived scale of norms concerning the relative pay structure.[5] While good consultative machinery may perhaps account for the high showing of Jaques' data, in this respect at least Glacier is a special case.

As intra-firm variation cannot be explained by the number of observations from each firm, there are two further directions that can be investigated. The first concerns the range over which we have time-span and felt-fair pay observations for each firm. The second concerns the *part of the overall time-span range* which is covered by observations from any single firm. What matters particularly for the sequel is whether most observations from a given firm fall onto the steep or the flat part of the Standard Relation, to the right or to the left of the kink in the middle of the time-span range.[6]

The range of observations on time-span and felt-fair pay was accordingly plotted against r^2 for each firm, but it is immediately clear from Figures 3a and 3b that the range of observations for each firm is not a major determinant of variation among them.

Turning now to the position of firms in the overall range, the question is more complicated. Figure 4 shows the range of each firm over the total and, in brackets, the associated values of N and r^2.

5. In that case, incidentally, Jaques' hypotheses would receive support, since one could then say that well-managed firms are well-managed because their pay structure responds to the felt desires of their work force.

6. Jaques has suggested that time-span measured in hours, days, weeks, etc., while natural as a way of conveying managerial decisions which are carried out in calendar time, is not necessarily natural as 'experienced' level of work. From the latter point of view he suggested a different unit of work measurement which corresponds to the concept of 'executive rank'. The distinction between the 'flat' and the 'steep' parts of the Standard Relation corresponds to low and high ranks of the latter theory, the inflection point between ranks 3 and 4.

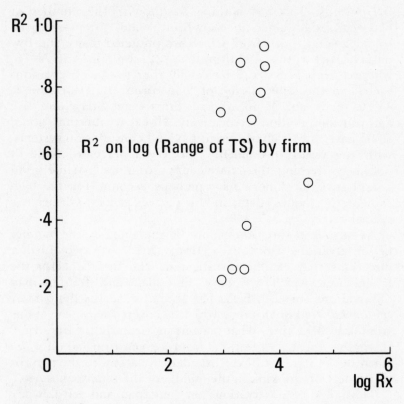

Figure 3a.　r^2 on log (range of TS) by firm.

Where N is small and/or the range in x is small, the linear expressions were used for the relevant r^2. Looking at overall ranges by firm does not however give a correct picture of the weight of each firm over a particular range, since each firm does not occupy its own range with any pattern. The picture of most firms overlapping about the middle of the range is sufficiently misleading to require looking at the scatter of each individual firm separately.

These scatters are plotted in Figures 5 (a-i) over the Standard Relation. From these figures it is possible to characterise each firm as lying predominantly to the left of the kink, on it, or to the right of it. Firms, 3, 8 and 9 quite unambiguously belong to the right of the kink whereas firm 6

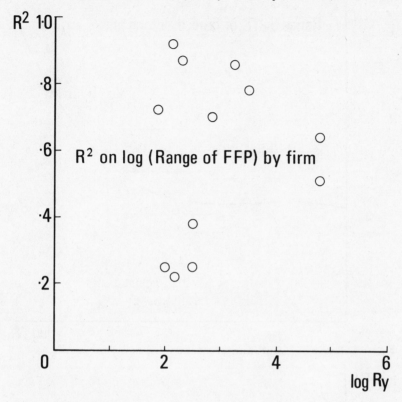

Figure 3b. r^2 on log (range of FFP) by firm.

is unambiguously to the left. The rest of the firms (1, 2, 4, 5 and 7) seem to fall mostly in the middle but with considerably more ambiguity.

If we now put values 1, 2 and 3 to represent left of, on, and to the right of the kink, we can obtain an idea of how position is related to the value of r^2.

There is clarity at the two extremes: the three firms that are towards the top of the range are uniformly high performers, whereas the single firm that is at the bottom is among the worst performers. But there is no pattern at all in the middle. It should however be noted that, while the bottom-left of the figure contains approximately one-third of the observations, all of them come from a single firm,

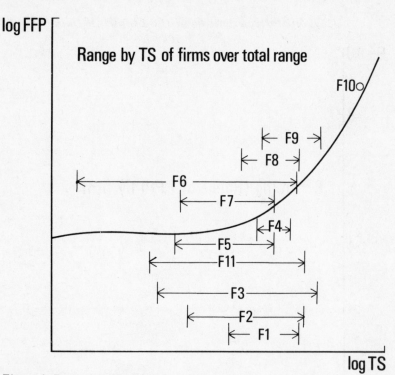

Figure 4. Range by *TS* of firms over total range.

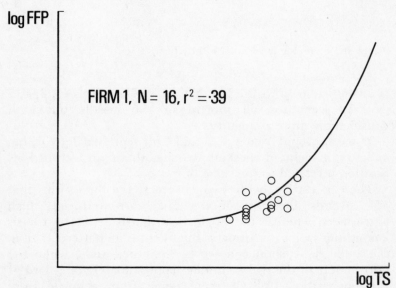

Figure 5a. Firm 1, $N=16$, $r^2 = \cdot 39$.

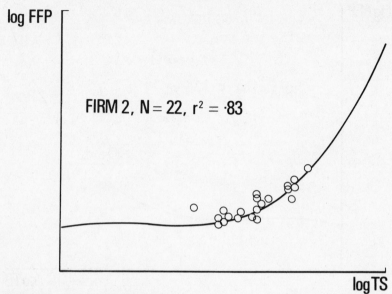

Figure 5b. Firm 2, $N=22$, $r^2 = \cdot 83$.

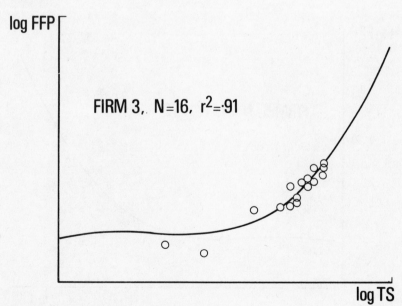

Figure 5c. Firm 3, $N=16$, $r^2 = \cdot 91$.

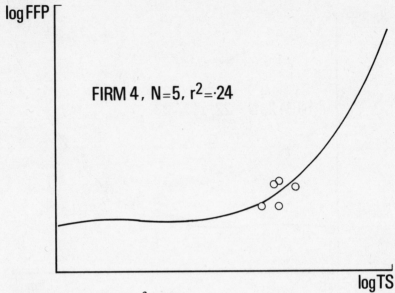

Figure 5d. Firm 4, $N=5$, $r^2=\cdot 24$.

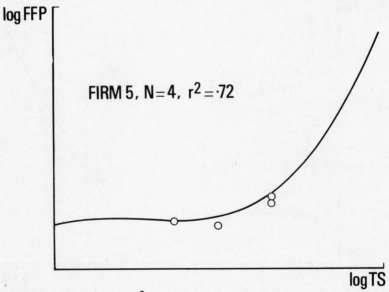

Figure 5e. Firm 5, $N=4$, $r^2=\cdot 72$.

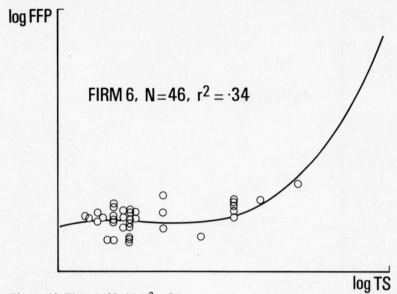

Figure 5f. Firm 6, $N=46$, $r^2=\cdot34$.

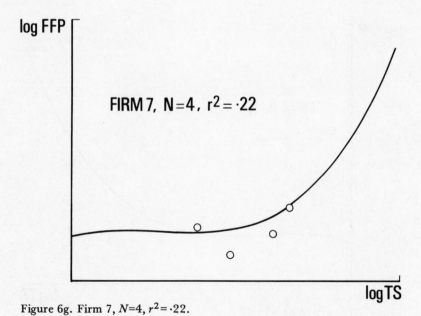

Figure 6g. Firm 7, $N=4$, $r^2=\cdot22$.

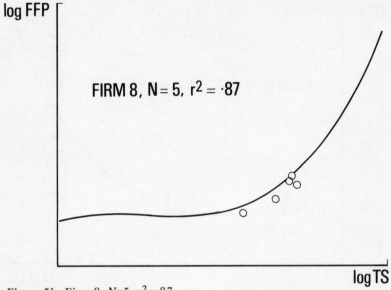

Figure 5h. Firm 8, N=5, r^2=·87.

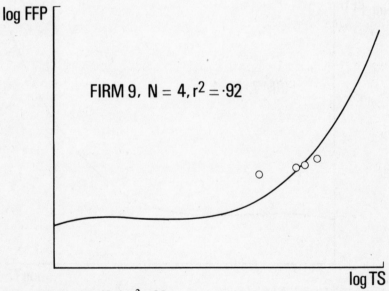

Figure 5i. Firm 9, N=4, r^2=·92.

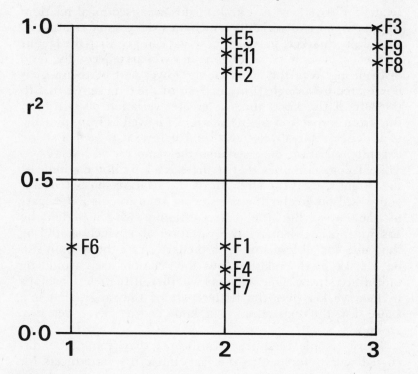

Figure 6.

whereas the top-right and the middle, again with about a third of the observations each, are represented by numerous firms. We are not therefore justified in concluding that the lower half of the range yields a weaker relationship between time-span and felt-fair pay inasmuch as the lower part effectively coincides with a single firm.

To sum up: there is nothing accidental in the new sample, in terms of the peculiarities of samples derived from individual firms, to make the overall relation appear good. Variation among firms is not related to anything systematic except, perhaps, to position in the overall sample. Since this last point is confused with one firm only, it is worth investigating more generally.

The problem can be put in terms of the kink on the overall curve. The data suggest two observations which may be

related. First, there is a kink in this cross-sectional relationship between two variables which must have some relation to
the labour market, in which case we can say that the labour
market is, in some sense, divided in two parts. Secondly, (and
discounting from the fact that the lower part of the range is
dominated by a single firm) analysis of the data shows that to
the left of the kink, there is greater variation of y given x.
But from inspection of the scatter[7] (as well as from plotting
confidence intervals, see section 4 below) it is seen that the
absolute variation of y remains the same for all levels of x.
This of course implies that if there is a kink in the middle of
the x-range, then the strength of the relationship between x
and y will be greater for the steeper than for the flatter part
of the curve. But the real question is why it should be
absolute rather than relative variation of y which should be
the same for all levels of x. In the latter case there could still
be a kink in the relation, but the relation itself would be
uniformly strong. One wonders whether, if the relationship is
in fact weaker over the flatter part of the range, that is a
cause for the existence of a kink and/or the other way
around.

These problems appear significant; they cannot be discussed with reference to the facts but rather as subjects for
economic analysis.[8] The disgression, however, suggests that it
would be meaningful to truncate the sample at the middle of
the range to investigate variation from an explicitly level-
of-work point of view.

3. Variation Between High and Low Levels of Work

The total sample of 195 observations was split at $x=1920$
hours which is equivalent to a one-year time-span of
discretion and corresponds to Jaques' Rank 4.[9] This mid-
range value was considered to belong to both subsets, partly
to increase the number of observations by firm and partly in
conformity with Jaques' theory of ranks, which are defined

7. See Figure 4.
8. They are taken up in Chapter Four below.
9. 'A Theory of Ranks' in *Glacier Project Papers*.

from their end points. Even with this device, there are only 24 observations above the one-year mark for all the firms in the new sample put together and only 13 for Jaques'. Table 3 gives a summary of the results.

Table 3

	Below 1 Year		Above 1 Year	
	N	r^2	*N*	r^2
Firms 1-10	109	49.95	24	90.58
Firm 11	61	87.5	13	87.59
TOTAL	170	49.02	37	86.75

Above the one-year mark the new sample gives better performance than Jaques', but below the one-year mark the new sample is significantly inferior to Jaques'. Thus the total relation looks significantly weaker for lower than for higher levels of work.

The same impression can also be obtained from Figure 7. Two straight lines are fitted for the two samples with $x = 1920$. While the confidence intervals about the mean of the fitted relation are equally tight for the two subsets, the confidence intervals about a random element are much wider about the flatter than about the steeper line, reflecting the approximate invariance with respect to x of the absolute variation in y. The analytical forms of these relations are:

For the left-hand subset ($x \leqslant 1920$ hours = 1 year)
$$\log y = 3.003 + 08239 \log x \pm t \left\{ \begin{matrix} 0.0025^1 \\ 0.009178^2 \end{matrix} \right\} -$$
$$- 0.0001602 \log x + 0.00004203 (\log x)^2$$

For the right hand subset ($x \geqslant 1920$ hours = 1 year)
$$\log y = 0.7955 + 0.7808 \log x \pm t \left\{ \begin{matrix} 0.032444^1 \\ 0.037996^2 \end{matrix} \right\} -$$
$$- 0.018539 \log x + 0.002661 (\log x)^2$$

---

[1] Constant term of confidence intervals about the mean.
[2] Constant term of confidence intervals about a random element.

The plotted curves were calculated with values of t for the 5% confidence interval.

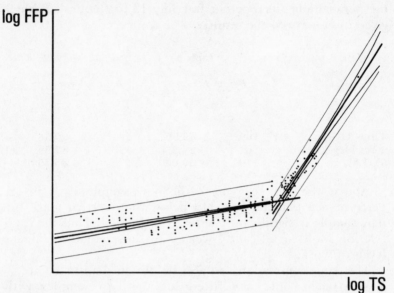

Figure 7.

The new sample is not however at all homogeneous. Regressions were run for each firm separately, see Table 4.

While no large firm attains an $r^2 = .875$, like Glacier, a sizeable number give good results. Discounting Firm 8 where $r^2 = 1$ as a freak, it is interesting that only two firms (1 and, as usual, 6) with a large number of observations are mainly responsible for the low value of the total r^2, whereas Firm 2 with 20 observations and Firm 3 with 7 give high values. With respect to inter-firm variation the picture is then mixed, the largest firm (No. 6) again being the worse performer.[10]

Having discussed variability among firms as far as the data

10. The reasons for the uniqueness of this firm in the sample must be indicated despite the general policy of avoiding detailed characterisation of establishments, which is a usual method of special pleading. Firm 6 was selected because it was the only firm which allowed investigation at the workshop level. A contributory cause of this was that the firm was not unionised, and hence did not require anybody's consent for the task-analysis exercise. A possible contributory cause for that state of affairs may have been the fact that the male labour employed in that firm was to a large extent unskilled immigrant labour. It may also have been of significance that one half of the processes studied were being modernised while the other half were due for modernisation. Finally, the

will allow, it is also useful to look at another aspect of the relation. It may be that the high closeness of fit at the upper half of the range imposes a non-existent relation on the lower half where there is none, in other words that time-span does not predict felt-fair pay for the range of time-span between twenty minutes (the lowest value in the sample) and some higher value such as six months or one year. In this case the true relation at the lower end of the range would be flat, i.e. have zero slope. It is therefore useful to ask whether the estimated slope for each firm is significantly different from zero.

Table 4 supplies the necessary information. The t-value of the estimated slope can be compared with the value at different levels of significance. It is noteworthy that firm 6 with r^2 = .1498 has significantly non-zero slope at the 10% level. Firms 5 and 7 do not yield significant estimates even at the 10% level but they yield a total of only 7 observations. Firm 2 as well as 11 (Glacier) yield significant estimates at the 0.1% level. As for the totals, both with and without Glacier, the slopes are significantly non-zero at the 0.1% level. It can therefore be concluded that, although from this sample it appears to be weaker at lower levels of time-span than higher up, the relationship is not spurious anywhere in the range. It is not possible to analyse the difference between high and low levels of work within each firm because there are not enough observations.

We can conclude that a weak (i.e. general) version of Jaques' hypothesis is not contradicted by the facts: there is a significant relationship at all levels of work and it has the postulated shape. The analysis of the data also suggests that the labour market is divided in two parts with respect to the time-span variable. This need not imply, however, that the two parts behave independently in all respects. It could well be that with respect to payment norms (relatives) over the longer period the labour market operates as one whole.[11]

---

incidence of women was highest in this firm, 23 out of 46. It may be the case that these factors taken all together account for relatively unclear reference groups and are thus an inadequate basis for comparisons for arriving at felt-fair pay. This does not mean, however, that either the time-span measurements or the felt-fair pay statements were in any degree less correct or credible than those obtained elsewhere.

11. See Chapter Four below.

Table 4
Results of Double-Logarithmic Straight Line Regression = Low Levels of Work

Firms	Estimated of Slope	t-value of Estimate	Levels of Significance				r^2	N
			(10%)	5%	1%	(0.1%)		
1	0.1529	2.05	(1.78)	2.18	3.05	—	24.5	16
2	0.1866	5.96		2.09	2.85	(3.85)	65.14	22
3	0.2134	5.45		2.45	3.71	(5.96)	83.22	16
4	0.2521	0.99	(2.35)	3.18	5.84		24.7	5
5	0.1261	2.27	(2.92)	4.30	9.92		72.05	4
6	0.0483	2.75		2.02	2.70	(3.5)	14.98	46
7	0.1108	0.76	(2.92)	4.30	9.92		22.47	4
8	0.3578	5.49		3.18	5.84		100.0	5
9	—	—	—	—	—		—	4
10	—	—	—	—	—		—	1
11	0.1455	20.33		2.00	2.66	(3.46)	85.7	70
1-8	0.749	9.16		1.99	2.62	(3.37)	43.95	120
1-11	0.824	12.71		1.97	2.60	(3.29)	49.02	195

We next turn to a stronger version of Jaques' hypothesis.

4. Jaques' Equitable Payment Scale

Figures 8 and 9 show confidence intervals for a random element and about the mean of the Standard Relation at the 5% level of significance.

The estimated relations are:

$$\log y = 3.067 - 0.00331 \log x - 0.03677 (\log x)^2 + 0.02128 (\log x)^3 \pm$$

$$\pm t \left\{ \begin{matrix} 0.0002024^1 \\ 0.006817^2 \end{matrix} \right\} - 0.0004911 \log x +$$

$$+ 0.001219 (\log x)^2 - 0.001273 (\log x)^3 + 0.0006235 (\log x)^4 - 0.0001449 (\log x)^5 + 0.00001296 (\log x)^6$$

[1] Constant term for confidence interval about the mean.
[2] Constant term for confidence interval about a random element.

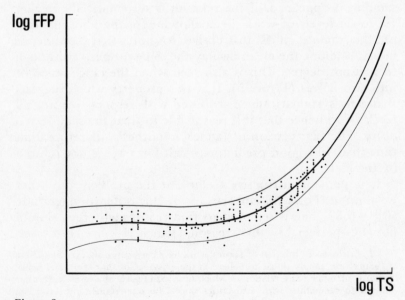

log FFP

log TS

Figure 8

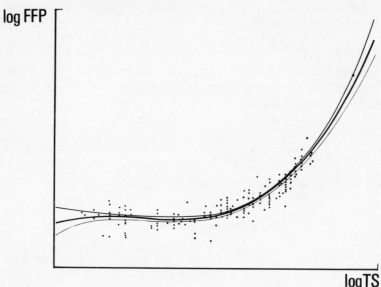

Figure 9.

Figures 8 and 9 confirm the visual impression that absolute variation of y is unaffected by x, so that, from this particular sample, it appears as if the relation is systematically weaker for lower levels of work. Even allowing for the idiosyncrasies of the sample, it is instructive to note that confidence intervals about the mean display the same property, although to a minor degree. This is also seen when the range was split into two halves (Figure 5). It is this property which suggests that y is systematically distributed with respect to x for all levels of x; hence that it is reasonable to treat the sample as a unity. The first version of Jaques' hypothesis, therefore, that time-span is a good predictor of felt-fair pay, is not refuted by the facts.

It is perhaps instructive to look at the problem the other way round. For with correlations of this order of magnitude ($R^2 = 0.89$) one is tempted to find reasons why they should not be perfect.[12] One reason, which I have not seen

12. Criticisms of this part of Jaques' work have been curiously extreme. There are some who simply refuse to believe in the existence of time-spans and hence cannot contemplate any relation in which time-span figures as a variable. It is not difficult to sympathise with such critics since I for one retained my scepticism until I tried to carry out analyses myself. There are others who do not dispute

elsewhere and which is pertinent over the whole range but more so with respect to the bottom half, is that while pay is for practical purposes a continuous variable, time-span is not. Tasks are assigned target completion times of one week, or one year, or one decade, not of 2,000 hours or 1.35 months. In view of this it is remarkable that the correlations are as good as perfect — and it is fortunate that at least the bottom half of the range behaves badly.

The natural discontinuities which are found in practice when measuring time-spans led Jaques to devise a scale for frequently occurring values. The 'Equitable Work-Payment Scale' is the strongest version of his hypothesis about the relation between the two variables we are examining.[13]

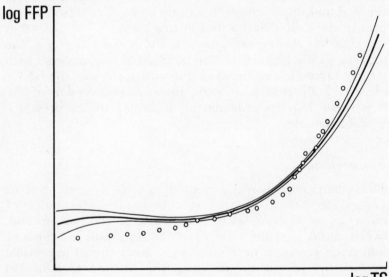

Figure 10.

that time-spans as such exist but consider that any relation with felt-fair pay is an irrelevancy since (in some sense) 'we know' that the time for which responsibility is carried has to do with the capacity to take decisions, that most decisions have to do with administration of property, and (somehow) it is not surprising that there should be correlation with what is thought of as fair earnings. The courts, for example, have developed penalties and rules of compensation on the basis of 'reasonable foresight', i.e. the time-span that should go with persons in the exercise of their social responsibilities. For people who think of this kind of relationship as some sort of a tautology, there is no reason why the fit between time-span and felt-fair pay should not be perfect.

13. See *Time-Span Handbook*.

Figure 10 shows the Scale in relation to the confidence intervals about the mean of the Standard Relation. It is clear that this version of the hypothesis cannot be accepted as it stands. Whereas 20 out of the 27 points of the Scale fall within the confidence intervals of the Standard Relation, the slope of the Scale is different both to the left and to the right of the kink. The scale thus tends to 'underpay' the low-paid and 'overpay' the higher paid, according to their own valuation of what constitutes fair pay for their work, at least as represented in this particular sample (including Jaques' own data).

It may of course be that the slopes of the average relation have shifted with time. There is evidence of flatter slope at the mid and upper ranges in a study by R. Richardson in one firm in the United States. But in that instance it appears that the kink has also moved upwards, and become flatter in the process, as if a higher absolute standard of incomes goes with greater homogeneity between the two sectors of the labour market.[14] Be that as it may, the strongest version of the hypothesis requires amendment according to the presently available sample.

5. Conclusion

The quantitative work presented here is a severe test of Jaques' hypothesis in that it covers a broader range of observations than his own, particularly at the bottom end, over a rather extreme variety of firms, locations and types of job. Such testing is necessary to get away from the possible peculiarities of the special case. The method of public in contrast to confidential analysis also brings the technique nearer to the hands of its natural users, the firms' management. This study therefore confirms that time-spans exist in the simple sense that they can be measured with objectivity and rigour. The three versions of Jaques' hypothesis are all confirmed with some amendment for the stricter one among them.

We can summarise the quantitative basis of Jaques' proposition as follows:

14. See Chapter Four below.

(a) The total of 11 firms, giving 195 observations, fit a cubic relationship with $r^2 = 0.89$.

(b) Jaques' original data (firm 11 in the Appendix and represented with circles in Fig. 1) fit a cubic relation with $r^2 = 0.94$ for 70 observations.

(c) The new sample (firms 1 to 10 in the Appendix and represented with dots in Fig. 1) fit a cubic relation with $r^2 = 0.84$ for 125 observations.

(d) Individual firms vary, in terms of closeness of fit, between $r^2 = 0.25$ and $r^2 = 0.98$, according to range of observations and position within the overall scatter.

(e) The relation can be presumed to fall into two natural parts, divided by the kink in the middle of the (logarithmic) range. The association between time-span and felt-fair pay appears generally weaker to the left of the kink, but it is not possible to attribute the cause as between the value of time span as such and/or characteristics of specific firms, as it is a single firm which dominates the lower range with 46 observations.

(f) Jaques' 'Equitable Payment Scale' falls mostly within the 95% confidence limit of the best overall cubic relation but has slightly different slope from it.

(g) Both halves of the relationship are statistically significant for all firms and all levels of work.

(h) Hence the time-span of discretion is a good predictor of felt-fair pay even if all other factors which may be considered to affect felt-fair pay are ignored.

Appendix A: The Data

(TS = Time Span of Discretion
FFP = Felt-fair pay)

FIRM 1

N	1	2	3	4	5	6	7
TS	160	320	320	320	320	320	640
FFP	1170	1200	1300	1400	1475	2080	1900

N	8	9	10	11	12	13	14
TS	800	960	960	960	960	1280	1920
FFP	1400	1500	1500	1600	2710	1800	1500

N	15	16
TS	1920	2880
FFP	2150	2900

FIRM 2

N	1	2	3	4	5	6	7
TS	28	80	80	80	100	100	120
FFP	1620	1150	1300	1300	1200	1530	1350

N	8	9	10	11	12	13	14
TS	180	200	320	400	400	400	400
FFP	1300	1500	1350	1290	1580	2000	2135

N	15	16	17	18	19	20	21
TS	480	640	1440	1440	1680	1920	1920
FFP	1800	2000	2450	2600	2000	2500	3000

N	22
TS	3360
FFP	3750

FIRM 3

N	1	2	3	4	5	6	7
TS	8	40	320	960	1440	1440	1920
FFP	900	750	1825	1950	2000	3000	2150

N	8	9	10	11	12	13	14
TS	1920	2400	2880	3040	3840	3840	5440
FFP	2400	3250	3500	3000	3300	4395	3800

N	15	16
TS	5760	5760
FFP	4500	4850

FIRM 4

N	1	2	3	4	5
TS	480	800	960	960	1920
FFP	1500	2350	1500	2500	2250

FIRM 5

N	1	2	3	4
TS	16	100	960	960
FFP	1100	1000	1600	1850

FIRM 6

N	1	2	3	4	5	6
TS	0.3	0.35	0.5	0.5	0.65	0.75
FFP	1300	1215	1144	1380	1250	780

N	7	8	9	10	11	12	13
TS	1	1	1	1	1	1	1
FFP	780	1150	1196	1300	1300	1300	1300

N	14	15	16	17	18	19	20
TS	1	1	1.5	1.5	1.5	1.5	1.5
FFP	1560	1664	998	1225	1250	1265	1440

N	21	22	23	24	25	26	27
TS	2	2	2	2	2	2	2
FFP	780	780	805	832	1040	1040	1065

N	28	29	30	31	32	33	34
TS	2	2	2	2	2	2.5	2.5
FFP	1100	1196	1196	1404	1475	1227	1404

N	35	36	37	38	39	40	41
TS	8	8	8	40	160	160	160
FFP	985	1380	1970	832	1280	1425	1584

N	42	43	44	45	46
TS	160	160	160	480	2400
FFP	1612	1716	1800	1800	2500

FIRM 7

N	1	2	3	4
TS	20	80	480	960
FFP	1248	702	1100	1900

FIRM 8

N	1	2	3	4	5
TS	240	960	1680	1920	2320
FFP	1200	1600	2350	2600	2200

FIRM 9

N	1	2	3	4
TS	560	2720	3840	6240
FFP	2850	3300	3500	4000

FIRM 10

N	1
TS	34560
FFP	25000

FIRM 11 (GLACIER)

N	1	2	3	4	5	6	7
TS	6	6	6	8	12	16	16
FFP	920	940	950	1020	1030	920	990

N	8	9	10	11	12	13	14
TS	16	16	20	24	24	26	32
FFP	1120	1260	1130	1060	1140	1010	1090

N	15	16	17	18	19	20	21
TS	40	60	60	65	70	80	80
FFP	1120	1210	1300	1500	1260	1220	1240

N	22	23	24	25	26	27	28
TS	80	120	120	120	120	120	130
FFP	1340	1240	1300	1360	1520	1700	1200

N	29	30	31	32	33	34	35
TS	160	160	160	180	200	240	280
FFP	1340	1360	1480	1260	1400	1720	1480

N	36	37	38	39	40	41	42
TS	320	320	320	400	480	640	640
FFP	1300	1450	1500	1780	1580	1620	1730

N	43	44	45	46	47	48	49
TS	960	960	960	960	960	1040	1440
FFP	1640	1680	1780	1840	1930	1840	1890

N	50	51	52	53	54	55	56
TS	1440	1440	1500	1600	1760	1920	1920
FFP	2000	2400	1860	2520	2050	2090	2150

N	57	58	59	60	61	62	63
TS	1920	1920	1920	2400	2400	2880	2880
FFP	2350	2500	2600	2620	2650	3550	3750

N	64	65	66	67	68	69	70
TS	2880	2880	3840	3840	3840	3840	4760
FFP	4150	4200	4000	4080	4100	5150	6500

Appendix B
Jaques' Equitable Payment Scale

RANK I	Time Span Natural Units	Hours	Felt-Fair Pay* January 1954	Mid-1960
1	15 minutes	0.25	588	755
2	1 hour	1	619	800
3	2 hours	2	635	825
4	½ day	4	650	845
5	1 day	8	697	900
6	2 days	16	728	940
7	3 days	24	765	995
8	5 days = 1 week	40	853	1100
9	2 weeks	80	874	1130
10	4 weeks = 1 month	160	967	1250
11	2 months	320	1024	1330
RANK II				
12	3 months	480	1090	1410
13	6 months	960	1240	1600
14	9 months	1440	1440	1840
RANK III				
15	12 months = 1 year	1920	1650	2100
16	15 months	2400	2040	2680
17	18 months	2880	2410	3150
18	21 months	3360	2860	3675
RANK IV	Time Span Natural Units	Hours	Felt-Fair Pay January 1954	Mid-1960
19	2 years	3840	3400	4400
20	3 years	5760	4300	5000
21	3½ years	6720	4900	6350
22	4 years	7680	5450	7000

* The pay figures were originally stated in weekly pounds and shillings for rank I, hence the strange yearly figures. (For a note on felt-fair pay see over.)

RANK V

| 23 | 5 years | 9600 | 6800 | 8750 |
| 24 | 7½ years | 14400 | 9750 | 12600 |

RANK VI

| 25 | 10 years | 19200 | 13500 | 17600 |
| 26 | 15 years | 28800 | 19000 | 24250 |

RANK VII

| 27 | 20 years | 3840 | 27000 | 35000 |

Note

Felt-fair pay figures are in answer to the question: 'What do you consider is fair pay for your job as you are doing it now?' Capacity felt-fair pay, which is referred to in Part II below, is in answer to the question: 'What do you consider fair pay for a job which would be just right for you?' The two answers may of course be the same — it may be worth pointing out that, as emerges clearly in Part II, actual pay seldom coincides with either felt-fair statement of pay and is as often greater as it is smaller than either.

CHAPTER FOUR

A Labour Market Interpretation

1. A micro-micro market

This chapter presents an attempt to construct an economic process of a labour market which can produce results compatible with Jaques' empirical relationship. It is possible to approach this objective with a standard supply and demand diagram, modified to contain as units those which have been defined in Chapter One and measured in Chapters Two and Three above.

Our first job is to show that these units can be fitted on a supply and demand diagram. This might seem superfluous after our extensive discussion of the time-span concept. A justification is required, however, because our labour input unit still lacks an important economic characteristic, that of existence under disequilibrium conditions. For the definition of the time horizon of responsibility in Chapter One is only valid as an equilibrium construct: under conditions of minimisation-maximisation, both from the supply and from the demand side, it is possible to reduce the n-dimensional delegated decision set for the individual worker on to the time axis which defines the task and its time-span.

But such conditions are purely logical; they can exist only in a static logical framework. In reality no role can be expected to be perfectly fitted to the man and no man can be expected to be perfectly fitted to the role. Further, no role as currently specified can be expected to be in equilibrium within and for the organisation. To construct a schedule of the supply and the demand for labour we must therefore reconsider the concept of the time-span of discretion in a context of time, which is to say in a context of forces at work which will tend, if an equilibrium exists, to the concept as defined and measured above. To do this properly we have to start from an analysis of the supply price and the demand price of labour in the short period, an analysis which, contrary to the usual practice, depends on short period interdependence between supply and demand forces.

Supply price

In a given short period the individual worker has a certain capital of skills and knowledge. He also has specific expectations of the type of work and the range of pay he is likely to get, expectations which are necessarily related to his past and particularly his recent experience. Regardless of the type and degree of organisation of the labour market, the individual worker is unlikely to know very much else.

Let us assume, for convenience, that the worker is already employed. His work, therefore, as defined by the organisation, has a task and time-span specification. Regardless of whether either the organisation or the worker is in equilibrium,[1] there is now an extant and measurable time-span. The worker is also paid a certain wage. What room is there for a concept of disequilibrium in any such given short period situation?

Dissatisfaction on the part of the worker may arise from either or both of two classes of phenomena. First, he may be dissatisfied with the prescribed content of his work. For example, the work may simply be too much. It may be too arduous, or the environmental conditions may be unpleasant. Alternatively, he may be dissatisfied with the level of responsibility he is allowed to carry. The content of the role, so far as he is concerned, may be fully integrated[2] in respect of physical arduousness and environmental conditions. Nevertheless it may be that the role is so defined as to carry a level

1. The concept of equilibrium in this study follows from the static characterisation of the task concept as a unit of labour input, in Chapter One above. The complementary notion of disequilibrium will be introduced below. There is no escaping from the fact that both notions are tentative. In what follows, the reader's sympathy is strongly requested to assist the process of groping towards a mechanism of interaction between the forces of supply and demand, through which we can also give meaning to the notions of equilibrium and disequilibrium.

2. The idea of an 'integrated' role comes from the observation of certain regularities in the prescribed content of work. For example, it is rare to find roles which have twenty one-week tasks and one two-year task. The idea is largely implicit in the analysis of the labour market but seems of sufficient interest in its own right. It is further discussed in Part II, which contains case studies in a more empirical context.

of responsibility other than that which the worker considers right for the job as performed or is perhaps performable by himself.

We thus make a sharp distinction between dissatisfaction which may be due to the knowledge component of the worker's ability to perform assigned tasks and the responsibility component of the role. We note also that these two types of disequilibria are entirely independent of any additional disequilibrium which may arise on the subject of pay. The pay may be right while the job is not. Or, the job may be right, while the pay is not. To construct a schedule of the supply of labour we must therefore show that there is a trade-off among the prescribed, the discretionary, and the pay aspects of a job.

To show the nature of the trade-off among these three sources of disequilibrium requires that we specify mechanisms which make the disequilibrium perceivable by the individual worker. We must, in other words, pose an information problem of the form, 'How does the individual worker get to know that his role is not integrated with respect to prescribed, discretionary and pay components?' We suppose that the information mechanism which is available to the individual worker is that of making comparisons with his peers. Each individual has a certain experience from working over a period of time next to other individuals. He comes to rate individuals as such, as well as the prescribed content of jobs around him, the discretionary content of these jobs and the associated pay. For the given short period the individual worker has already made these comparisons. He knows whether, in his opinion, he is getting the right share, for himself, of the three components of the job situation. We do not imply that there is anything objective, or rational, or anything else, about these opinions. They are simply held and are valid for the individual worker for the given short period.

We postulate a trade-off between prescribed and discretionary components of work such that the more prescribed delegation is assigned to the job the greater is the responsibility that will be demanded to cope with the additional load of prescribed content. This positive trade-off is of course the opposite of the usual postulate associating utilities with disutilities. In the present approach, however, *work as such is not considered as a disutility.*[3] Work for the individual is part of his natural social condition in the given cultural set up.[4] Disutility arises from the wrong share of work, or of some component of work, *vis à vis* the individual's working peers.

When comparing load of work as between the prescribed and discretionary components, therefore, the individual can only proceed by comparing himself, component by component, with those other individuals with whom he considers it fair to rate himself. If, from a given position, he is given more prescribed content without any change in his discretionary component, then of necessity the borrowing of time he can do as between shorter and longer tasks is reduced. He has less slack than in the previous situation and so cannot achieve the fair standard of quality which rates him as equal to other individuals. To preserve his position at the level of the given quality with which he associates himself he has one recourse, to demand greater discretionary authority so that he can borrow to the requisite extent.[5] The supply of one kind of work, the prescribed component, therefore goes with greater supply of the other kind of work, the discretionary component.

We next postulate a positive trade-off between the discretionary component of work and pay. For now the discretionary component must be associated with a public fact of industrial life, namely pay. If the individual worker only has comparisons with other workers as the means of information concerning his position, then the comparisons must have a publicly known component. There must be something that stands, as it were, objectively in the view of others concerning this particular individual's social position. There would be no point in the individual worker being able

3. This statement is independent of whether or not the individual worker has more than one available opportunity for work.

4. This view of work, as part of an individual's normal social life, is of course very similar to that held by Marshall.

5. An individual worker may demand a greater time-span in two senses: first, he would simply like to have more discretion. But secondly, he may actively ask for more discretion by all the processes of pressure and consultation available in the culture of industrial life. The model we are considering permits all sorts of interactions between demand and supply, other than the price of work.

to compare himself favourably with himself if others, in turn, cannot be made aware of whether this individual compares as before or not. But the prescribed content is highly multi-dimensional, so that the information-flows concerning its content are necessarily incomplete. The time-span of discretion, if measured, is perfectly communicable, but generally it is highly implicit and can only figure in the individual's comparisons with others as an experienced, or felt, variable which cannot therefore be easily communicated to others. Pay, on the other hand, is extremely clear cut. Regardless of how it is arrived at, as a flat rate, or as overtime, or as danger money, or whatnot, it remains that there is a specific pay packet at the end of the short period which is public knowledge. The discretionary content of work and the pay component are therefore also related by a positive trade-off: more of one means more of the other.[6]

It now follows from the complementary relationship between the prescribed and discretionary components of work that, regardless of whether or not the role is in equilibrium in respect of these two components, it suffices to use the third measurable component, the time-span of discretion, as sufficient proxy for the unit of labour input supplied. It also follows that, insofar as the time-span of discretion and pay (or the supply price of work) are concerned, the positive trade-off means that we postulate an upward-sloping supply curve of labour for the elementary, nuclear level of the labour market. So far, then, the argument is that there is a range in which time-span and supply price vary together so that there is rising supply price of labour, as in the orthodox treatment.[7]

6. The argument is meant to be general and should not be confined to the environment of the workshop. We have no reason to constrain the information available to the individual worker to fit into any particular environment. Some individuals find the workshop too large as a referent group, while others find the world too small. We return to the question of information in Sections Two and Three below, where we attempt to distinguish different types of relevant information for the process of adjustment of supply to demand, and vice versa. For the moment the argument abstracts from the range of environments where it can be valid, an abstraction which is compatible with the assumption of overall tranquility; see below.

7. Equilibrium labour input for the individual worker means that he is on his trade-offs between the two components of work, the prescribed component and the discretionary component. In conditions of equilibrium, input supplied is therefore fully represented by the time-span of discretion. Rising supply price is

We may note in passing that strictly rising supply price may be an unduly restrictive construction. If the short period were one of tranquillity, if in other words it was expected to be roughly as it turned out to be, then there is nothing wrong with postulating rising supply for labour. If, on the other hand, the short period is planned as a transition from one state of affairs to another, there is nothing contradictory in supposing that there is also a range of falling supply price. An instance of this would be, for example, when in a given short period an individual worker is opting for a better job in spite of lower pay, because he expects that this better job will sooner or later put him where he is truly fitted to be in relation to his peers, and that sooner or later the pay component will also come to justify this new position. It is convenient for the analysis, however, to assume a state of tranquillity, so that the addition (aggregation) of individual workers' supply curves does not pose any problem of weighting as between the two possible directions of supply price. (We make use of this assumption to discuss the operation of a 'local' labour market in Section Two below). The x-axis of these supply curves is calibrated in calendar time units representing the time-span of discretion which, as we have argued above, represents all the other components of labour input by virtue of the postulated positive trade-off.[8]

The next step is to consider the factors which affect the elasticity of the supply curve for the individual worker. We can bring here another given for the short period, a variable which can be thought of as a stock and refers to the level of responsibility which an individual has been prepared to undertake by his past experience. This is the individual's *capacity*, and it plays the role of an upper bound beyond which the responsibility content of work becomes a disutility. We can then say that the elasticity of the short period individual supply curve depends on how close the given short

strictly associated with labour input as the trade-off between equilibrium labour input and pay. We may, however, also associate rising supply price with disequilibrium labour input, provided we hold to the weaker requirement of general tranquility; see below.

8. This postulate is not, of course, arbitrary. Rather it is a formal expression of the argument developed in Chapters Two and Three, as well as being supported by the weight of the qualitative evidence presented through the case studies in Part II.

period time-span is to its capacity value. The closer it is to this capacity value the greater the increase of supply price that will be required to induce an individual to proceed from a level of responsibility which yields utility to a level of responsibility which eventually becomes disutility.

Independently therefore of the environmental range of comparisons the individual is making with his peers,[9] there are also internal or subjective constraints which prevent him from carrying the comparison unrealistically too far. That is to say, we assume that the individual has the measure of his own capacity which defines the range of his comparisons. He compares himself with other individuals who, in his view, are of equivalent capacity. He responds more elastically to price the farther he is from his perceived capacity level and continues to respond so long as the increment of responsibility still lies on the utility side. As responsibility is increased and approaches the disutility level supply price must rise faster so as to compensate for the emerging disutility component. Supply price is therefore rising at an increasing rate.

Next we consider the possible range of the two variables, work and pay, for a specific individual in a given short period. We postulate that the range of variation of the labour input variable is contained within a qualitatively homogeneous quantum of responsibility. In one of his most original papers[10] Jaques has suggested the concept of an *experienced*, as distinct from a *measured*, level of responsibility. This experienced level of responsibility is defined on the managerial hierarchy but does not congruently correspond to the time scale. The units for the experienced level of responsibility, the 'ranks', refer to the level of abstraction which corresponds to the exercise of responsibility at a certain level and therefore also to the substantive managerial ranks in the organisational hierarchy. The argument of that paper is too rich to be summarised here. Suffice it to say that on the strength of that argument Jaques is able to suggest an entirely psychological hypothesis of social-managerial stratification. This is because there is a linear association of the ranks with

9. See note 6 above.
10. 'Notes Towards a Theory of Managerial Ranks' in *Glacier Project Papers*.

the logarith of felt-fair pay,[11] a phenomenon analogous to the psychological law concerning experienced sensations and their valuation proposed by Weber and Fechner.

For our purposes, what the theory of ranks suggests is a sequence of *discontinuities* of the experienced level of responsibility superimposed on the continuous range of cardinal responsibility. In the short period the capacity level of the individual is given. Under tranquillity conditions the individual worker is approximately where he expected to be. It follows that his capacity in the short period is within a homogeneous experienced segment, marked off by discontinuities of quality rather than merely by size of level of responsibility carried.

The superimposition of non-homogeneous ranks on the diagrams of Chapter Three yields a suggestion for the value of the elasticity of supply. Jaques' ranks become bunched on those diagrams towards the higher end so that the segments of homogeneous qualitative level of responsibility are longest at the origin and become progressively shorter for the higher ranks towards the top end of the curve. If we add the assumption made above, that individuals consider work as utility up to their capacity limit, it follows that the elasticity of labour supply is greater the lower the rank as well as the lower the time-span. We shall make use of this suggestion from a more aggregative point of view when we consider situations of market disequilibrium in section three below.

To characterise the limits of variation of supply price we have to bring in additional considerations. In the given short period the individual has a reservation price derived from his past experience. In the case of an individual who is already employed, as in our present argument, this reservation price is of little importance. Under conditions of tranquillity we can therefore say very little about it. We must nevertheless ask what the individual considers to be the principles whereby he would arrive at his, so to say, long-period reservation price. For regardless of the present state of employment and the expected prospects, the individual

11. This association is meant to be as broadly applicable as the time-span-felt-fair pay association examined in Chapter Three. No specific field work, however, was conducted for this study, and accordingly the concept of 'rank' is used is the present argument only in a heuristic sense.

worker will still have a view of the rock-bottom price he will be prepared to accept if things turned out to be entirely wrong.[12]

To discuss the rationale of the reservation price we have to consider the alternatives open to the individual. Insofar as these alternatives are in any sense close to the present situation, we would expect that the reservation price will be quite close to the current wage. For, under conditions of tranquility, the individual worker envisages a normal pattern of labour turnover and therefore has an expectation of normal jobs and normal pay more or less ready to hand. If, on the other hand, the situation turns out to be (progressively) worse than expected, then the alternatives which effectively present themselves will also be (progressively) further removed from the present situation.

How quickly an individual worker will adjust his reservation price will depend on his ability to finance his search, his expectations about the duration of untoward conditions, etc., as well as the specific institutions of the labour market. Regardless, however, of the speed of response to the evidence of adversity, there is one price which for the worker must surely be subsistence.[13] This is the price that he could obtain by opting out of the industrial system altogether. Under conditions of general macro-economic collapse this price could well be zero and subsistence would simply mean starvation. Under conditions of tranquillity, however, there is an alternative open to every category of worker in an industrial society, and that is self-employment. The availability of subsistence alternative employment is a modern phenomenon, in that it presupposes a substantial tertiary sector, parallel to the industrial sector of the economy, where self-employment with little capital and almost regardless of skill can yield a living wage to virtually every category of worker.[14]

12. As before, the argument is intended to be general and therefore abstracts from institutional facts such as social security, etc.

13. The idea for this treatment of the reservation price comes from Lydall's 'one man firm' in 'A Theory of Distribution and Growth with Economies of Scale', *Economic Journal*, March 1971.

14. Joan Robinson's original analysis of a two-sector labour market is in her paper 'Disguised Unemployment', reprinted in *Collected Papers*, vol. 4. Her argument contains the, to my knowledge, original hypothesis of a 'dual' labour market structure. The emphasis in that paper is on the macro-economic

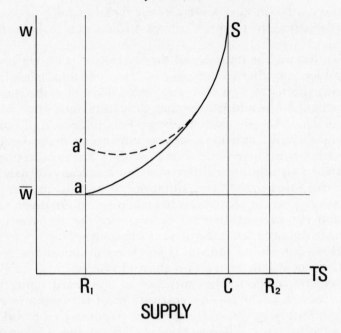

Figure 1.

We postulate that the self-employment alternative is available for every level of responsibility, because the size, complexity, and vigour of the tertiary sector provides some parallel in that sector to every industrial job for virtually every individual participant in the labour market.[15] We shall make use of this two-sector feature of the labour market in the analysis of relative wage movements below. For the moment we just take the existence of a service sector as a sufficient condition to provide each worker, under conditions of tranquility, with a reservation price not much below the price he is actually getting for his labour.

implications of a subsistence wage mechanism as a substitute for unemployment, whereas the present argument concentrates on the micro-economic effect of expectations concerning the 'ultimate' margin of labour mobility. The similarity between the two arguments is that neither considers work as an alternative to leisure — where people may starve. Supply price is bounded below by subsistence when this is available, not by the disutility of not giving up leisure, as leisure is by itself not available at all.

15. For example, in the two cases presented in Chapter One, the chocolate-bar lady could become a cleaner whereas a shipping managing director could become a consultant.

The argument on the individual labourer's short period supply function can now be summarised in a diagram (see Figure 1). The vertical axis measures the money wage while the horizontal axis measures the time-span of discretion in time units. The horizontal dimension is marked off by two lines, R_1 and R_2, which denote discontinuities in the quality of responsibility carried or managerial ranks. Within the R_1 R_2 effective labour input range we mark off by C the given perceived level of capacity of the individual. On the vertical axis we mark $\overline{W}$ as the reservation wage, as defined above. The supply curve then starts at the inter-section of W and R_1 and climbs progressively more steeply until it reaches the capacity level, where it becomes perfectly inelastic. The supply curve embodies the current expectations of the individual worker concerning the fair position for himself in his social comparisons, both for this short period and through time.

Demand price

We turn next to the consideration of the factors determining demand price. The first point to note is that, whereas supply refers to a specific person, demand is concerned with an impersonal role holder. Supply refers to a totality of commitment and a totality of social relations. Demand refers to the specification of the job which is satisfactory for the organisational and other objectives of the firm, whose pay is also satisfactory from the viewpoint of the firm, but which can be filled by any odd individual who accepts the job and can do it satisfactorily. The social relations that enter the demand side are of course also important, since in defining jobs and filling them with particular individuals the firm cannot ignore the implications of the existing job structure on the other individuals working within it. Such social relations are nevertheless secondary. The firm specifies requirements, it fills in a slot in a pattern, it is not interested directly in the satisfaction that people will receive: the firm is not really fitting round pegs into square holes, it is willing to leave at least half of the adjustment to the pegs. Let us see this two-sided adjustment process as a short-period micro-micro labour-market mechanism.

In the short period the requirements, or the required content for a job, are of course given. The job exists from the past and is performed at some level of responsibility within a more or less integrated job structure. But the firm has considerable flexibility in adjusting the job within the short period. It may marginally vary the prescribed content, it may marginally redefine the qualitative component and it may marginally alter the time-span of discretion. It may do any or all of these things either for reasons directly arising from the demand side or in response to supply. It may wish, for example, to adjust the role to the cluster of the organisational hierarchy around it. It may equally wish to adjust the role in response to evidence of disequilibrium from the side of supply, e.g. feelings of dissatisfaction communicated to the firm by the job holder.

Now the individual worker may also offer to adjust his behaviour to the requirements of the firm under conditions of tranquillity. His expectations about the prescribed, the discretionary and the pay components of work are not absolutely rigid. There is a range for each component which represents to him tolerable departures from the equilibrium position of his trade-offs, tolerable in the sense that his expectations are not altered at least for the current short period. The individual may even revise his trade-offs as between the components of work in response to short period comparisons with his peer group. But under conditions of tranquility such revision will again be marginal and will not disturb the short-period expectations.

In summary, then, both the firm and the individual job holder may, within limits, vary the short-period requirements and offers related to a specific job. Demand and supply are at least partly interdependent within the short period.

Whereas, however, the individual only adjusts himself through his social comparisons, the firm must also take account of the impact of change in any individual job on the rest of the hierarchy. The firm must therefore have a longer horizon, it must commit itself to more specific expectations about the evolution of the job structure, it must have a strategy concerning its organisation and part of this strategy is the development of manpower. It follows that the firm may be in more than marginal short period disequilibrium

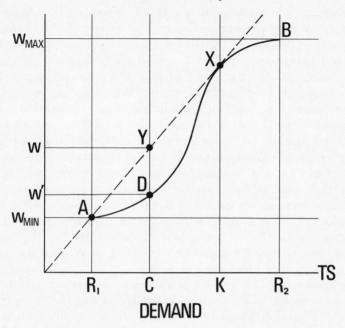

Figure 2.

with respect to any particular job taken by itself. But such localised disequilibria will still be marginal in relation to the overall policy, meaning by 'policy' the rational level of abstraction for the level of the firm. The firm, in other words, may in its view over-pay or under-pay a particular individual to a greater extent than a particular individual may feel under-paid or over-paid because the firm has to administer a whole structure of internal wages. Equilibrium for the firm and equilibrium for the worker operate at different levels of abstraction and this is one of the characteristics of asymmetry between the two sides of the labour market. We shall see below how these asymmetric forces acting on demand price and supply price work to determine market price.

We now turn to a diagrammatic presentation of the demand curve (see Figure 2). We assume, for convenience, that the job concerned is already filled and that the firm is generally satisfied with the job holder's performance. We also assume that the firm has designed the job within a range of

homogeneous quality of levels of responsibility independently of the present occupant. In Figure 2 this designed
range is represented by the two extreme lines R_1 and R_2.
Within this range the firm is tooled up for the job, not only
in relation to specific types of capital equipment required as
a complement to human effort but also for the other
complementary functions, including the informational and
control set-up, around this particular job. The firm considers
that its tooling up corresponds to a level of responsibility
marked in our diagram by K. This does not, however, mean
that the firm must necessarily employ complementary labour
input at level K so as to minimise the costs of its tooling
up. The manner of defining K simply means that the firm
thinks it is tooled up roughly right for roughly that level of
responsibility. Since the job is already filled, in the firm's
view satisfactorily, we can give meaning to K with the same
rough degree of precision.

The demand for labour is therefore expressed within the
range from R_1 to R_2 with special reference to the range close
to the capital component K. (For purposes of illustration we
also assume that the individual's capacity is below K and
mark C accordingly.)

We can think of the movement of demand price over the
broader range R_1 R_2 as well as in the narrower range close to
K. The firm knows, in the same manner that the housewife
knows, that cut-price workers are not worth the having.
There is therefore a minimum level of pay, W_{min}, which
corresponds to the minimum level of work the firm would
consider worth having for this type of job, in the broadest
homogeneous range that the firm considers as relevant.
Similarly, there is a maximum demand price, marked
W_{max}, which corresponds to the maximum wage the firm
would consider for any job holder within this range of
responsibility for this particular job taken by itself, i.e.
ceteris paribus. (For a rigorous general proof of rising
demand price see the paragraph on relative pay in Section
Two below.)

The range from A to B, however, is too large from the
viewpoint of the short period under tranquility conditions.
To the extent that the firm has concrete views about its
capital investment K there is a maximum price the firm is

prepared to pay for judgment exercised at this capacity level. We mark this point X on the vertical line from K. Suppose now that the present occupant works at his own capacity level C and is paid Y. Y could of course coincide with D in Figure 2 but is actually drawn above D. Is this possible? In what sense can a firm be paying more than its own demand price? Simply in the sense that strategic considerations, beyond the immediate environment of the job whose demand price for C is D lead the firm to pay a higher wage Y. In due course, that is to say beyond the current short period, this discrepancy between D and Y may lead the firm to redesign the pay structure or change other objectives. Similarly, if the firm is prepared to pay more for more work, say X for K, there may be changes in manpower policy, in tooling up, or in other modifications of the organisational structure to enable the firm to approach its objectives more closely.

Accordingly demand price for a single job need not be equal to market price for that job in the short period. The only thing we can say is that demand price is rising throughout the range R_1 R_2. The proposition of rising demand price within a rank of homogeneous labour input units follows from the definition of labour input we are using which makes it equivalent to output.

The observed short-period wage is not necessarily an (equilibrium) demand price for the job taken by itself. The extent of the disequilibrium which does not lead to short-period demand responses depends on the firm's strategy and in particular on its concept of tranquillity. The line W_{min}, the cut-price pay for a given level of work, does not of course play any part in the determination of wages and employment. Its inclusion in the diagram is meant to stress that in the present analysis the firm is not an active short period cost minimiser, in the sense of wishing to pay as little as it can for any given level of work.

Thus the firm may be in disequilibrium with regard to the wages it pays out in the short period. None the less, the firm has a list of maximum demand prices depending on the level of work it can extract or appropriate from particular job holders. In deciding on this maximum demand price the firm has to consider the implications of this particular wage on everything that might go wrong in case it over-pays or under-pays in relation to the complex of the hierarchy around the job. Disequilibrium simply means that some of the firm's expectations turned out to be wrong.[16]

We may now consider whether there are criteria determining the price elasticity of demand. An assumption which is consistent with the definition of K is that the price elasticity of the demand curve reaches a maximum at the demand price X which corresponds to the firm's tooling up. The firm, in other words, is prepared to pay at a rising rate as the job holder performs not merely satisfactorily but also at the level for which the job was designed. By taking C as lower than K on the diagram, it is implied that the individual job holder cannot perform at level K. The job holder is in equilibrium but the firm is not, for it has a greater elasticity of demand for someone else who could fill the job as it was designed.

Market price

We can see, then, two types of disequilibrium for the firm, even considering the level of work as the unique component in the firm's plans. Firstly, the firm's demand price may be different from the pay actually given to the present job holder. Secondly, the firm may be getting maximum work for given pay but would nevertheless have preferred to get more work at higher pay.

The analysis of supply and demand, by the individual worker and for the individual job, does not have to be built up around a concept of equilibrium. The supply and demand curves are transitory positions of rest. Even if the individual or the firm happen to work and pay on their respective short-period curves, there is no guarantee that this will be more than a temporary situation. For within the given short period the information on which the various comparisons of the two participants are made is bound to change. Experience of equilibrium, i.e. being on one's curve, within a short period need not therefore lead to the expectation, or indeed

16. Product prices are taken as given in the analysis so far. Period-to-period variation of wages and prices will be considered in the market analysis of the next section.

the desire, that the experience should be repeated in the next short period.

Under conditions of tranquillity there is nevertheless a presumption that the closer the current position is to equilibrium the less are expectations likely to change.[17] A small difference between the current position and equilibrium is an indication that there will be more active search by the workers and the firm to improve the situation. Only if the difference reaches 'threshold' proportions do expectations get revised so as to shift the curves or lead to a change of employment. We can therefore find use for the supply and demand apparatus as an indicator of the various ways in which the labour market is, so to say, in perpetual motion.

In Figure 3 we plot the two curves for supply and demand. (To change the previous illustration, the capacity level of the

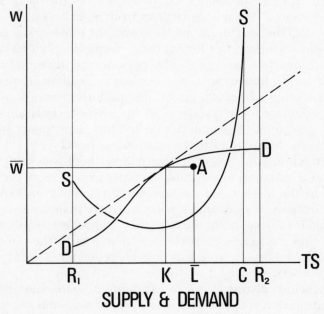

SUPPLY & DEMAND

Figure 3.

17. This assumption is analogous to the treatment of investment demand by Joan Robinson (*Essays*, 1960); the response of investment to the current rate of profit is stable within some limits, even though current investment is not equal to desired investment.

individual is now greater than the tooling up of the firm.) As drawn, the curves intersect twice. Suppose that the job is currently operated at the level *A*. There is (some) disequilibrium here for both sides of the market. The firm would be willing to pay more for that level of work. On the other hand the firm would be happier if either the design of the job at *K* were closer to *A* or if the individual were such as to perform closer to *K*. The individual is dissatisfied that, although he gets more pay than he asks for the work done, he is much below his capacity *C*. Yet when all has been said and done there is no reason that there should not be a margin, such as indicated in the diagram, whereby point *A* is quite acceptable in the given short period to both sides of the market. It is in this proximate sense that the firm and the worker can consider the position satisfactory. More specifically, the position is satisfactory if it does not lead either side of the market to modify its behaviour in the next short period *because of* these departures from equilibrium.[18]

Putting the matter in another way, in this market which exists in historical, not logical time, people simply don't take equilibrium *too* seriously. The presence of disequilibrium, within some limits, does not necessarily lead to immediate modifications of behaviour. By disequilibrium within overall tranquility we mean a state of affairs where there is generally no implication of overall action by the participants in the market to change the situation as soon as possible.

Yet within the range of tranquillity there is considerable room for variation of individual components of work on both sides of the market. We cannot therefore infer from Figure 3 that, because at *A* demand price is greater than supply price, we shall witness in the next period a change towards more work and pay, i.e. a change where *A* moves to the right and upwards. For apart from this possible tendency there are also many others.

The chief characteristic of the *micro-micro* level of the labour market is that *supply and demand decisions are highly interdependent*. The informational institutions of the labour market make it possible for flexibility to be exercised from

---

18. This is a notion of equilibrium closer to Hahn's recent suggestion than to the traditional GE concept.

the supply or from the demand side, which does not involve mechanisms analogous to the Marshallian stabilising tendencies. Even within the short period the firm has the ability to re-deploy its labour force within some limits. Now re-deployment means changing people around jobs or changing jobs around people. Considering how complex the specification of any one job can be, the effective flexibility available to the firm is quite considerable. On the other hand, it appears that, in practice, the flexibility that can be exercised by individual workers within the institutions of any establishment is also quite considerable. Going slow or fast or at a medium pace is one expression of such flexibility. Sharing with other people *via* informal arrangements is common practice. The modern factory or organisation is a sub-culture where information-flows about items other than price are direct, continuous and evolving.

Of course, all this does not mean that pay does not enter the information circuits of the employment sub-culture. But it does mean that pay is only *one* of the infinite ingredients that compensate for the social comparisons which operate on the supply side and for the continuous plans of re-organisation which go on the side of the firm. For it may well be, on the one hand, that the macro-economic information-flows concerning alternative job opportunities and pay are extremely inadequate, an assumption which has been made much use of in the discussion of 'The Reappraisal of Keynesian Economics'. It is not however contradictory to this assumption, which refers to the world in the large, that the very opposite assumption should be appropriate for the world in the *very small*. The worker who is unemployed and is looking for a job may indeed be highly deficient in reliable information so that he can base his plans accordingly. The search for him is a blind man's buff.

The worker, however, is normally not unemployed. Yet he normally *is* in a process of search. This is not because he is primarily active in finding another, 'better', job. It is simply that he is alive and working in an evolving environment. He cannot help knowing what is going on around him. And the firm similarly cannot help knowing that whatever arrangements it may arrive at are bound to be temporary. Given, then, that the search goes on all the time from both sides of the market, it is not suprising that gross turnover is infinitely greater than net turnover. General tranquillity, in other words, is perfectly compatible with infinitely many disequilibria in the very small. The notions of interdependent supply price and demand price are acceptable in this interpretation of the real world at the present, elementary level of disaggregation, since both sides of the market have views of what is the right sort of pay for a given level of work.

But the approach here takes nothing as given for good. Even the tooling up, the capital component offered by the firm, and capacity, the capital component offered by the individual worker, must be thought of as approximate and changing constraints. They are, in the last analysis, social data, data of social experience, not of engineering. The tolerance limits around these constraints are therefore a matter of expectations. In a world of technical change it is inconceivable that any organisation should not experience continuous disturbances, mainly in the small, which enter its plans for reorganisation. But for the supply side, also, there are endless disturbances, if only because historical conditions of relatively full employment have been realised long enough to permit extensive mobility of a particular kind, mobility which may be called 'sideways' rather than 'upwards'. It is simply that the culture of modern industrial society permits an immense amount of information to flow quasi-freely and a great amount of movement to occur relatively costlessly, together with, and partly in response to, continuous disturbances from the side of technology and the product market.

In such a world equilibrium can only have the meaning of *a state of rest*. Disequilibrium will therefore be used in the sequel to mean exclusively a situation where expectations have been so drastically disturbed that they lead to a change in behaviour pattern. Such situations are, for example, when men leave their jobs because there is no hope of achieving equilibrium within a given organisational set-up, or when men are dismissed from their jobs because they cannot be accommodated within the tolerable changes of the system. Such disequilibrium in the small is of course quite possible within overall macro-economic tranquillity. The break-up of tranquility in the large obviously reinforces disequilibria in the small, and this may, in turn, have bearing on the overall situation.

To sum up so far, we have constructed the supply curve for the short period for one individual participant in the labour market and the demand curve for any one of all possible holders of a specific job. The interaction of these two curves has essentially taxonomic significance. It permits us to draw up a list of the factors which qualify a state of rest and indicates the limits to that state. We next consider an aggregation of individuals from the supply and demand side in order to say something more about policies of recruitment and promotion. This will lead to our discussion of the determination of relative pay. The argument will be conducted on the basis of a rank in the level of work, independently of any associated skills. In other words, equilibrium among the various components of work is implicitly taken as given.

2. 'Local' labour markets[19]

Given the distribution of skills and the tooling up of firms,[20] there is, in the short period, a level of demand and supply, measured in manhours, for each individual qualitatively homogeneous component of work (measured as TSD) by firms individually and in the aggregate. Figure 4 refers to one such managerial rank or a sub-set of it. The number of manhours demanded vary inversely with the money wage, given the price of the product. This is so because, for the firm, the price of labour is relevant only in relation to the price of the product. This demand function may refer to an

19. The level of abstraction for the 'local' labour market is left deliberately vague. A crowd seen from a helicopter looks different from the same crowd at worm's eye level. There are other 'eyes' that can watch the same crowd: the traffic policeman, the ambulance driver, the mother who has lost her child, the platform speaker, the stewards, the provocateurs, etc. The notion of labour input advanced here does not oblige us to look for operational labour markets, which alone exhaust some phenomena, viz. internal-versus-external, local-versus-national, wage-contoured or product-contoured, etc. Such 'markets' are not considered non-existent: they can simply be assumed away from our purposes.

20. Firms tool up in accordance with the expectation of wage rates and availability of labour. Whatever these expectations, in the short period the tooling up is given.

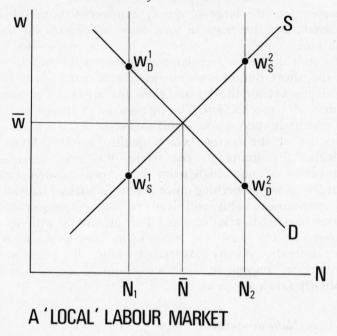

A 'LOCAL' LABOUR MARKET

Figure 4.

individual firm, to 'the' industry, to the local labour market, to the region, or to the economy as a whole. The operation of the labour market as described so far enables us to be entirely general on the range of validity of such an aggregate demand curve. Similarly, the supply of manhours is an increasing function of price by individuals in a given trade, or in many trades, working in one firm or in many, in one local labour market or in the economy as a whole. The result of the previous analysis therefore is to present an entirely conventional-looking supply and demand diagram for the traditional variables of the labour market.

There is nothing conventional, however, about the oper-ation of this market. Suppose, for example, that in the given short period the market is in conventional equilibrium: this need not mean that any of the individual participants are in equilibrium as well. It simply means that, with the expect-ations and prospects that they hold, individuals and firms settle for the time being in that position of rest. There can therefore be no presumption that where demand price is greater than supply price there will be a tendency towards equilibrium at greater levels of manhours and pay nor, conversely, where supply price is greater than demand price that there will be movement toward less manhours and pay. *What tendency there will be for the aggregate market will entirely depend on the distribution of disequilibria at the micro-micro level.* For example, where demand price is greater than supply price, firms, disappointed that they cannot obtain the manpower they have planned for at a given price, may dilute jobs downwards in order to make use of thereby acceptable entrants. Similarly, where firms find that they can obtain all the labour they want at wages lower than expected for any given level of work, it does not follow that they will increase employment. On the contrary, they may well up-grade jobs in order to make use of more acceptable entrants. The operation of the aggregate market, in other words, reflects firms' and individuals' information concerning the *quality*, as well as the availability, of jobs to match the supply as particular levels of pay.

The operation of this aggregate market tells firms what to do about their manpower development policies as much as how they should develop their technical basis. With prospects of rising money and real wages, which in our context are taken as given exogenously, firms may have a long period view of capital investment through which the relationship of the money wage to the price of the product can guarantee adequate profits and growth. Additionally, however, firms obtain from the labour market information concerning the availability of particular levels of capacity to yield responsibility, regardless of the type of technology installed. These two types of information have to be considered together by the firm when it revises its short period plans.

The type of information conveyed by the aggregate labour market to the supply side is quite different. Basically it is information on whether people who have a given level of capacity are *employable* at that level of capacity and its associated pay or not. We· take up this point again in Section Three of this chapter.

We now assume that there are as many 'local' labour markets as there are homogeneous ranks of responsibility in the industrial sector.[21] We recall that a rank defines the limits within which firms and workers consider job specification. As time-span is continuous in cardinal units, such ranks are also continuous, regardless of the skill component of work. There is no loss of generality in assuming further that the ranks are the same for all skills and do not overlap among them.

We use these assumptions to argue, first, that *over time, supply is what demand decides to make it*, and, secondly, that *supply price adjusts through time to demand price for each rank*. Contrary therefore to the human capital theory approach, which gives primacy to the notion of individual utility maximisation through time, we say, that it is the progress of industry that decides on the shape of supply which is compatible with it and then makes the price of supply acceptable to the suppliers.

Relative pay

We first take up the matter of relative pay. We have seen that, for the individual worker and the individual job, price and work go together for most of the relevant range. We must now show that, for any individual rank, 'market' work and pay also go together,[22] whence it follows that adjacent ranks must have the same relation. Supply price presents no difficulty when we go beyond the 'local' labour market, for rising supply price would obtain if we were to combine two ranks and form one. The tendency of rising supply price has all the more force when we consider the division between two consecutive ranks to be one of qualitative difference. The difficulty concerns the proposition of rising demand price which, as we shall argue below, is the primary determinant of market price.

To see labour input, as defined in this study in decision-making units, as the primary explanatory factor for pay differentials, it is necessary to relate the distribution of decision capacity supplied to the firm's intentions concerning

21. In an attempt rigorously to define the concept of rank and to measure it, Jaques arrived at the figure 7 for managerial hierarchies, as they have developed in the United Kingdom and the United States. But there is no reason to stick to any specific figure for the purposes of our analysis.

22. Rising supply price in Figure 3 permits us to infer rising supply price in Figure 4, even though the quantity unit shifts from time-span units in the former to manhours in the latter.

the structure of technology, that is to say to investment. The investment decision, like all others, is of course taken at a particular point in time but it has long-period implications. It is with this in mind that the firm must make an estimate, not only of the level of future labour costs in general, but also of the structure of these costs as a complement to, or substitute for, the types of investment that may be undertaken.

We assume that the firm has some choice concerning the relation of labour costs to capital costs which are embodied in alternative pieces of capital equipment it is intended to purchase. There is, in other words, an *ex ante* isoquant giving the points representing the input mix of expected labour cost and capital cost which will produce one physical unit of output. This is a standard neo-classical construct (cf. Salter, 1960) which we now use as a heuristic basis for our discussion.

Now labour costs, in our treatment, are not simply manhours. They are essentially like alternative types of capital equipment. The investment decision by the firm therefore represents alternative structures of physical capital and labour decision-making components, all of which to-gether give a point in cost space. For simplicity, we assume that manpower is of two types, which are distinguished by capacity levels falling into adjacent ranks. Machinery comes designed for a specific type of manpower to operate it. We can think, in an *ex ante* sense, of alternative designs of machinery producing the same physical output, these designs differing precisely in the type of manpower they are designed to be operated by. It now follows from our definition of work as decision-making responsibility that *there is a negative trade-off between manpower costs and capital costs.* Since this is the only static proposition in this theory we must investigate it with some care.

We first suggest the existence of an *ex ante* isoquant, *ex ante* not only to the investment decision but also prior to the existence of capital equipment as such. It is an *ex ante* isoquant in the design sense. Design engineers are told that machinery to produce a certain physical product must be specified in alternative ways,[23] so as to give choice to

23. Two alternative types of machine and two types of labour are sufficient for the argument. We do not need continuous smooth isoquants.

entrepeneurs who want to buy and use this machinery, not only in the context of a technological structure of production but also within a social sub-culture, a local labour market. The supply price of each type of machinery we take as given. The demand price of firms for alternative types of machinery will therefore depend on the overall calculus of profitability for each type of machine, depending on the operating, or labour cost, component attached to each. What can we deduce about the demand price by firms of alternative types of labour for alternative types of machine?

The reduction of the machine unit to the isoquant concept permits us to say one thing and one thing only. Labour input, measured in units of responsibility, *complements* machinery which has precisely that level of responsibility *left out* of its design. For any level of responsibility can be removed from the human operator by being designed into the machine. Given that the output is the same, it follows that machinery which is designed to be operated at a low level of responsibility must contain a higher 'embodied' level of responsibility. This embodiment of responsibility into the machine must be costly. We can presume that the greater the embodiment the greater the cost. The higher therefore the supply price of machinery, the lower the responsibility of manpower which is needed as its complement, and hence the lower the demand price for this type of labour. Insofar as there is choice in the design of machinery, therefore, and if we can reduce the size of machinery to the isoquant basis, we can establish a negative trade-off between capital cost and the demand price for labour. Accordingly, the schedule by firms of the demand price for labour input is a rising function of the quantity of labour, measured in units of responsibility, that is required.[24]

Demand price and market price
We have thus established a schedule of rising demand price regardless of rank and range of the level of responsibility. The

24. The process of automation, which requires more top-rank employees as well as low-rank operators while making the semi-skilled redundant, is not relevant to the above argument, which is conducted on the isoquant basis, i.e. that each 'machine' can be associated with output units independently of the structure of technology around it. If we reduce the process of automation to discrete alternatives we get the same answer as in the text.

next point to consider is whether demand price is particularly significant for the determination of market price. We argued in the previous section that neither supply nor demand price can be presumed, in the short period, to determine the market price for each individual job. The present argument, however, is conducted from a different angle. We are not faced with a given short-period situation, where capacity in terms of tooling up is fixed, but rather with the design of this tooling up from the point of view of the firm. The firm, in other words, now contemplates a situation which will gradually emerge as its investment expenditure takes physical shape. The evolving technological environment requires it to plan its structure of manpower intake as well as to develop its existing manpower to match.

The jobs in such a situation are likely to be somewhat new, in the sense that there is, strictly, no given supply price for these jobs. No job is, of course, absolutely new. Some existing skills and some capacity levels given from the past necessarily enter the picture. The conditions of supply, as in the previous section, are not here also independent of demand or conversely. Plans of demand are necessarily constrained by the firm's expectations as to the elasticity of supply.

There are, however, two reasons why we may presume that, in the context of the investment decision which we are discussing now, the demand side is the stronger determinant of market price in every period. The first reason is that the firm is necessarily the prime mover: 'effective' supply presupposes a certain design of jobs and a demand price for them. The second reason is that there is necessarily greater slack, more flexibility, on the supply than on the demand side. There is an asymmetry between the organisation of the firm, which is subject to powerful technological forces, and the organisation of the social sub-culture from which the supply of labour is drawn.

When conditions are tranquil there is a definite short-period structure of market wages which more or less corresponds to decision-making levels. The short-period behaviour of the firm does not reconstruct the labour market from scratch. To the extent that the firm is a prime mover, however, both by hiring labour and investing in new technology, its behaviour reproduces but also adopts the structure of differential pay. The schedule of demand price of firms makes and re-makes differentials in any short period. Under conditions of tranquillity the capacity levels of individuals fall close to the designed capacity level of firms. To the extent that capacity levels for each local labour market are in elastic supply, it is demand price which fixes or reinforces the pattern of relativities.

Having established the short-period schedule of rising demand price we may now drop the static characterisation, in terms of the isoquant, of the investment decision. The introduction of technological evolution as a powerful determinant of the variables in the labour market takes us to the second reason why market price is primarily determined by demand price. We can view technical progress as a combination of autonomous scientific factors and induced responses by firms to their expectations of markets, sales, prices, and wage costs. The firm, in other words, does not take part, at its level of aggregation, in the shape and pace of technical progress. It has no power to exercise a demand price as between alternative designs of machinery. Investment for the firm means shopping from a list of already constructed machinery.

This diminution of choice for the investment carried out by the firm, however, is compatible with our previous deduction concerning the rising demand-price schedule in the choice of labour. Faced with given machinery and with a given structure of market wages, the firm can exercise effective cost-minimising choices only by designing jobs according to the preferred capacity levels. It may not be able to obtain, say, engineers at a price other than that dictated by the market. But it can design jobs for engineers which fit its own machinery and can therefore exercise effective choice by demanding engineers of the requisite capacity to fill them. As jobs turn up through time in a technologically envolving environment, suppliers of labour are necessarily ignorant in one and every short period, not of the prescribed component of jobs, but of the level of responsibility required. They have no option but to respond elastically to the level of capacity performance required. The greater the technological dynamism of the economy the less tranquil are conditions in each local labour market. There is of necessity turnover of labour. There is also simultaneously 'learning by doing'. Supply price rises to meet the level of capacity demanded. Taking one short period with another, supply price responds to demand price.[25]

Supply price and employment
But the converse need not also be true. Demand need not respond to supply. Firms simply don't have to; they are not obliged to employ individuals at the capacity already attained. If the pay they offer does not produce disequilibria for the firm, the firm need not worry that the responsibility *not* offered to specific individuals is for them a source of disequilibrium. The firm may simply have no use for the capacity available in the market. If this is true of all firms in a local labour market, because of the nature of general technical progress, there is simply nothing that the suppliers of labour can do about it. Or, rather, there *is* something: they can reduce their own perceived level of capacity, they can accept being socially demoted — they can reduce their supply *price.*

It is at this point of the argument that the explanation of the distribution of pay and decision-making capacity in the population differs from that offered by Jaques. His hypothesis is that capacity is fundamentally a psychological phenomenon. The non-homogeneity of capacity ranks suggests that, if measured, capacity is multi-modally distributed in the population. With this hypothesis about the facts of the case there is no disagreement. The point at issue is, rather, *How does it happen that the distribution of capacity levels which exist in society matches so closely the distribution of capacity levels demanded by the industrial structure? Is the structure of work and pay in industry primarily determined by the availability of the given distribution of capacity levels, or is it rather the evolution of industry that creates, through time, a distribution of capacity levels to match?*

To prevent any misunderstanding, the above does not suggest that, in Jaques' view, there are say 10% of potential virtuosi on the violin, who will simply push themselves on to

25. This point is taken up in Section Three below.

the world's concert halls, and that their psychological characteristics explain the musicality of present society. Nor do I claim that the demand for violinists to fill the concert halls already constructed will produce the supply thereof. The argument has nothing to do with the level of skills or the type of skills. Both Jaques' and the present argument assume that the supply of the skill component of work is elastic over time. If there is sustained demand for any one skill, industrial society will find it advantageous to invest in the education of people in that skill. Both Jaques' and the present argument are concerned entirely with the level of responsibility-component of work which, as we have argued, is empirically, as well as analytically, sufficient to explain differential pay.

Jaques' explanation is supply-side oriented. The present explanation gives primary importance to demand. We say that it is the supply price that adjusts through time to demand price, for each rank and level of work. But this primary role generally accorded to demand is not incompatible with the suggestion that mechanisms also exist whereby supply price over a certain range induces capacity to adjust as well. To see this asymmetric interdependence between the forces of supply and demand in determining differential pay, we will shift our viewpoint in Section Three below to consider forces relating the whole of the labour market with the aid of a 'dual' labour market hypothesis. By contrast, the forces of demand operate with clarity in the 'local' labour market context.

What happens if a local labour market is in disequilibrium?[26] If demand price is above supply price for a sustained period of time, we expect that supply will respond elastically in terms of the capacity level required. It is, generally, in the interests of industry to help such a process. We may have witnessed this phenomenon recently with the industrial training boards, which increased the pool from which higher capacity response could also be expected. This type of

26. Disequilibrium in a local labour market is the state of affairs which leads the participants to alter their behaviour in the next short period. It is a qualitative rather than a quantitative situation, such as would be reflected, for example, in the figures for registered unemployment or unfilled vacancies. The quantitative evidence suggesting our notion of disequilibrium would relate to gross turnover and wage drift rather than net turnover and gross earnings.

phenomenon does not contradict commonsense, at least of the optimistic variety.

The other side of the coin may be less acceptable. For where supply price exceeds demand price for a sustained period of time it is unfortunately plausible to assume that supply *price* will fall. To consider this phenomenon, it is necessary to enlarge our view of the operative local labour market. The depression of the thirties, for instance, witnessed vast movements of labour in search of jobs that would prevent it from lowering its supply price. The local labour market in such conditions tends to become enlarged. Perhaps we should no longer speak of overall tranquillity. Yet it is precisely a shift towards another type of tranquillity: it is the expectation of labourers whose supply price is persistently above demand price which induces them to, so to speak, 'devalue' their own labour.[27]

There are two ways in which labour may devalue itself. The first, and simpler, is to cut its supply price. But generally this would mean accepting a lower differential. We may consider that this will be a short-period response. Let us, however, shift our attention to developments over a considerable period of time. Let us suppose that technical change continuously displaces people of a certain skill, employed at a certain level of capacity, and replaces them with people of different skill, employed at a lower level of capacity. This may have happened in coal-mining since the war. The older workers may still be capable of learning the technical component of the new skills. But there is only one way in which they can find a supply *equilibrium* in the new technological situation, and that is by lowering their own *experienced* level of capacity. The secular transition from craft to industry was precisely such a long-term historical phenomenon. In a general way, all we are arguing is that the industrial system has had power over men of no independent income such that they have been fitted, over a period of time, into the positions that the industrial system had

27. The relative devaluation of supply price is not necessarily connected with Keynes' macro-economic proposition, that a fall in money wages does not cause employment to increase, since prices follow money wages downwards faster than effective demand increases. Keynes' argument, however, provides an environmental context leading to a cut in relative supply price.

interest to evolve.[28]

The argument that the supply of capacity gradually and under conditions of tranquillity adjusts to demand price is not meant, therefore, to apply only to partial phenomena, such as older workers, obsolete skills, declining regions or industries, etc. It is meant to be understood as a general law of the operation of the labour market. Demand calls the tune because the firms, and through them technical progress, call the tune. The prime mover of the economic system is investment demand, not only at the aggregate level but right down to our micro-micro level of disaggregation.

We may note now that our two fundamental propositions from this interpretation of the labour market are compatible with three empirical phenomena on which there seems to be general agreement. The first of these is the distribution of pay which has remained relatively invariant since the 1880s. The discussion of this regularity by Dr Routh led him, in the conclusion of his book,[29] to consider Jaques' hypothesis for the determination of pay. The present analysis, which uses Jaques' concept of work, suggests that the invariance of the distribution of relative pay through time is a natural phenomenon, because it does not depend on the occupational structure considered by skill but on the occupational structure measured by the level of responsibility carried.

The second phenomenon which is compatible with the above analysis is the response of labour to economic incentives, as seen in the movements of labour through time towards higher paying occupations. Higher-paying occupations, as well as regions, can only be such on the basis of greater technical dynamism which yields to such industries and regions a different structure of manpower whose average capacity and pay are higher.

The third phenomenon compatible with our analysis is the persistent differentials of pay by firms according to size. Size and technical dynamism are intimately related, and the above explanation would account for these disparities of pay within the logic of the theoretical analysis offered.[30]

28. This, I understand, is the central thesis of the novel approach to the notion of the division of labour proposed by Professor Steven Marglin; see references.

29. G. Routh (1960); see references.

30. It is not sufficient to explain higher relative pay by firms' size as the

3. A dual labour market

The analysis of this chapter follows the empirical properties of Jaques' relative work and pay curve. So far we have established the reason for the existence of a subsistence structure of wages for the whole range of the curve as well as for its minimum and the existence of relatively invariant differential pay according to the level of responsibility. We now come to the peculiarity of Jaques' curve, which appears as a kink at approximately the middle of the range measured as a logarithm of the time-span unit. Why is there a kink, and does it matter for the movements of the level of wages in the average through time? It is the presence of the kink that enables us to bring the forces of supply into the determination of relative pay.

It is, first, important to remember that the halfway mark on the curve divides two very unequal sizes of population. Below the halfway mark there lie probably 90-95% of people in industrial employment. We are thus involved here with the mass of workers in the commonsense usage of the term. Above the half-way mark lies what may be broadly called management. A large number of these people, in total perhaps 5% of the industrial population, are virtually self-employed, in that their relationship to the industrial structure is one of consultancy.

The argument of the previous section was that all people are basically moulded into their social position, into the selection of terms of reference defining their peers, by the evolution of the industrial system.[31] We now distinguish two categories of people, of which the bulky one is moulded rather more effectively than the other. We suggest, in other words, that the presence of the kink on the empirical curve denotes a *dual* labour market. This dual labour market is distinguished by two principal characteristics. The first of

consequence of relatively higher output per head. Since our unit of work cannot be restricted to manhours, productivity differentials cannot explain anything on their own. Higher profitability permits higher pay because it is itself a result of higher quality of labour input, the latter being the complement of technological dynamism.

31. The argument from now on is conducted from the viewpoint of explaining the period-to-period upwards movement of the whole curve and the agents behind such movement.

these derives from the nature of the industrial system, or from the nature of technical progress. The second has more to do with the social structure surrounding the modern market economy. Since the second is simpler to describe we start from that.

Social dualism

The level of subsistence was defined as that which any individual in the industrial sector of the labour market could obtain by opting out of the industrial sector and entering the service sector where self-employment is technologically and financially possible. The question then is: what cut in pay would an individual suffer as a result of joining the tertiary sector? Our dual labour market hypothesis suggests that, for those individuals below the kink, the cut in pay would be large, whereas for those above the kink the cut would be small if not insignificant.

The reason for this asymmetry derives from two factors. The first is that the financial ability to enter self-employment is very much higher for those who are employed in the industrial sector above the kink. The range of job opportunities for those people in the tertiary sector is therefore correspondingly larger. Secondly, however, people above the kink in the industrial sector are skilled in a different way from those below the kink. Their skill, or 'capital', is not only to take different types of decisions but also to take them with different types of people. The product which they offer outside the industrial sector is quite similar to that which they offer within it. Their demand price depends on the type of market to which they address themselves. By opting out of the industrial sector they don't opt out of the social condition of their life in it. The situation is drastically different for participants below the kink in the industrial labour market. The social sub-culture in which they live has no demand for their services outside the industrial sector. Their skill, or 'capital', component is virtually useless outside the industrial sector. The product that they can offer in the service sector cannot command a demand price above that of the entirely unskilled, truly subsistence, labourer. Put somewhat crudely, the argument is that managers may become consultants whereas workers may become redundant.[32]

Labour market dualism and technology
These social characteristics of the two labour markets are vastly reinforced because of the specific complementarity-substitutability relations that different types of labour have with the technological apparatus of industry. As we shall see in a moment, there is a curious reversal of these relationships when we proceed from the short period to events taking place through time.

In the short period, the lower the rank of manpower we consider, the greater its *complementarity* with the technology installed. At low ranks of the labour hierarchy manpower is a strict complement to the capital capacity installed, as well as to the informational and control structure of the organisation. At higher levels of responsibility this relationship is less strict. This is because higher management operates at a higher level of abstraction and is, thereby, necessarily less closely coupled with the technological set-up of the firm. The informational and control processes at the top are necessarily more supple and therefore permit swift changes in supply. Putting the matter in another way, in the short period the firm can accommodate relatively less disequilibrium at its lower ranks. Not only will electricians be replaced by electricians. They will also be replaced by technicians of approximately the same rank. It is the design of machinery that is primarily responsible for imposing a requisite structure of manpower to man it. But machinery is less of a constraint when the processes involve decisions rather than operations. The decisional component, as it were, takes over from the more mechanical or technical aspects of the firm's work.

But looking at the matter through longer periods of time reverses this complementarity-substitutability correspondence. Manpower at lower ranks is now seen as essentially a *substitute* for machinery. This is because the investment decision, *inter alia*, embodies a choice of technique. To the extent that technical progress is autonomous of the existing

32. The term 'workers' here covers people currently earning up to £3,000 per annum, in which so-called middle management figures prominently. It is perhaps this marginal component of the work force at large which provides the best

distribution of individual capacities, it is these capacities, we have argued, that will be induced to be supplied in due course. The decisional component we use to define work does not alter the long-period proposition that in a world where investment, technology, and the structure of industry are the prime movers, labour is a substitute not a complement in the process of accumulation.[33]

In the process of accumulation, however, the demand for higher-level manpower is not a substitute but a *complement*. This is because the process of accumulation requires managerial manpower to occur at all. The dimension of managerial judgment becomes fused with the characteristic of entrepreneurship as the decision level of responsibility is increased towards the top of the range. It is precisely these people at the top of the hierarchy who are responsible for the pace, the character, and even the institutionalisation of the accumulation process. It is *their decision*, in the last analysis, *that labour other than their own is a substitute for accumulation.* They are themselves the agents of it and are therefore complementary to it. It is not, then, in this view surprising, that the cut-off point between the two ranges of Jaques' curve should be the one-year mark, the mark dividing line managers from people virtually uninvolved with the operation of machinery.

We now argue that the complementarity-substitutability relationship of the two types of manpower to the process of accumulation has implications for the market price of their work. Specifically, we argue that, over time, the lower levels of work cannot dictate their supply price but must, on the contrary, accommodate their supply price to the given demand price. By contrast, the higher levels of work have, in a sense, monopoly power *vis à·vis* the process of accumulation and can therefore dictate their market price from the supply side.[34] The demand price of the firms must of

illustration for the argument in the text. Redundant middle managers are virtually unemployable because their middle level of decision-taking function goes with extra-specific skills and a highly constraining social position. This limits their local labour market alternatives to effective retirement.

33. This view is in conflict with the proposition known as Verdoorn's Law. I take it that the Verdoorn Law was simply an empirically valid tendency over a period of time but is no longer true; see Cripps and Tarling (1973).

34. Supply price is, again, in this instance limited by the reservation price that these people can obtain if they opt out of the industrial structure.

necessity approach their supply price.

The discontinuity of pay differentials which distinguishes the two sectors of the labour market arises, therefore, from the reversal of supply and demand elasticities, which is the result of the asymmetric relation between labour and physical capital. In the long period, low-level work is a substitute for machinery, and so the demand is inelastic while the supply is elastic; whereas high-level work is a complement for machinery, and so the demand is elastic whereas the supply is inelastic. The proviso, *ceteris paribus*, for these static propositions to hold is that the macro-economic forces of accumulation and distribution are given.

Labour market dualism and the process of accumulation

The question now arises as to why the category of high-level manpower can *maintain* through time such a high supply-price differential as is represented by the kink in Jaques' curve.

We can adduce two reasons for the maintainance of a discontinuous differential. The first, and in my view more important, reason comes from the development of the firm as a historical institution. The firm emerged as an organisational entity under the control of an owner-entrepreneur-manager. It was natural that, in the origins of the firm, profits, rent and salary should be confused. The pattern of salaries and wages which evolved historically can therefore be thought of as 'filling in' the continuum through Jaques' curve from the two extreme ends. Unskilled and, at that time, low-decision-level manpower gradually evolved and, through the progress of educational institutions, acquired a pay distribution filling in the various managerial ranks up to the one-year level. Simultaneously the growth of the joint stock corporation, together with the progress of science and technology and its relations to production, devolved the powers and respon-sibilities of the owner-manager-entrepreneur downwards to professional managerial strata. There thus came to be constructed, so to speak, a continuous spectrum of levels of responsibility.

Where the pay levels 'joined', however, there remained a discontinuity, because of the *qualitative* difference of the manpower so evolved with respect to the complementarity-substitutability characteristic relating it to the accumulation process. In high levels of responsibility as in low, it is demand that makes the supply, both in terms of the manhours made available by skill and in terms of managerial rank. But the supply of skills, levels of responsibility and manhours is one thing. The influence of the conditions of demand on supply *price* is another. It is a condition of accumulation that supply of the bulk of the work force should be elastic to demand *price.* The substitutability characteristic of low-level work makes this possible, since supply price thereby adjusts to demand price.

But when we consider the top end of the 'dual' labour market, it is neither a condition for the process of accumulation, nor indeed possible within its institutional context, that the demand should have this overwhelming influence on supply as in the lower ranks of work. There may indeed be a range around the one-year mark, composed of middle-aged, middle-rank managers, where supply price adjusts to demand price. The forces of complementarity, however, soon take over. At the top of the firm there remains a confusion between profits, rent and salaries. Nowadays this confusion has to do with side payments in kind. In the rapid progress of industry the complementary component of accumulation is necessarily in short supply. The firms can simply not afford to adjust differentials above the one-year mark to those below the one-year mark. The upper managerial hierarchy is a tight sub-culture; information within it is plentiful. Social comparisons would make for excessive disequilibrium. Competition among firms therefore dictates the keeping of differentials from the top to the one-year mark undisturbed in relation to differentials below the one-year mark.

Thus our first reason concerns the historical growth of the industrial corporate sector. The second reason has to do with the historical evolution of the distribution of income and the formation of the social classes that receive this income. The tertiary sector, at the level of responsibility corresponding to the higher managerial ranks, is broadly speaking the professional classes. The product of these classes is of course consumed by the same type of income classes as belong to the higher managerial ranks. The other customers of this product are the corporate sector itself and the state. Such services therefore have an inbuilt tendency to higher relative price. Once this price is accepted, intake into these professions assures that the costs of acquiring the requisite skills cannot be accommodated if this relative price falls. Thinking of this class of manpower in general and not in relation to specific skills, we can say that the prices for the products of these services are matched through time to the cost of reproduction of the manpower producing them. Human capital theory is, as it were, turned the other way round.

The operation of the 'dual' labour market thus also characterises a division of the social processes for reproducing labour power. At the lower side of the division, labour power is reproduced to suit the process of accumulation. At the higher end of the division, the reproduction of labour power is itself a cause in the process of accumulation. Through its relation to the process of accumulation, this higher-level manpower is able to appropriate some of the characteristics of the corporate sector itself. It has a degree of relative autonomy and can dictate its share of income in real terms. Management can hardly be distinguished from shareholders, who can command a value of dividends in real terms as a condition for the survival of the corporate system. High-level manpower can decide how much to get. Low-level manpower is given what the process of accumulation can afford.

4. Pay relativities and the share of wages

In this last section we examine the mechanism of wage increases through the interplay of wage differentials. The analysis concerns a sequence of short periods, where the strategy of corporations with respect to growth and profits is given in relation to a state of expectations about effective demand, from which follow the decisions of firms concerning prices, product differentiation, selling, etc. We confine the present discussion to the work concept defined in time units.

Disturbances of pay relatives in a given short period can come from two sources. The first, and preponderant one, is the progress of technology. Additionally, however, there is the overall process of social and demographic change. A specific pattern of differentials may be disturbed for any one of an immense number of reasons. The short-period shortage of a given skill may press firms, competing against each other, to offer abnormal wage increases. Strong union organisation may lead to exceptional increases in pay for one group in relation to others. New entrants into the labour market are bound to disturb the equilibria concerning differentials for those already employed. Under conditions of general tranquillity it is to be expected that the major mechanism for adjusting for short-period disequilibria will be 'sideways' mobility, accounting for the permanent presence of high gross turnover through the industrial structure.

Short-period excess demands for various types of skill and capacity can, under conditions of general tranquillity, be considered as random disturbances. The ability of industry to pay, in real terms, will dictate at least partly whether such temporary disequilibria can be allowed to produce a rising level of real pay throughout the structure.[35] Our discussion concerning the flatter part of Jaques' curve suggests that these random disturbances can be accommodated by industry without fundamentally affecting the elasticity of labour supply to the process of accumulation.

The same cannot however be said about the higher managerial ranks. The maintenance of relatives for that range of Jaques' curve requires that salaries adjust to the growth of profits. Since profits in real terms are a function of accumulation, it follows that the steeper part of Jaques' curve will rise in proportion to the rate of accumulation and profits. But it also follows that, to the extent that differential comparisons by lower income groups are made not just locally but in relation to the whole range of Jaques' curve, the rest of the wages structure will also rise with the growth

35. Rising money wages leading to rising real wages have been explained by Professor A.H. Turner by differential pay policies of firms. Progressive firms pay higher wages and social comparisons compel other firms to follow suit. Such a mechanism, however, does not explain why rising real wages preserve the same relative structure. The argument below subsumes the Turner hypothesis concerning money wage increases under the hypothesis concerning social comparisons between the two sectors of the 'dual' labour market. Needless to say, our mechanism of social comparisons operates within each of the two major sectors of the labour market. As the social comparison is now well accepted in explaining wage negotiations on the sequence of claims of, for example, drivers and electricians, we say no more on the matter but concentrate on social comparisons which span the whole of the pay structure.

of profits, thus keeping the share of wages relatively constant. (The presently rising share of wages can thus be seen directly as the result of attempting to change relatives between the two sectors of the 'dual' labour market.)

To see this essentially macro-economic mechanism at work we must enlarge our view of social comparisons. In deriving the micro schedule of supply price we made use of a set of social comparisons involving a specific individual and his peers. It would seem at first sight far-fetched to say that the peer group of any one individual extends over the whole of society. But it is not necessary to think of the problem this way. The comparisons we now think of do not involve a given short period but a sequence of spot comparisons through time in the context of modern industrial relations. In such a context, individuals in the lower ranks on the labour market are highly organised. The information available to the individual concerning pay does not depend merely on his own range of perception. It is possible for agents of groups of workers to be considerably better informed about the range of pay in the economy at large. Secondly, comparisons about relative pay need not derive from knowledge of pay but can be directly inferred from knowledge of consumption patterns. It is in many ways more natural to compare housing with housing, entertainment with entertainment, holidays with holidays, transport with transport, durables with durables etc., then pay packets with pay packets. It is harder for individuals to compare tens of pounds to thousands of guineas than it is to compare bicycles with private motor cars, or council flats with private mansions. It is also the growth of the tertiary sector of the economy which has, *inter alia*, contributed immensely to the diffusion of knowledge of consumption standards throughout society. There is wages push because of consumption push, not the other way around. Thirdly, individuals spend a period of time together in relatively equal surroundings before they enter the labour market. In a society with considerable social mobility, individuals know, after they have joined the labour market, about the progress of other individuals whom they knew as more or less equal before.

The latter point is of some special importance. A direct implication of the kink in Jaques' curve is that while individuals may start their life time careers at approximately equal levels of pay, differentials increase through their life times. Pay progression and job promotion imply a notion of human capital which grows as a function of time: it 'depreciates' the wrong way around. But it increases at highly differential rates.[36] Entrants at the lower ranks of the labour market cannot expect to reach beyond its elastic segment, i.e. beyond the kink. Entrants into the higher ranks will expect to climb according to the much steeper slope of that part of the curve, i.e. above the kink. Therefore, interpersonal pay comparisons through time also constitute information about the inequity of any given set of differentials.

It is all these forces in society that through time determine relatives of supply price. Supply price is simply the name we give to the concept of fairness. Fairness as a force determining pay relatives may not appear sharply or clearly in all circumstances. Nor may it appear to everybody as social integration, a Good Thing, that dockers should raise questions about the salaries of managers of private banks. It suffices for our purposes that some key groups of workers, or their unions, should be aware of the movement of pay in the higher managerial ranks, even though the individuals employed at lower levels of work are not aware of company balance sheets, profits and, therefore, what firms can afford to pay them. As profits rise because of accumulation and productivity growth, so do top salaries and, therefore, eventually, all wages and salaries too. The inflationary component, or wage push, is due to the top, not to the mass of wage claims. Excessive claims on output in real terms are an indication of the power of a social group to exploit its peculiar complementary relationship with the process of accumulation. In the higher managerial ranks we have effectively an equivalent of the Ricardian landlords, who had a prior claim on output and whose decisions to exercise it in turn constrained the process of accumulation itself.

But it is difficult to maintain generally that the growth of managerial salaries is a necessary, or a sufficient, condition for successful accumulation. Insofar as accumulation is subject to the laws of technology, the remuneration of

36. See the appendix to this chapter.

managers has little to do with it. Insofar as accumulation is governed by powerful historical traditions, its pace and character is in any case dictated by these traditions, and so are the salaries of the top managers. But there do exist in society other social groups who may perform the function of organising accumulation rather better and require less of the product for their own use. The development of the modern corporation has created coalitions of interests which are effectively representative of the rentier classes rather than of the scientific and technological establishment of the community or, indeed, of the mass of the people.

Part I has attempted to show that it is social rather than psychological mechanisms, related to the process of accumulation in a capitalist economy, that determine the social value of labour power — a conclusion which is also no more than a hypothesis. The strength of the hypothesis, however, is not only dependent on the strength of the analytical discussion. The hypothesis essentially derives from the real world, insofar as the method of work measurement permits us to see reality. The case studies in Part II should give some evidence in this regard.

Appendix

Management Education as a Resource Allocation Problem, or how to choose whom to educate and what to do with them afterwards*

1. Summary

In the process of economic growth, firms have to 'progress' their manpower and make it fit for new tasks. But while people may 'grow' on the job, it may also be necessary to expend resources in order to provide manpower with additional qualifications and thus develop potential that would otherwise be wasted. Management education can be defined as the activity that enables people to 'grow' faster than they would otherwise do on job experience alone. This appendix presents a model scheme which attempts to embody the essentials of the practice followed by business firms in manpower development and pay. The scheme is then used to formulate the choices pertinent to expenditure on management education and defines the costs implied by, and the benefits to be derived from, these decisions. The formulation is then applied to some hypothetical cases so that the logic of the scheme can be seen to be simple and convenient, although of course it is *not* a substitute for management decision-taking ability. Finally, some theoretical implications of the formulation are presented in connection with what has been called 'the economics of human capital'.

2. Introduction

The field of management education has expanded rapidly in recent years, perhaps proving that the 'demonstration effect' operates powerfully in advanced as well as in underdeveloped countries — on the production as well as on the consumption

---

* This appendix was originally written separately at a stage when I was trying to clarify my own ideas. It is reproduced with minor changes as it relates to the material of Chapter Four.

side of the economy. Whatever the micro-forces in this expansion, there is little doubt that the intellectual climate which justified it derived from the discovery and quantification of the 'residual' factor in economic progress.[1] This climate may now be changing.[2] But there is need for some framework to analyse the costs and benefits of management education at the micro-level where many if not most of the pertinent decisions are made. For while firms are bound by current legislation to contribute to the Funds of the Industrial Training Boards, they must still decide *which* managers to send to training, *what* type of training to demand, and *what to do with* their managers once trained.

The present paper takes it for granted that, as witnessed by the pioneer work of Professor H. Rose's report,[3] there will be more systematic scrutiny of the effects of legislation, on the volume of resources that is to be allocated to management education nationally and by sector, and on the types of management education that should be offered by various academic and other institutions.[4] The scheme, however, is independent of progress in other areas, as it is concerned with what the individual firm must do to attain its own objectives, given the environment in which it operates.

From the firm's point of view, expenditure on management education must, like all other expenditure, be justified by the firm's overall 'optimising', 'satisfying', or whatever decision-making criteria operate. The allocation problem for the firm consists of two interdependent choices: (a) what budget to fix for management education in relation to other fields of 'investment' expenditure; and (b) how to allocate this budget by persons and courses. To simplify, we assume that (a) is substantially given for firms (by legislation, etc.) and we confine our attention to (b). This has the advantage

1. E.g. R.M. Solow, 'Technical Change and the Aggregate Production Function', *Review of Economics and Statistics* (1957); E.F. Denison, *The Sources of Economic Growth in the United States and the Alternative Before Us* (1962).

2. Now that this particular neo-classical *deus ex machina* is on the decline, there are in the air the beginnings of scepticism as to the pay-off that has been more or less assumed to be associated with 'investment' in education. It would be a pity if the good baby were to go with the original bath-water.

3. H. Rose, *Management Education in the 1970s*, NEDC (1970).

4. Some of the above issues may be fruitfully discussed in relation to the model scheme presented below.

of concentrating on the relatively underdeveloped field of resource allocation *within* the firm.

The model-scheme can be thought of in two ways: first, as a convenient diagrammatic short-cut, which permits simple graphic treatment of problems that become unmanageable if treated in plain English; secondly, as deriving from an (at least) partly tested dynamic theory of work organisation which underpins the particular diagrammatic short-cut.[5] The first alternative is made use of in the text for reasons of brevity. For those who like their 'plausible' abstractions rather more fully worked out there is a short note at the end of this appendix.

3. *Differential earnings histories: a hypothetical example*

We proceed to construct a diagram.

Plot the age of a manager in years on the horizontal x-axis and his gross pay in pounds per annum on the vertical y-axis. Take an actual manager you know of, who has reached maturity in his career and although not near retirement age is yet not expected to advance any further. Record his earnings (total gross emoluments received before tax, plus the monetary value of any perquisites that went with the job) year by year from the beginning of his career to the present.

The first preliminary step in the exercise is to construct an earning history which consists of *comparable* money values in some relevant sense. To see the meaning of this, assume that your selected manager earned, say, £3,000 p.a. five years ago. But these £3,000 p.a. are not 'equivalent' to £3,000 had he earned it ten years ago, or to £3,000 *now*, were he earning it now. This is because all manner of relevant facts change through time: e.g. his 'experience' has grown, his 'responsibility' in the affairs of the firm is now greater, his 'peers' in the firm and outside are earning more, his family has grown in terms of expenditure demands upon him, his outside social commitments have risen, etc., etc.; but, also, the cost-of-living index, manpower productivity (in his firm, in the whole sector of industry he knows, and in the economy as a

5. 'Glacier' Theory, as the work of E. Jaques and his associates has come to be called, has so far found little sympathy, perhaps on account of its being *depaysée* in the Anglo-Saxon cultural context. A brief exposition is given in the note at the end of this Appendix.

whole), all earnings, etc., have risen as well.

It follows that, if we wish to plot *his* earnings 'history', we must decide which of these or other factors must be used to deflate the actual figures so as to make them 'equivalent'. For purposes of the diagram we use the index of total earnings in money terms (which is published in the Department of Employment Review). If this index rose by 10% over 2 years and his salary rose from £3,000 to £3,300, we would say that he is *now* obtaining 'equivalent' earnings to what he obtained 2 years ago. While he is 10% better off (in money terms) with respect to himself 2 years ago, he has remained *relatively* at the *same* point in relation to the national average. His age, experience, responsibility etc. have *not* advanced him relatively to the social average. He has coasted along with everyone else and is *not better* off but *as well* off.

It is obvious that there is a vital distinction between one's *own* advancement and following the general average. The formula suggested is a clear-cut way of separating (and ignoring) *general* social advancement in order to concentrate on *differential*, relative, faster-than-average, personal advancement.

Other formulae can of course be used to make figures that extend over time comparable among themselves in some sense or other. But each such formula implies assumptions about social behaviour.[6] Some formula, however, there must be, and we proceed on the basis of the one proposed.

This manager's (assumed) career history, in terms of his gross earnings, gives the following plot (see Figure 1). His actual earnings in current gross figures as he received them at the time are the points graphed *ABCDE*. Assume a story which goes like this: His first employment was at the age of 23 (*A*) after discharge from National Service. He then followed a part-time course at University during which he

6. The point is of importance for any theory of the labour market. A 'relative' position or movement cannot be assumed as significant apart from a theory of behaviour of people in relation to some variables which can in principle be measured. The assumption in the text implies a theory which considers relative income position as a strategic variable. Such a theory may be more pertinent to long-run (i.e. historical) rather than short-run analysis. It is also implied in the text that the relative *structure* of earnings with respect to some useful measure of 'level of work' or 'responsibility' remains invariant through time, so that *differential* movement is more specifically defined. These important topics are abstracted from in this paper; see references.

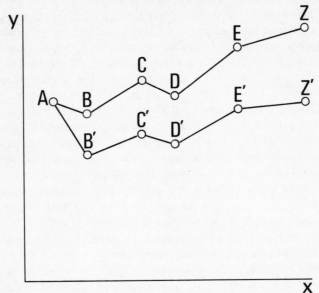

Figure 1.

received no promotion in the firm. (*AB*). Upon graduation he became a highflier (*BC*) but then got stuck as head of Accounts (*CD*) until it was almost too late for him to advance to the Group's Headquarters. The Clapham Bus created a vacancy for his rescue and he has been Group Accountant since (*DE*). He expects to remain there until retirement.

Meanwhile, however, total earnings in the economy have also been growing.[7] The average nationwide rate of change is

7. The table below shows the movement of the index of earnings for recent years:

Year	Index	% rate of change from previous year	Year	Index	% rate of change from previous year
1959	100.0	–	1965	141.3	8.4
1960	105.6	5.6	1966	147.4	4.3
1961	110.8	4.9	1967	154.2	4.6
1962	117.0	5.5	1968	163.9	6.2
1963	123.4	5.4	1969	176.5	7.6
1964	130.3	5.5			

Source: *Department of Employment Gazette*, June 1970, p.548.

6-7%.[8]

This manager's 'real' earnings are plotted as the line $AB'C'D'E'Z'$. During two periods of his life he fell below the average improvement experienced for the economy as a whole. During his university course (AB') he took a current cost as an 'investment' in the future $(B'C')$. But then he got stuck $(C'D')$ and did not resume his personal advantage until rather late $(D'E')$. From now to retirement he is high enough to be satisfied to coast along.

For present purposes the reason for converting current into 'real' earnings is two-fold: (a) the firm should relate its own payment policy to national movements, even if only to decide to depart from them; (b) in making plans for the future, the firm must also distinguish between the 'inflationary' — or *general* — and the 'real' — or *differential* — component in the growth of its wage bill and the individual salaries it pays out.

4. Future earnings profiles

The above example sums up the method of constructing the diagram from real-life histories. The method can however also be used to *project* future earnings 'histories'. Obviously such a projection will be subject to error with respect to any number of factors: there may be no vacancies for promotion, the individual may leave the firm, early promise of mental and moral development may be disappointed, *other* individuals may develop differently or there may be newcomers, the firm's growth plans may change, and the demand for the potential of this (type of) individual may shift etc., etc. Such uncertainty is however in the nature of all projections. What matters is that firms actually do decide about manpower

8. Actual gross earnings need not of course be confined to salary. They should in principle include the current money equivalent of all remuneration given in kind. There is a complication here in that the cost to the firm of providing such 'earnings' in kind need not be the same as the employee would incur to obtain these same commodities in the market. This is part of a larger complication, involving the effect of taxation on firms' payments policies and the possible consequent effects on the supply side of the labour market. I ignore all these issues here, which is why I am talking of gross earnings, as if taxation and other factors do not matter to the argument, which I believe they don't all that much for present purposes since they remain relatively stable through time. But see below, on the 'pay-off' to management training.

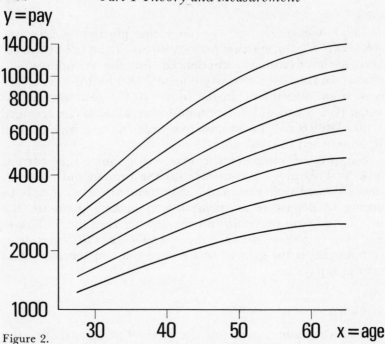

Figure 2.

development and pay in the face of such and other uncertainty. They decide if only by default. We proceed to use the diagram for the subset of these policies which concern management education. For this we shall transform our diagram into a *formula*, or generalised plot of *all* past and future earnings histories, *as if* all such histories are subject to a *pattern*.

Figure 2 presents such a 'plausible' pattern. The rationale for this pattern could start by saying that, as everyone knows, there are 'high fliers' and 'low fliers'. There are also middle-fliers and all sorts of other intermediates. Of course every individual may be one thing at one stage of his life and a different one at another. Nobody believes that neo-capitalism, neo-communism, or anything else, provides the fantastically flexible operation of the labour market required to produce smooth and continuous historical career patterns (which look so suspiciously like a system of parabolae produced by a computer's plotter package),[9] for this would

9. The diagrams are in fact so constructed. I have borrowed the diagram from my colleague J.S. Evans; see note 17 below.

mean that all round pegs and all square holes are continuously and perfectly adjusted. Nobody knows a person who has followed any one 'normal' career path, and most likely no such person exists. But all this is irrelevant. We are presenting a pattern, that is to say an *abstraction*, not a *fact*. We argue its *plausibility* as follows:

(a) There is no pattern before some age, say 25, because people are searching and making mistakes about their careers.

(b) There is *coasting* after some age, say 55, because there is objectively and subjectively little mobility after this age, at any rate at this time and in our culture as we know it.

(c) The *rate* of growth in relative terms is continuously decreasing between the ages of 25 and 55 because mobility is restricted by the *objective* and *subjective* properties of the 'groove' each individual has entered at around 25. The 'groove' comprises at least two dimensions: one is the *technical* expertise that goes with the job; the other is the much more elusive one of the total weight of a personality at the time of selecting — or being selected for — a particular 'groove'. In other words: either because society makes us so, or because we are innately so, there is a crucial point beyond which we stop experimenting and *settle* into a pattern whose future evolution is reasonably predictable and reasonably satisfactory to us and to our mutually selected group of 'peers'.[10]

(d) It follows that high initial growth rates of 'real', i.e. relative, earnings dominate the future even more than the present. *Absolute* differentials increase with age and life histories increasingly differ in total quality, as well as quantity, of earnings profiles.

Supposing now that this extremely simple pattern exists, we turn to its use for manpower planning. A firm's management hierarchy must be plotted on top of this pattern. An example is shown in Figure 3(a). This is kept simple, to illustrate just two points. In usual organisation

10. This paragraph makes light of what undeniably is a big question. I use figurative language in order to emphasise that I am speaking in terms of *plausible* reasoning, which is addressed to experience and intuition rather than logical truth. For those interested to pursue the matter a list of references is provided at the end.

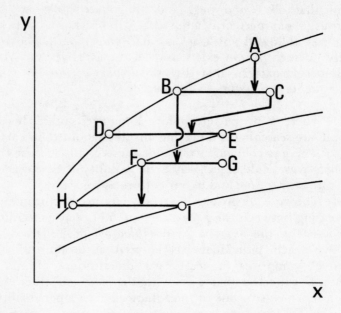

Figure 3a.

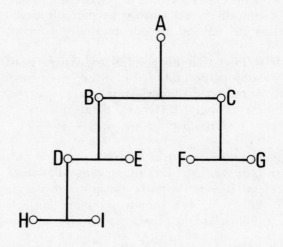

Figure 3b.

chart form, as in Figure 3(b), there is *no* systematic portrayal of 'distance' between levels of the hierarchy, nor is inform- ation directly incorporated about the *dynamics* (i.e. the evolution through time) of the changes in personnel of the various roles. If the same persons are plotted on the age-pay diagram, the neatness of the organisation chart obviously disappears. It looks as if hierarchical and communications wires become crossed. But this of course is not so. What is gained is a clear pictorial representation of the dynamics.

Assume that the facts of our example are as follows: *A* is the managing director aged 50, *B* and *C* run different departments, say development and accounts. *B*, who is on the same 'groove' as *A*, can be expected to succeed him. But *D*, who is on the same groove as *B*, is an accountant, not a development engineer, while *F*, who is of quite the right age to succeed *B*, is on a different groove. *H* will of course succeed *F* while *D* may succeed *C* (if *C*'s job is up-valued in terms of responsibilities as well as pay in order to fit *D*'s 'groove'). Problems in the growth of the firm are to provide for the succession of *B* and *E*, a replacement for *D*, and so on. And this presumably is the sort of manpower planning all managers do, without (or perhaps with?) the diagram.

The changing rate of pay progression
Suppose now we draw a tangent at point *D* (Figure 4). This represents the instantaneous growth rate of pay *y* at age *x*. Point *D* is the current value the firm puts upon the services of this individual. For the firm, the tangent represents the rate at which these services increase. Thus the groove, curve *T*, represents the value of the services that the firm can appropriate from the individual as well as the pay that the individual can obtain from the firm.[11]

Suppose now that we look at the situation from before it

11. We are speaking in terms of an abstract pattern, and hence do not have to worry about the complicated manner in which pay is actually arrived at and the forces that determine it.

On the other hand, it is theoretically legitimate to identify pay with marginal value product. By assumption the curve *T* represents the 'level of work' an individual is capable of performing, hence his 'physical' product. Now the firm does, presumably, both cost the employment of some resource and determine the pay-off from it. We assume that the services of that particular individual *are* demanded. Hence the firm knows the maximum it can afford for this individual's services. We have further to assume a competitive labour market so that at

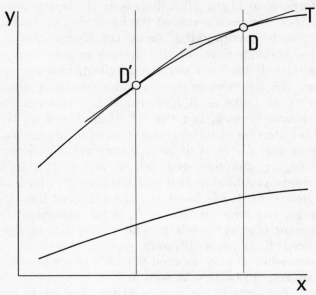

Figure 4.

happens. Five years earlier, today's individual D was at D', *by assumption in the same groove*, paid (absolutely) less but at a higher instantaneous rate (of climb) than now. The firm's interest is to keep D on the groove, not to allow him to drop to a lower groove. This is because a drop to a lower groove not only diminishes his pay at any given age (which is his concern, not the firm's) but also correspondingly diminishes his value to the firm. Given the groove, and D' five years ago, the firm's interest is therefore to keep the tangent from sloping less than at D by the time D gets there. If the firm did not know the groove it would seek to maximise the rate of climb from D, or to minimise the rate of fall from D'. If the firm knows the groove, it has a solution for the allowable 'normal' rate of fall from the tangent at D' which keeps D on the groove throughout his career. Given two points such as D' and D, the difference between the two tangents represents the *cost* to the firm of obtaining the tangent at D. If the firm

_____

equilibrium the firm cannot get away with paying less.

The above does not imply that the implicit use of the 'utilisation' function concept at the level of the firm at a given point of time carries over either through time or at the aggregate level, as is indicated below.

has to incur that cost and no more for keeping D on the groove from which he would otherwise have dropped, then the firm is getting a maximal return on its expenditure.

This in a nutshell is the simple logic for allocating expenditure for manpower progression and hence also for management education. We are now in a position to discuss the three problems posed in Section One above: whom to train, how to train them, what to do with them afterwards.

5. Manpower progression

One problem for the firm in real life is to push individuals up from their (apparent) present path; another is to prevent individuals from leaving (or going downhill) because there is no room at the top. The model-scheme can be usefully restricted to cope with some important cases of 'disequilibrium' which the firm may encounter in the ordinary conduct of its affairs.

First, the firm plans about the future in some relation to past experience. Let us restrict the *time-dimension* by cutting

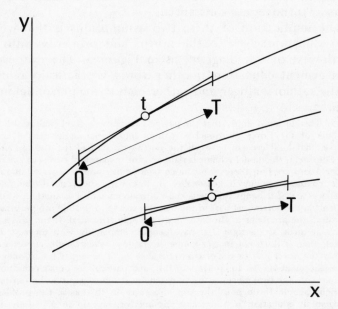

Figure 5.

off some time in the past beyond which experience is 'irrelevant' and stopping to look ahead beyond some time in the future where uncertainty becomes 'forbidding'. Call these *O* and *T* respectively and assume for the purposes of this discussion that they are five years either way from the present, denoted *t* in Figure 5. For each one of its managers the firm can now think in terms of a simplified situation: we *know* how much he was worth to us at *O*; we *think* we know that he is worth to us *now* as much as we pay him; let us try and figure what he might be worth to us at five years from now.

Secondly, the *coverage* of the exercise can be restricted to those management strata (or individuals) where mistakes in or lack of proper planning might be *costly*. The costs of 'induction' can be measured by asking: what is the value of the resources the firm has to spend before the new employee is fully 'in' the job?

This definition has a counterpart in the cost of *losing* a man's services to somebody else. Some of these manpower-turnover costs may be high, others may be negligible. We are only concerned with those strata and individuals where the costs of turnover are substantial.

The implication of these two assumptions is that we are restricting ourselves to the north, and primarily onto the north-west of our diagram, as in Figure 5. The exercise of management education, in other words, is practically relevant to the rather younger and rather high-flying personnel in the firm.[1][2]

12. This does not imply that the pay and manpower development policy for the bulk of the firm's personnel is without importance or interest. There are however major differences between the north-west part of the diagram and the rest. For one, if the model scheme is right and the 'expansion' curves of the rest in *relative* terms are flat, there is not much *relative* pay policy to worry about if a firm's payments policy is reasonably in line with the rest of the relevant industry — and if it is not they will know it soon enough. For another, while the problems in the north-west part of the diagram are, so to speak, both personal and structural, the problems at the lower part are only structural. If the firm has got its management strata right and pays people comparably with the rest of the market, then it does not matter *whom* it employs wherever the curves are flat (mainly the lower half of the diagram) because the *opportunity* cost of induction and replacement is *low*. In contrast to this, and particularly under conditions of rapid growth, the firm must get the management structure right at the top *and* get the right people throughout the top structure. In this sense the problem of management education is practically relevant for, say, up to 5% of the firm's personnel.

We assume that the firm has a plan for its management structure as a whole from now to *T*. In other words it is in a position to *define* the jobs that it would like to see done at *T* in the future. The firm can now proceed in two ways. From the 'supply' side it can project the evolution in maturity, judgment, skills, etc., of its present employees and see whether any one individual hits upon any of the jobs outlined (projected) for year *T*. From the 'demand' side it can scan 'backwards' to see what type of evolution is presupposed for graduation into any given job which will become available at *T*. In reality firms are likely to do both. It can nevertheless be expected that in a world where the labour market is fairly accessible to expanding and progressive firms, it is the firms' expansion plans which have priority and so the 'demand' at *T* can be considered as given. Let us take one individual's projected 'history' to see the problems that may occur.

He was hired five years ago and given salary A, see Figure 6. Actually, he was worth to the firm less, say *A'*, but mistakes are always possible. It would have been inconvenient at the time to replace him, so he was kept on. In fact, he surprised the firm because he turned out to grow with the job and was soon promoted, so that — it must be confessed — he is worth more to the firm now than they actually pay him. Of course he knows this and is rather restive. The job seems to fit him well, but he would have left were it not for his expectation that there is big promotion ahead according to the firm's expansion plans. The firm's top management are, however, worried. They have no objection to raising his actual pay to match his worth to them and to keep the two more in line in the future. But they are not sure that his evolution will take

---

It should also be emphasised that in this appendix I am concentrating on a narrow problem and seeing it only from the view-point of the firm. The problem of rising productivity, good labour relations, etc., are entirely abstracted from here. So is the bigger national problem of inflation which has, in the short run, more to do with appropriate pay structures for the lower part of the diagram. From the longer-term viewpoint firms must have appropriate manpower and pay policies for the *whole* of their employment structure including the shop floor. Finally, the area of middle management is only now beginning to be investigated, and the apparent flatness of the growth curves at *those* levels may be the result of the *lack* of management education and other opportunities for developing potential, rather than an argument for not bothering because there is no pay-off to be obtained.

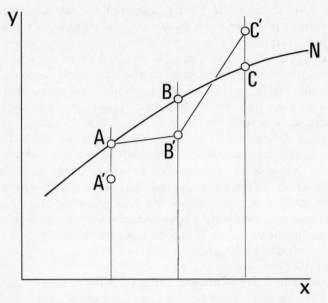

Figure 6.

him as high as C' five years hence. They *think* that his 'normal' growth curve is N, but they aren't sure, because it is only since last year that he has been worth as the curve indicates. Specifically, it is not known whether he can make the *qualitative* move one step up the executive ladder, which is concealed in the difference between C and C'. At C' he would be in charge of *two* departments, whereas in C he would be the deputy in charge of *one* of them. Now the problems of co-ordination of two different departments are vastly different from *just* running one, etc.

One should perhaps stop and ask the firm whether the difference between pay C and C' is sufficiently great to account for the qualitative difference of the executive strata they have just described and, if not, whether they are indeed different qualitative strata. But leave that on one side. We have the case of a firm which (a) would like to use some simple rule, such as provided by the model scheme, (b) operates under uncertainty on how to fit the specific case to the general rule, and (c) is not all that clear about its objectives (to redefine the job, to risk losing the man, etc.). Perhaps a typical firm.

6. *Management education*

But the firm has a further option: to spend resources on developing its personnel. The firm is in fact committed on the *total* amount it must spend on education, so that it cannot forgo the costs which are already given by legislation. The two decisions it faces, assuming it can choose among *different* types of education and *different* persons to educate, may be to some extent interdependent: a given individual may benefit from very specific types of education so that the two in practice go together. Additionally, some types of education may impose *opportunity* costs to the firm.

For our purposes choices about management education can be characterised by two factors only: (a) the value of services forgone due to a person's attendance of a scheme plus any other opportunity costs, (b) the increment in his worth to the firm (and presumably, or possibly, also his pay) which would result from the scheme.

It would be misleading to say that if a manager is, say, absent for a month on a course, the *additional* cost to the firm is one month of his salary. The true cost is the total cost of 'making do' without his services for a month. In all firms there is some degree of slack. The cost may vary from nothing to a month's salary, to the loss of important orders, to anything whatever. This cost is of course additional to any out-of-pocket costs that the firm may also have to incur in the process. But the firm should *not* add its out-of-pocket expenses which result from legislation, since these are 'by-gone' costs, which would have to be incurred whether it decides to educate its managers or not.

The return from a specific type of education scheme is best looked at in relation to the specific person selected. The firm must have a view as to whether it wants to *keep* a person and if so whether it will be able to offer that person work consonant with his ability, experience, etc., in the future. If yes, it must then have a view whether this person will be able to cope in the natural course of his development with the further avenues of promotion which the firm will make available to him. The question now is of the type: will the person be able to cope with the (assumed) *discontinuous* advancement from *B* to *C* in the future *without* something

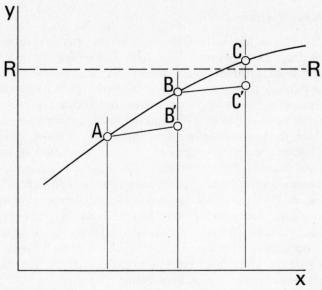

Figure 7.

extra to normal work experience, or will the firm have to fit job *C down* to him at *C'* for some time, as it (perhaps) had to do when he reached stage *B*? See Fig 7. Remembering now that the curve *N* is only a *general* rule and hence only a tentative forecast for the specific individual, may it not be that something extra can push this individual *up* from his too-normal possibilities of growing on the job by themselves? The firm must take a decision about what the answer should be, as for example: (a) the worth to the firm of this man *without* management education shall be *C'*, (b) *with* education it shall be *C*. The difference is of course the returns to education.

Having found a way to estimate costs and a way to estimate returns, it is of course simple to compute any measure of the *rate* of return or whatever else one may like.

7. Limitations of the scheme

The firm maximises returns if it selects those management courses and persons which yield higher returns than any alternative package of courses and persons.[13] The existence of a simple rule, such as presented in this appendix, doesn't however mean that reality will be that simply strait-jacketed into it. There are two good reasons why the *scheme* is more useful than the rule. The first is that when there is the degree of uncertainty involved in imputing costs and returns it is unlikely that any sensible firm will just compute *via* a rule *and* accept the verdict. Firms should obviously compute as much as possible, particularly when there are many variables involved, in order to educate their minds to the problem. But there is no way in which they can delegate their judgment of the *total* situation to a formula.

The second reason has to do precisely with the 'total' situation. It is sufficiently well known that various patterns of (de)-centralisation, various ways of 'marrying' an executive tree-like hierarchy with the circularity of the communications and information process, various ways of communicating and being affected by the environment, etc., all have *external* effects on one another. The dynamic, rapidly growing firm is precisely breaking the 'norms' of average behaviour, in the field of manpower progression as everywhere else. Such a firm could still benefit from using the 'normal' parabolic version of the scheme which represents average behaviour. But surely, what makes a firm dynamic is the total mode of operations rather than the individual bits, which, on the contrary, can hardly be comprehended apart from their relation to the whole.

8. 'Human capital'

Let us finally look briefly at some of the economics of 'human capital' which is related to the model scheme. The return on management education appears not only as an increment of the individual's marginal value product to the firm, but also as an increment in his own ability to earn in the future. Two things are happening at the same time: there is an increase in the scarcity-worth of this man, and there is

13. Ranking of alternatives could be done either by defining a rate of return or by comparing present values of the alternative income streams. I do not see the point of discussing the theory of such alternative measures, as I do not see the point of presenting formulae, in a field where spurious rigour can only be harmful.

also a change in his asset-value. Asset value has increased, in the sense that the individual can *expect* higher earnings in the future. The twin increase of income and 'capital' does not however belong to the firm alone, for a man, unlike a machine, carries his growth with him. It is 'society' which receives an 'external' payoff, by virtue of the curious fact that human capital depreciates 'the wrong way round', i.e. it *appreciates* with time, independently of the specific firm which employs it. Imputation of marginal products then vanishes by virtue of 'technical change' and the consequent increase in asset valuation of (very) embodied human 'capital'.

But the increased asset value of the firm's employees not only is a non-appropriable externality. The more a manager is trained by a firm, the more 'specific' a factor of production he becomes for the *firm*. But the more they need him the less he needs them: his *position* in the firm is part of his asset value which is enchanced in the market (provided of course he is still young enough to have more climb ahead of him). As his transfer price increases within the firm, so do his quasi-rents because of *alternative* employment outside the firm. As he ceases to be substitutable *within* the firm, his value to the firm is defined by his asset value in the market and not the other way round. The more rapid the expansion of management strata the greater the effect of asset values on supply price and the more powerful the profit-linked cost-push from the top of Jaques' curve. Managerial capitalism indeed.

14. If top-flight specialists in 'management' obtain a market price from the services to rapidly growing firms which define value in terms of growth potential rather than current profits, then the asset price of these specialists can well exceed, if expressed in terms of current return, what value they could offer to more average slow-going firms. But how are these average firms to know what marginal value product is for them when employing a non-substitutable specialist? It seems to me that such a mechanism may often be at work in the case of new specialist occupations, such as high level computer programmers, together with the more often discussed short-term excess demand for such services which explains apparently high salaries — whatever that may mean in the absence of some well-defined measure of labour input. It may be that such a mechanism is at work generally at the higher echelons of the pay scale which have received attention in relation to incomes policy discussions. Pay increases thus generated at the top of the payment scale may then lead to pressures from lower levels in an

Note

The 'normal' progression scheme used to present this particular resource allocation problem stems from the work of Elliott Jaques.[15] The reader who is not content with the 'plausibility' argument offered in the text may want to know the following summary of his theory:

Job satisfaction is defined according to (a) the harmony which exists, at a point of time and through time, between labour input required by the firm, i.e. job specification, and a generalised measure of decisional ability, and (b) the harmony between own pay and the pay of referent groups. Insofar as society runs tolerably well, one would expect, as the theory predicts, that pay and labour input will be closely associated.

One may also expect that general ability and work roles go well together. But this is a much more difficult relationship to test. There is indirect evidence that this may be so. As for direct evidence of the nature of generalised ability, there are preliminary results from psychologists' tests that such ability is multi-modally distributed.[16] I would for my part guess that this is so, but that the external manifestations, particularly concerning the growth of such ability, have as much to do with the overall political and cultural levels of social reality as with individual psychology. For a *given* society I would conjecture that generalised ability is strongly associated with labour input hence also with (relative) pay. Accordingly any one or all three of these variables can figure on the *y*-axis and all of them can be expressed in cardinal terms as pounds per annum. In the argument of the appendix I used all three at various points to give more heuristic value to the examples.

The *x*-axis simply measures age in years. The *x-y* diagram can therefore be interpreted in three different ways. From the point of view of the underlying theory, the ability-age

effort to sustain 'differentials' — quite independently of increases in productivity, the cost of living or general pressures in the labour market.

15. E. Jaques, *Equitable Payment*; *Time-Span Handbook*; *Pay and Progression Handbook*; and 'Towards a Theory of Managerial Ranks' in *Glacier Project Papers*.

16. Psychologists' tests; reference by E. Jaques.

relation is the fundamental one. From the point of view of *economic* theory, the own-demanded pay (the supply price of labour) work-level relation is the more important. Finally, from the point of view of empirical work, the pay-age version is more important. Jaques started off with 600 earnings profiles on which he attempted to fit a pattern. J.S. Evans worked on more than 100,000 such profiles and has devised methods for observing average behaviour.[17] I would further expect that the rate of growth of firms, and perhaps their size, may be significant in producing variation of the kinds I have indicated in the text. Further, the more it is true that the micro-dynamics exhibit variation, the greater is the practical need for a model scheme such as the one presented above, provided we know that a simple 'average behaviour' pattern exists.

Taking the multi-modal distribution of ability (which is the psychological leg for a 'rank' theory of managerial hierarchies) on the one hand and the pay-progression pattern on the other, we can obtain a system of 'normal' dynamic change which can be adequately represented by a system of 'nested' parabolae. A parameter taking the units from 1 to 7 gives the 7 management 'ranks'. Each 'rank' can be sub-divided into 3 to give 21 pay-scales by age; and it is a very convenient visual aid to one's thinking if a firm's hierarchy is plotted on a chart of this kind. This is the method Jaques and his associates have employed.

What I have done is to take this material over and fit a specific resource allocation problem to it. A simple mathematical treatment of the rules discussed is of course possible. Of more interest, I think, is the theoretical identification of costs and payoffs to management education. This may please the soul of the marginalist — perhaps infuse new inspiration into the neo-classicist searching for the market in which 'human capital' is traded, but eventually (as I have tried to argue in Chapter Four) turns to the gratification of (as usual) Cambridge.

17. J.S. Evans, 'Tracing Salary Patterns', *Personnel Management*, December 1970; and 'Career Travel in Works Management: The 1970 Survey', *Personnel Management*, January 1971.

PART II

Work Measurement in Practice

CHAPTER FIVE

The Pilot Project at H. Ltd.

(March/April 1968)

This report covers interviews which took place at the P. factory of H. Ltd. during March/April 1968. Fifteen roles were interviewed in total. Of these, I myself did nine. Interviews took place in two production departments and in quality control. Each role in the diagram is numbered and the interviews are suffixed with *A* if done with the manager and *B* if done with the occupant of the role. The order of presentation here is the same as the order of the interviews.

1. Interview 8A. Discussion with Mr. M. on the role of Mr. K.

The occupant of the role is a foreman and has been in the role for three years. According to his manager he is fully doing the job. As things now stand, the occupant does not get all the supporting services which he needs and for this reason is perhaps over-loaded and under some strain. The manager considers the responsibility he is given as 'approximately right' despite the failure of supporting services. The manager considers that felt-fair pay should be of the order of £2,300-£2,500 per annum. In his view, the occupant has higher capacity than required for his present job and, at least potentially, his felt-fair pay ought to rise to £2,750 per annum. The manager did not wish to discuss the question of the meaning of a 'long job' for his subordinates. He did not quite understand the question in the abstract. He did however spend considerable time discussing the meanings to be given to terms such as 'immediately' etc. This meant one hour or less. 'As soon as possible' meant during the day; 'soon' meant a couple of days; 'in the fairly near future' meant within the week; 'when you have time' meant nothing since the manager never used this expression; 'no hurry, give it plently of time' would mean approximately one week, although this is not an expression the manager would often use; 'we don't need this for quite some time' the manager would never use because it is too indefinite; 'this will be a long job' would mean in the manager's mind about one month. The manager would select his expression to give time dimension to an instruction according to his own assessment of the possibilities. In his words: 'I, myself, project myself into other people's jobs.'

Considerable confusion had been caused in this organisation by a major exercise of setting 'objectives' for each job in the firm. Everything was expressed in terms of general responsibilities and it was much more difficult for people to find the concrete expression in terms of tasks. The tasks I finally extracted are as follows:

Task 1. The foreman is responsible for meeting a production target given by a quarterly plan. Production in this department is quite complicated as it involves approximately 700 operations. The quarterly programme which is given to the foreman is broken down into weekly schedules. This is, however, only as a help to the foreman, who is not bound to any one week's target. There is a 'danger level' of prescribed character: in order to maintain the quantity schedule, he must be up to two weeks ahead of demand. This is considered the safe inventory level. But this is only a lower bound. The foreman is not constrained to two weeks on components generally. On certain components he can be up to seven, eight or ten weeks ahead of demand, if he has got the storage space, which is left to his own judgment. But since storage space is probably the scarcest factor in this factory such extension ahead of time is rather exceptional.

The manager digressed to say that, under exceptional circumstances, the foreman would be allowed to plan for up to twenty weeks ahead. This would however come under the manager's own veto. Besides, the question is rather academic since the schedules remain very much alike. In conclusion, the role as defined by this task is of the order of three months. Note that this is not accidental: the reorganisation carried out in this factory was particularly aimed to raise the level of the foremen so that they could deal with a quarterly production programme.

Task 2. This arises from the general responsibility of dealing with safety and tidiness in the shop. The task is short, perhaps of the order of one day. It involves applying the recommendations of the six-monthly Ministry of Labour review into safety procedures. The manager confused his own role with that of the subordinate concerning this task, since he thought that the responsibility lay only between Ministry reviews.

Task 3. This task concerns applying a monthly budget. The purpose of this budget is to check on what is called indirect efficiency. The foreman has certain freedom of operation as to how he will employ his labour and particularly service labour. There is no check on direct efficiency of the use of resources apart from meeting the quarterly schedule and keeping to the prescribed standard of using labour and the standards of machine utilisation.

Task 4. This concerns the training of subordinates. The foreman is given up to one month for training qualified personnel and much less for unskilled people.

Comment: The major difficulties of this first interview originated from the fact that it was the first. Further, the manager was insistent on giving general responsibility headings instead of tasks in reply to questions. For example, he said that the foreman was encouraged to propose methods for improvements; that he was expected to propose innovations within the year; and many such others, which seemed rather forced in his own mind.

The interview made the manager think of the role much more deeply. Towards the end of our discussion he proposed all sorts of amendments, none of which, however, affected the three-month measurement. Examples of these are: at the weekly production meeting of foremen, the manager would expect foremen to originate new tasks over specific problems, particularly concerning machine utilisation. The manager said he was also concerned about 'important' jobs, by which he meant jobs which were most urgent. Even though in terms of value-loaded language the manager considered the quarterly schedule to be the '*raison d'être*', as he called it, of the foreman's role, it was difficult to get him to accept that the length of tasks was of a different status from the urgency of specific problems. I also found it difficult to keep the manager to the same level of abstraction during the length of the interview. He often confused his own responsibilities with those of his subordinate. He also stressed that he was judging performance 'continuously'.

I distinctly felt that part of the confusion was due to the management-by-objectives exercise the firm had carried before. Beyond this, the technological characteristics of this firm seemed to play a part. The very short period of through-put and limited storage facilities got the managers to thinking in terms of 'spinning the money around' and therefore they judged the contribution to the firm's objectives by the speed of this 'spinning' to which 'everyone' contributed. I did not feel then that this particular characteristic should be in any way related to the time-structure of the organisation. One could however, in due course, consider this statement as a testable hypothesis of the form: 'Should the time-structure have anything to do with the technology of the organisation?'

Towards the end of the interview, the manager was quite content to think of the time-dimensions of roles. A certain thought struck him as interesting: that this particular occupant could do this particular job; whereas five years before, the foremen used to work to a weekly schedule. In the manager's view, they were very 'different people'. Finally (and crucially in the light of the changes in method introduced after the pilot exercise) difficulties arose from isolating *one* role from those of the supporting engineering service roles with which he had most to do. The task specification would, I feel, be a lot more complete if we had analysed those engineering services. The characteristic 'frantic' running-about of the foreman's role would then be substantially explained.

2. Interview 10B. Discussion with Mr. G. concerning his own role

Mr. G. is another foreman. This second interview is in some

ways the most interesting in showing up the difficulties of the method used for the pilot run of the project.

The occupant is aged 47, his father was a wet miller in a cement factory. He went to elementary school, then to the Royal Navy from 1941-6, and stopped all formal education at the age of 14. He has had 23 years of experience in the H. factory and has always been in the London region. An event which prevented further education was illness in the family; in particular this prevented him from taking an evening technical course at the Acton College of Technology.

The occupant has been in his present role for 2 years and he thinks he is doing the work fully. Concerning the quantity of work he has got to do, he felt that he had rather 'too much'. Concerning the responsibility content of his work, he felt that he has 'not been getting quite enough' responsibility. From that question onwards I felt there might be a discrepancy between his own view of his job and his manager's 'decision' about it. My doubts strengthened over the next question concerning felt-fair pay. The occupant thought that his actual pay was fair for his work but that others who in his view were doing 'equivalent' jobs to his (in terms of rank, etc.) were being over-paid. He justified this by saying that he was in fact doing 'more work' than normally goes with the role. He explained that he was in charge of a 'very large' department, in fact about twice as large as the other comparable ones. The complexities of dealing with such a large number of people on the shop floor made the role considerably larger. Because of this he has to work longer hours than other people: he has to be there very often during weekends, he has to take work 'in his mind' at home and often does not sleep nights. Further he expressed concern about faults which arose away and beyond where his own responsibilities ended. This in turn made him unhappy that he 'did not have enough authority' to deal with people in other parts of the factory, particularly engineers, at those levels where his problems could be solved.

The feeling that his job should be bigger found expression in his view of felt-fair pay. He named his capacity felt-fair pay as between £2,500-£3,000 per annum. One year from the interview he felt he ought to be getting between £2,000-£2,500, in three years £2,500, in five years £3,000 and at the age of 55 over £3,000 per annum. These figures seemed all to be beyond the likely prospects of career development in that particular factory.

At the pilot stage there was an experimental 'short-cut' question to the measurement of time-span. The question was: 'Which of the problems or tasks you are presently concerned with do you expect to be with you longest? What would the total length of time be?' The answer to this single question dispelled hope that there was such a short-cut. This occupant's answer was in terms of a general responsibility. The thing he expected to stay with him the longest was 'communicating with people'; this particular 'problem' would stay with him forever. If that particular problem did not exist, the one that would come up as the longest would be the break-down factor of equipment used in his shop. He could keep worrying about this problem for a whole year, although he expected that some parts of it would be resolved within the year. When I said that something which would stay with him forever was not really a problem as such but rather an area within which problems would occur, he understood the point and replied, 'You didn't want me to say that. You are interested in other things.' These other things he would be prepared to offer if the guidance were more precise: one question was too general a stimulus and it drove him off beam — a battery of questions might do the trick.

Questions as to the meaning of language, such as the terms 'quickly', 'immediately', 'soon' and so forth, interested this occupant considerably. He said that such terms would never be used out of context. The manager giving the instruction would know the context and this would automatically give different meaning to the instruction. Having said this, however, he interpreted 'immediately' to mean '*start* on the job at once'. No intermediate terms in the scale would ever be used, because they were too indefinite. 'This will be a long job' may be used from time to time, and then it would mean a couple of months.

His actual pay, which he also considers as fair, is £1,750. He receives no extras of any kind and has the normal four-week holiday. He had a very good memory concerning his earning history. He is married, has one daughter of 22 soon getting married and no other dependants. The task specification of his job is as follows:

Task 1. This concerns the quarterly production programme. All targets are expressed in terms of general responsibility, such as 'being responsible for supervising the performance of men and machines over his shop so as to meet the programme schedule of requirements'. Now this is a man who has been at his present job longer than my previous subject, and it is interesting that he started his description of the quarterly programme by saying it was a *weekly* programme. To this he gave the title of a 'master'. He then went on to say that this master forms part of a schedule which is now given to him in quarterly intervals. He was not at all clear how long his responsibilities lay since the quarterly schedules changed very little, a characteristic on which he put great insistence. Shorter tasks originating from the quarterly schedule involve keeping the records every day and consolidating them before returning them every week. Others are: to plan his quarterly target of labour requirements and to report accordingly; to plan his day and night workings of the machines according to the given formula of machine utilisation; to start requisitions for labour if he needs more and initiate proposals concerning further machine requirements; if necessary, to increase the load on his machinery so as to ensure that supplies are forthcoming to the other departments.

Task 2. This concerns cleanliness and safety of the shop. I got this task more clearly from this interview because the occupant offered the information that there is a factory safety inspector who comes through every department about once every week, as a supplement to the Ministry of Labour review which takes place every six months. The foreman specified that the Ministry Inspector did not deal with him but with his Manager, so the foreman's safety task is one week long.

Task 3. This concerns managing labour. The foreman is clearly the full manager of his men because he has a veto over hiring and firing. In managing labour he has to co-operate with the work-study people in the wages department concerning bonus and rates. At this point of the analysis the occupant went into a straightforward 'illusion' about his role. The sub-task concerns man-power review. He said that he keeps labour under 'continuous' review and thought that this was connected with the yearly review of performance in the factory. With respect to this review, the foreman's job is to fill a merit card for the year. He felt that his view about a man's performance would be normally accepted by his manager but complained that he did not possess sufficient authority. He felt that the yearly review was his own task and was not open to the suggestion that it was really his manager's and not his.

Task 4. This concerns training of labour and is of one month like in the previous case.

Task 5. This concerns a monthly budget, again similar to the previous foreman's.

Task 6. Unlike the previous foreman, this occupant suggested that he also had a number of projects. The first of these has to do with changing the system of records. He had started 'thinking about it' five months before the interview took place and had just got it finished. Nevertheless, the project would continue for about six more months. When I dug into this, it appeared that for the previous twelve months he had been claiming that the system of records ought to be changed. On his insistence, the manager had given him the task to change the system and had given him six months in which to do it. But the manager was not interviewed by me, so that it was impossible to check on the accuracy of this.

Task 7. This project had to do with co-operating with the work-study people for the review of bonus and rates. My impression again was that the occupant confused his own role with that of his manager, but I could not check on this. His explanation did not seem convincing because the task, as he described it, was too similar to those he had already described under his everyday short-term routine. His own strong feeling, however, was that this was a one-year job.

Task 8. A jumble of projects came out all together and I could not disentangle them beyond a certain point. There was, first, a production problem which involved ordering new machinery. This would take about one year to complete. A related production project involved changing the layout of part of the shop and his job in this was to put over-time production right. Finally, in relation to the above two, he had to submit expenditure estimates for one year ahead. (Smilingly he said that one had to 'cheat' and over-demand necessary labour and components in order to get what one actually needed: sociologists, please note!)

Comment: I most certainly got the very honest perceptions of what the occupant of the role considered to be his responsibilities. Interestingly enough, it was not difficult for him after the first hour of the interview to express his job in task form, to give the beginning and end and to identify the results precisely. What continuously appeared, however, was a form of worry that, even though he was responsible for producing such and such, his 'authority' to proceed was not commensurate with his 'responsibility'. It was very difficult to pinpoint him as to what were the real limits of his own role and where his descriptions overspilled into the role of his manager. My initial reaction to this interview (before we held a seminar on our first results) was to consider that considerable fantasy had crept into the description by the occupant of the limits of his responsibility. This was particularly so when after 2½ hours of discussion the occupant was getting tired and speaking of whole areas of problems, jumping from any one of them. Several of the tasks he half-described seemed distinct and real, particularly some having to do with co-operation with work-study people and labour performance review (which he described as a yearly task). A number of others had to do with projects such as changing the layout, changing a particular design, thinking how overtime would work out so that certain buffer stocks could be achieved, even a capital expenditure project which was related to the layout problem. All of these stretched over six months and did not appear at all unrealistic; and, on the face of it, there was no reason to believe that six months' tasks could not exist in this role. Inconsistencies which appeared in the felt-fair pay questions were also probably due to language rather than to fantasy creeping in.

Since then my view is that we have from this interview not

a problematic job but rather a test of the method then used, which considered time-span to be measurabŀe as a separate perception by the manager *or* by the occupant, of the tasks assigned, and this method can clearly give two *different* perceptions. I ought therefore to say now that what we got in the pilot project was the descriptions of role specification in task form, as perceived *subjectively* by the manager *or* by the subordinate. Whether the descriptions are themselves the time-span or whether this method contaminates the data we are trying to get, was of course the main methodological problem which arose from the pilot project.

3. *Interview 5B. Discussion with Mr. W. on his own role*

Mr. W. is a quality controller. He is 52 years old and his father was a painter. He is a Londoner and went to the Highway Central School in Limehouse. He received some technical education up to scholarship level and finished his formal education at the age of 15, He then went to the Institute of Foremanship and his present technical title is A.M.I.E.I. He thinks that there have been factors holding him back in his career and in particular that some individual in the firm withheld promotion which was due to him. His present title in the firm is 'V'. Quality Controller. He gave Mr. Pa. as his manager. According to records, however, it is Mr. P. who is his manager, whereas Mr. Pa. is Mr. P.'s manager. This minor point proved indicative of general feelings of 'disequilibrium' expressed throughout the interview.

Mr. W. has been in the role for two years and he is certainly 'in' the job. He considers that, in terms of quantity of work, he is getting a little too much. His level of responsibility, on the other hand, he rates as about right. With respect to felt-fair pay he gave £1,800 to £2,000 as his present felt-fair pay and his capacity felt-fair pay was the same figure. He added that he should get over £2,000 if promoted. Clearly the felt-fair pay statement here is contingent on his view of his prospects of promotion, which he considers to be nil. Questioned as to which jobs are long, he said that labour problems are the longest. Then he realised that this was a general responsibility and he went on to 'urgent' matters or things which he considered to be 'important'. Thus there could be a 'bad patch'; it took perhaps one week to sort out this major problem. In the same manner, for faulty machines it would take up to two weeks at the most for some of his longest jobs. All these 'important' tasks are very much smaller than the tasks that came up later.

On the significance of his manager asking him to do something 'quickly' he said that this meant he would be *doing* it right now. The term 'immediately' meant right away, the term 'as soon as possible' meant the same day, and the same held for 'soon'. The term 'in the fairly near future' meant about a week. 'When you have time' meant about a month, but this was an unlikely statement. 'No hurry, give it plenty of time' would be over a month, but he had never heard his manager say this. 'We don't need this for quite some time' was not used. As for 'this will be a long job', he now came up with the answer three months, *but not six*, as emerges later. His present gross earnings are £1,900. The length of his annual holiday is four weeks. His first job was at the age of 15 when he was engaged in a sliding-door gear firm in the City. He worked there for five years. At the age of 21, in 1936, he was engaged at H. starting at £2. 10s. per week. He has always worked at the P. Factory. He is married, has no children; his wife works part-time as a shop assistant earning from £2 to £3 per week. He has no other income.

In describing his job he outlined five general responsibilities which were a summary from his statement by objectives. They are as follows:

(a) To ensure that good quality articles reach the assembly floor from outside suppliers.
(b) To control the labour force in his department.
(c) To liaise with outside suppliers and to travel over the country to do so.
(d) To maintain quality records of suppliers.
(e) To train subordinates.

The majority of his routine recurring tasks are generated by the first general responsibility. Examples are as follows:

1. To check subordinates' work of the previous day, every

day in the morning. This is a very short task of approximately one hour.

2. To check rejects from the floor and to arrange for the return of these rejects to the suppliers. This sort of task can last up to one week.

3. To query whether progress-chasers are dealing with urgent matters. This is approximately one day.

4. To report on his own rejections, again within the day.

5. To answer suppliers' queries within the day.

6. To test materials or components that have been rejected or are under query. This would be a longer task, taking from one month to six weeks.

7. To prepare a weekly report on components, which would be a one week task.

All these tasks would involve taking the material into the laboratory and writing reports for Mr. Pa., or Mr. P., or someone else involved. They are rather short and are always 'urgent' because the through-put in the factory is short. There are a great number of reports and undoubtedly this is the source of his feeling rather strained in his work.

He then gave me a planning task which is of a project nature. He said that obtaining a piece of testing equipment would take him from six months to one year. In describing this task he made it appear rather unlikely. He didn't quite believe it and let it drop.

He then got on to the main part of his job, which is operating the V. quality control system. This is a new system according to which the firm does not inspect materials bought outside on arrival but enforces a system of quality control on their suppliers. Mr. W.'s job in relation to this is to classify the supplying firms into three classes, the A, B and C streams. Since there are fifty types of materials and approximately 5,000 component parts and 330 suppliers, it is impossible to check all the suppliers all the time. The object of the classification into streams is to ensure that the majority of the firms operate the V. quality control system and therefore can be put into the A and B classes, which absolves the firm from testing their supplies themselves. Mr. W.'s job is to ensure that most firms continuously qualify for inclusion in the A and B streams. In order to do this he keeps record cards of each supplier and these are checked each quarter. He visits firms to inspect the quality control system on the spot. His aim, which is the prescribed limit to this task, is to keep over 75% of suppliers in stream *A* and over 15% in stream *B*.

The precise tasks that are generated in doing this work are:

1. A monthly report on the programme, which is a month's task.

2. A quarterly report on suppliers' grading, which is a three months' task.

3. A six monthly report on inspection.

This was done only once so far, but he hopes it will be done again. It involved him into some changes of the system of keeping records and took six months. The task appeared very plausible the way he described it. He then jumped on to say, however, that another report had just been assigned to him and he was given a year in which to complete it. The yearly task did not ring at all true and he quickly dropped it.

We returned to the six months' task, which he now viewed as a sequence — he thought about it in the previous January and he took a month to write it. He was then authorised to repeat this in six months. If he doesn't do it in six months he thinks that Mr. Pa. (this time) would notice that he has not repeated it and would expect it and ask for it. It is a rather short document of two or three pages.

The V. system has been operating three years. Simplifying the records system and changing every six months was the kind of major improvement very much expected by his managers. Mr. W. expects that six monthly improvements are quite possible and he would like to think a year ahead, but he 'hasn't the time'. Here he changed his expressions. If he had the time he would like to make some improvements, but he needn't really think one year ahead to do so.

The disequilibrium feelings mentioned at the beginning of this report of the interview concerned his relations with his immediate manager, Mr. P. From time to time Mr. W. appeared to think that he was responsible to Mr. Pa. directly and therefore the tasks he was given to do were confused in his perception with the tasks given by Mr. Pa. to Mr. P. This did now, however, appear to be the case with his six months report on the V. system.

Note that Mr. W. is a fairly senior foreman and would very likely have got Mr. P.'s job. In fact Mr. P. was brought in from another department and the whole situation is in disequilibrium because Mr. W. has been in the department much longer than his immediate manager. To make matters worse the manager of the department, Mr. Pa., has been in the role even less that Mr. P.

In spite of all his strong feelings of personal 'disequilibrium' in the role, as presently fitted in the hierarchy, the interview went well and was conducted throughout in a friendly tone. Mr. W. was very colourful in his description of the way in which he ensures that firms comply with the quality control system and procedures favoured by H. In several cases he used the expression 'using my loaf' in spotting things that were wrongly designed in other firms' quality control systems. He thought of himself as a very experienced man who need not receive '*any* instructions' about how to conduct his work.

4. Interview 7A. Discussion with Mr. T., Manager of the P. site on the role of Mr. M. (one of the two superintendents of production)

Mr. M. is the manager of Mr. K. and a description of Mr. M.'s role provides some interesting parallels with what he had himself previously said on Mr. K.'s role.

The manager described the occupant's quantity of work as rather too much. He thought that the level of responsibility given to the occupant was also rather too much. He considered the worth of the occupant, in felt-fair pay terms, as between £2,500-£3,000 per annum. The actual salary was £2,015 per annum. Mr. M. was a fairly senior person who could very well have got Mr. T.'s, the manager's, own job, but Mr. T. thought that while Mr. M. had the experience and ability, on the whole his career had been narrower than his own. The felt-fair pay for Mr. T.'s job would be in the region of £3,400-£4,000 per year.

On the question of what kind of job would be considered a 'long' job for Mr. M., the manager replied that this would be of the order of two years. He gave an example of one such task which will be discussed below. The manager was not particularly happy about questions concerning the time-dimension of instructions but nevertheless replied to my questions. The instruction 'quickly' would be 'by tonight' (!); 'immediately' would be 'now'; 'as soon as possible' would be 'in two or three days'; 'soon' would never be used; 'in the fairly near future' would be 'in three to six months'; 'when you have time' would never be used; similarly with 'no hurry'; 'we don't need this for quite some time' would never be used either; whereas 'this would be a long job' would mean *one* year. At this point, interestingly enough, the manager gave me the *same* example which he had previously considered as a two-year job.

This fourth interview was the second with the manager rather than with the occupant of a role. There was already little doubt by then that interviews with managers were much more clear-cut. Once some initial difficulties of terminology were overcome, the description of tasks was concise, precise as well as extremely plausible. The task analysis of this role was given as follows:

Task 1. The routine recurring production task came under the general responsibility of 'supplying components to the assembly floors, at the right time, at the right cost, at the right quality, according to the requisites of stores'. Production was organised according to the quarterly master plan which, however, was issued to superintendents one month ahead of the quarter. This required the occupant to plan the deployment of labour and utilisation of machinery four months ahead. This then was a four months' task.

Task 2. The efficiency of operation was computed by a 'standard cost' system. Bonus was calculated in terms of output, and the records of bonus would describe Mr. M.'s achievement on direct cost standards. From this there was also computed an efficiency ratio. Indirect cost was controlled by a budget on machine repairs and setting, and another budget on supplies, tools, materials, etc. Each department operated on a monthly budget, but Mr. M. was not held down to this. He was expected to operate his indirect costs on a yearly budget. He could shift from month to month according to how he felt maintenance should be carried out. The responsibility of keeping indirect costs down thus produced a yearly task, keeping to a budget expressed in monthly terms but extending over one year. Through these indicative monthly budgets the occupant would in turn control the indirect cost performance of his foremen. (This then was a check that the tasks of a superintendent and foreman *did* link up and that the manager once removed could exercise overall control.)

Task 3. This task concerned the capital budget which came up in August of each year. There was then a review of capital expenditure requirements for one year ahead, the yearly capital budget being then a constraint on the occupant's future action. We thus have two tasks of one year.

Other shorter routine recurring tasks were as follows: One concerned the efficiency of new jobs. The manager had a task of approximately one to six weeks in which to 'standardise' new jobs. Standards were also reviewed at the end of every year and this responsibility generated a short task of approximately one month. There was also a responsibility related to the Ministry review of safety measures which took place every six months. In between these reviews the occupant was responsible for safety.

Task 4. We went on to examine the occupant's projects. There was one project in operation at the time of the interview. This concerned the area of machine supplies and maintenance for which there had been very high expenses in the past. In August 1966 Mr. M. had asked for various new items of machinery and for changes in layout. He had also asked for similar changes three years before, but then his proposals had been rejected. At the present instance the manager approved of a two-year plan which is to go ahead. The two-year plan, however, had to be split into two phases. The reason for this was that even the manager could not by himself approve anything extending for over a year. Even the yearly capital budget is not approved by the manager of this role but elsewhere in the organisation.

I tried to probe into this in order to distinguish formalities from real decision-taking. Mr. T. was quite clear that Mr. M.

was not responsible for simply completing the first phase. Each phase had no more than accounting significance. Formally one had to comply with regulations and construct proposals falling within one budget. According to Mr. T., Mr. M. was held accountable for completing the whole change of layout by the end of the two-year period. My conclusion was that this project was in fact a two-year task. Nevertheless, I did not feel very happy about it. It felt as if the two-year task was the manager's own to a very large extent. It is this situation which cannot be resolved unless one confronts this evidence with that from the occupant and perhaps then again with the manager once removed.

Task 5. We then came to the category of training manpower. When it came to new appointments, the manager said that for three years there would be vague thoughts, for two years there would be grooming of people for promotion, and for about one year persons would be short-listed. At this point he would give Mr. M. one year in which to train the new occupant. Upon questioning the meaning of the various terms used, such as 'vague thoughts', 'grooming', etc., Mr. T. said that he would expect Mr. M. to take 'action' two years before he needed a person fully in the job. He would be expected to short-list, select, appoint, groom, train; and all this would have to be completed within two years. There was, however, again some disquiet as to whether the two years were continuously under Mr. M.'s own responsibility. For example, would Mr. T. not have any say in the appointment, thus splitting the two years in half? Mr. T., however, was getting a little impatient, and we had to conclude that on his evidence this was a two-year role. An attempt to get him back on the two-year project failed to produce further response. I just managed to slip in that the gap between the two-year role held by Mr. T. and the three months of his foremen should be noticed. The manager, however, was not involved any more, and the interview finished at this point.

5. Interview 3B. Discussion with Mr. P. concerning his own role

Mr. P. is one of the two quality control superintendents. (He is the manager of Mr. W. whose interview is recorded above.) The occupant is 48 years old; his father was a tram-driver; he went to elementary school and finished all formal full-time education at the age of 15. He later went on to various training part-time courses and presently his qualification is I.E.D. graduate. His direct manager is Mr. Pa. whose title is Quality Control Manager. Mr. P.'s title is Quality Control Superintendent. He only entered the role on 1 August 1967 but considers that he is fully doing it. He had a little too much work due to a new model which was being introduced and presented a lot of snags. He considers the job still new in some respects, somewhat inconsistently with his previous answer. He feels that his responsibility is rather too much, but when he gets more familiar with the job he expects to be delegating more. The distinction between quantity of work and amount of responsibility involved did not strike him as important.

His present felt-fair pay is £2,600-£3,000 per annum. His capacity felt-fair pay at the present time is the same figure. In one year's time, however, he expects to get £250 more per year. Thus, after one year, he should be getting £2,800-£3,000, in two year's time he expected to get another £250 increase and in five year's time he thought he should be over £3,000 per year. At 55 he should be getting about £3,500.

He came up to the meaning of a long job very quickly. This would be about one year. Every other verbal instruction produced very confused answers: 'quickly' could be anything from one week to six months; similarly for everything else. Then he returned to a 'long' job. His answers this time were very blurred. It could be two days; it could be three months, two weeks, five days, anything at all; at which point the discussion became very confused.

His present salary is £2,250 and he gets four weeks' holiday a year. He joined H. in May 1947. He has always worked at the P. factory. Before joining H. he went to school in the London area and worked for a tool-manufacturing firm in London. He is married and has a boy of 21 and a girl of 16. He has no other income and his wife does occasional agency work.

The interview with Mr. P. further showed how difficult it is to obtain satisfactory time-span measurements by the 'split-type' of interview adopted on the pilot run. The discussion had in fact to be continued for a further session because after three hours of argument Mr. P. got far too tired and was not further interested in elucidating the nature of his work. A second interview was arranged for the day after, in which he explained most points satisfactorily, partly because he was considerably more relaxed. This write-up combines both discussions. The tasks he described were the following:

Task 1. He had to produce a monthly report concerning the operation of the V. system, part of which had by now evolved into an Insurance System to suppliers. His report concerns the percentage of increase of suppliers operating the Insurance System. This was a clear-cut monthly task.

Task 2. This and the following task explains the tie-up between this role and that of his subordinate I described above. The second task has to do with salvaging equipment for machines producing faulty parts. The faulty parts are rejected and the machines must be repaired. It is sometimes worthwhile for the factory to salvage the rejected parts. These are given to Mr. P., who operates a small salvage department. The task originates with a 'form' which tells him that he must salvage a certain quantity of faulty products and is given a maximum of five weeks to deliver these products back to the production departments.

Task 3. The other task concerns the repair of the machines that produce the faulty parts. In this case he has to get in touch with the engineers and tell them what is expected of the machine. His job is through when the engineers put the machine right and he re-tests the product. Such tasks are usually over in about three weeks.

Task 4. Mr. P. is also responsible for the operation of the inspection system inside the prime manufacturing sector. His job involves producing a monthly report. The Quality

Controllers inside the production departments, particularly in the prime manufacturing sector, are responsible directly to him. His monthly report describes the way in which they operate. In some cases he is involved in action across two monthly reports. Such action, on which he may have to report separately, may take up to six weeks. This task is therefore up to one and a half months long.

Task 5. The occupant is responsible for operating within a yearly capital budget. He has to submit estimates for this budget and once this is approved he is responsible for operating within it. He turns in monthly reports on capital expenditure but is not held to any monthly totals. At the end of the year he submits a yearly report on the use of funds. When he described the details of the operation, however, it was less clear that he was involved with a one-year budget.

Task 6. This originated from his responsibility over man-power in his department. He started by stating that he was responsible for planning manpower requirements one year ahead. By this time he had fully understood the point of my questions. Pressed further, he said that he had to take action six months ahead of trouble. Next he said that this sort of trouble could be forecast with virtual certainty in this factory. This then is a six month task.

The operation of the V. quality system is worth analysing in more detail. He gets triggered off by a monthly report he receives on the record of supplies and the assessment of suppliers, including the number of rejections and complaints. He then puts these records in the form of a graph, issues a monthly report on the progress of quality control operations outside of H. and explains the reason for any hold-up due to supplies being inadequate. From his graphs he forms a view as to how the maintenance of an efficient control system can be achieved. He ensures that the suppliers maintain their own quality control system by sending his own man, Mr. W., to visit them. He also operates the insurance system to the suppliers. Somewhere around this part of the discussion I felt that there was a longer task which he could not describe and which had probably to do with this six months' change and improvement of the V. quality control system which had been previously described to me by Mr. W. Mr. P., however, was reluctant to say anything directly on this matter.

Task 7. Immediately after this hesitant discussion, Mr. P. gave me an excellent description of the operation of Form 143 with respect to the standards room. This form concerns the vetting of a new part which has not been produced before. Whenever a new part originates, Mr. P. gets hold of a sample or the model and does dimensional tests. He does not do any live testing. He then passes out his tests to his collateral for assembly control and does the same for product testing in final form. All reports from assembly and production come back to him. His decision then involves accepting, approving, or rejecting the part.

We spent one hour charting this procedure in detail. On further discussion he is not triggered off by the sample. Sometimes he didn't get the samples through normal processes and had to 'find' them. Asked how he knew of the existence of such an item, he replied that he received minutes. These minutes were a green form communicated to him from the development engineers. On getting hold of the minutes he would then try to find the samples, sometimes with some difficulty, and then put the item on the standards room for the various dimensional tests. On being satisfied with these tests, he filled his Form 143 and sent this to the buyer for ordering. Copies of the form were sent to the other quality control people concerned. Another copy went to the goods inward inspection, guiding them on the item and the particular supplier.

He then gave me an example of the procedure on Form 143. This concerned a large mould which was produced by a tool of Italian manufacture which had been purchased outside. Note here that the tests Mr. P. is responsible for do not involve the machinery which produces components but rather the components themselves. According to changes on the components, changes are demanded of the machinery one way or the other. The particular sample component was in this instance sent directly from Italy. Mr. P. checked the component, approved of it partly and recommended some changes in the tool. After the machine tool was bought and installed, a production sample came back to him. He then did further tests and produced another Form 143, authorising provisional acceptance of the product but again recommended further changes. The first Form 143 was issued on the October before the interview. A new sample was produced at H. and then came to him in December (before the interview) and three days later he produced another Form 143. Two weeks after that he got another sample, did further tests and again provisionally accepted with another Form. He also did some salvage and complementary parts related to the job. This was repeated for some further batches of initial production. He finally approved the product with a 143 Form on the week of the interview.

We thus have a whole series of small projects generated under the general responsibility of vetting new parts and components. In this example, between the first minutes which triggered him off and the relevant, that is to say, the first, Form 143 which he signed, there lapsed a span of seven months. The overall length between the first minutes and the final form is obviously much longer, but these were different projects and each one of them originated outside Mr. P.'s role. The task then, properly, is each project on its own, the longest of these being seven months. This was the nicest example (which I got) of a task sequence arising from a general responsibility.

A confusing area in this department was that of manpower, training, promotion, etc. All members of this department were concerned about the manpower situation, which was natural in that the majority of the employees were getting very old and near retirement age, whereas most of the managers were very new appointments. There was thus a discrepancy between what the managers considered their own normal career prospects and their lack of experience which, in turn, would be difficult to get in view of the manpower situation inherited. This to some extent explains Mr. W.'s view, that it would take him six months to train a subordinate, whereas Mr. P. who was his manager thought it would also take him six months at the very most before he would take any action in respect of subordinates. The problem of ageing manpower was met by instituting a yearly prospective of talent, a development started by the new manager of quality control. This was not however Mr. P.'s own task.

6. *Interview 6B. Discussion with Mr. B. on his own role*

The occupant is responsible for the quality of outgoing *c*. products. He comes into operation after production checking of the various products and before they get despatched. His authority is to stop them. His recurring tasks occur in this area and they take up most of his time.

Task 1. He is triggered off by the arrival of the finished products from production checking at a particular place in the factory where he has access. I asked how much time the various products would be in his hands and he replied 'from Thursday afternoon to Tuesday morning'. He has a number of fairly elderly workers to do the checking for him. If he is in some way unsatisfied with quality he will issue a work order to bond the batch and will then report to the works manager, Mr. T., *via* the quality control manager Mr. Pa. Once again I met a role occupant who does not refer to his own immediate manager, Mr. H.

Task 2. Another small routine recurring task is checking on the weekly report from his subordinates and judging their performance by it. This report, plus his comments, he then passes on to Mr. H. After some thinking and re-thinking, he qualified his weekly report to Mr. H. as his 'prime' function.

As is recorded here, at this interview I tried to get some tasks out before I went through the lengthy process of biographical comments, etc. This certainly seems to pay. But now I turned to the side questions. Mr. B. was born in 1912; his father was a Post Office sorter. He went to elementary school and stopped all formal full-time education at the age of 14. He felt that his ability would qualify him for higher posts, but his lack of formal qualifications has prevented this. His present title is Senior Quality Controller and he has been in the job for two years. His quantity of work and amount of responsibility he considers as not quite enough to not enough at all. He felt a job of this nature or an 'office' of this kind is actually worth £2,700 a year. His capacity felt-fair pay he gave me as £3,000 a year. The question concerning a 'long job' he considered a very clear one, and his answer was directly 'six months up to one year'. He was thinking of a specific example concerning a changeover of the quality control system. His present gross earnings are £1,950 a year. He has been at H. since 1934. He is married, has a daughter of 32 and a son of 21. His wife is employed and earns approximately £16 a week.

Either because the sequence of the interview (covering the then form of the questionnaire later in the interview) is a better method, or because this occupant was not in a particular rush to go back to work, this interview went a lot better than the others. Very leisurely, he described to me his routine recurring tasks and gave me more examples than I really needed. Gradually a certain feeling of bitterness came out as he was describing the very limited prospects of promotion. The vagaries of fate which had prevented him from getting formal qualifications and the fact that even when he was doing some job which he liked and considered important it was snatched away from him just at the time when it was sufficiently ready to be presented to his managers (once removed) made him unhappy. Such jobs originated from two projects which were as follows:

Project 1. This concerns the introduction of a new quality control system for outgoing products which is called the *d.* system on points. The idea of this system originated with Mr. B after some visits he had paid to other factories. The problem was to eliminate the need for detailed checking by his own men on each production batch. The object of the new system was to introduce some sample testing which would then be so tabulated as to be a guide to the production superintendents for the avoidance of these particular kinds of sub-standard results. It was the beginning of October when he was allowed to proceed with this new system and he was given to the beginning of February to complete it. (This was a few days before the interview took place.) Having completed this four-months task, he expected that his manager would let him do a two-months follow-up, to introduce the method to the production superintendents. He described to me how this would work, how errors would be classified as critical, major or minor. However, since his paper had been finished, his manager, Mr. Pa. (this is again the manager once removed), 'snatched it away from him'. On top of this, the manager had simply sat on the report and done nothing about it. Mr. B. had therefore decided to give the write-up himself to the superintendents and thus trigger Mr. Pa. into action. (I was later able to check on these facts with Mr. Pa., who gave me a rather different description of how the project had been planned, but, interestingly enough, agreed to the *false* proposition (as it turned out) that there had been assigned a four-month freak of a task. In such a situation, it became extremely difficult not to be a participant in the debate.)

Project 2. This concerns devising a new control system. The procedure sheet for his own employees, according to which his subordinates did the sampling before the goods reached despatch, required revision. This project originated whenever there was a new product or a new model for which the tests performed by his quality controllers must be different to whatever existed before. One year before a new model is due for despatch, he is triggered off by his manager and asked to produce a prototype of the new procedure sheet for testing on this model. He is given six months to do this. The prototype is then checked by his manager, who in turn gives him another three months to produce a finalised procedure sheet. At this point he is finished, and there are three more months of grace before the new model is due in and the procedure sheets will be utilised.

Project 3. This concerns the compilation of a rejection form. This form is not unlike the procedure sheet described above, and it can often be derived from an existing procedure sheet; hence the time-spans are rather shorter. Usually, after the compilation of a procedure sheet and approximately one month before production, he will start producing his rejection form. He can start even later, so the maximum for this task is one month.

Task 6. The occupant's final task falls in the area of training of subordinates. In this department as well as in others the manpower was getting near retirement age, so the specific example was the replacing of a foreman. The task came out very easily, the instruction being to find, appoint and train a new foreman within six months.

There are no other tasks. There is no separate budget for

the department and the occupant operates to a part of the department budget.

Comment: The atmosphere of this interview seemed to me entirely realistic. All tasks given by the occupant were clear-cut and all appeared plausible. The time-span of the role was *six months*.

7. *Interview 9B. Discussion with Mr. T. on his own role*

The occupant's title is Assembly Superintendent. The occupant is 47 years old. His father was a tram driver. After elementary school he went to technical school for 1½ years and then for six years to evening classes, weekend studies, a management course and then to three resident courses, the latter during his career at H., which were of six weeks, four weeks, and two weeks apiece. His formal education stopped at the age of 15½. He also spent six years in the R.A.F. between 1939 and 1945, where he was employed as a fitter. Factors which have held him back in his career included leaving the technological school for family reasons. His present area of authority is to superintend the assembly of the first and the second floor. His current manager is Mr. T. The occupant has been in the job for almost nine years.

In terms of quantity of work he is getting rather too much, because of the size of his department, which is approximately twice as large as the production departments. He would not answer the question on the level of responsibility directly. He wished to make a distinction between responsibility and authority. Whereas there was responsibility to deal with 'every' problem under his province, he did not have sufficient authority to deal with other collateral managers, particularly in the service departments, and this made it all the harder to discharge his own responsibilities. He felt that the authority of the superintendent had historically diminished, whereas his responsibilities had not. I questioned whether this was a matter of language. He countered that he was obliged to deal with his manager on more matters, but manager's approval did not absolve him of any responsibility. I could not resolve the matter at that time, although it was obvious that there was some inadequacy of task specification for his own work.

(I also felt that abstracting from the system of communications in the department probably diminished the value of the interviews, a subject upon which I will comment later.)

On the matter of felt-fair pay he gave a range for the job. Starting fair pay would be £2,600 or £2,700 per annum, going up to £3,100 up to £3,250. His present salary was £2,000 per annum. In answer to a question about his capacity felt-fair pay, he replied that it would take over £3,000 per annum to induce him to leave his present job. There was a problem of (the absence of) vacancies at the top in his own firm. He had in fact been offered a job elsewhere but did not take it up even though a car was thrown in. But he did not rate the prospective job at any more than his present job. In order to leave he would really want a production or works manager job. With respect to the evolution of his capacity and pay over the next three years, he expected to be worth £300 more per annum. His projection would willingly go over the next five years but, in his view, such a projection would not be realistic in that the question was not about growing capacity and pay. It rather mattered whether the vacancies were there and whether promotion prospects were realistic.

The occupant then speculated about the pleasure one gets from one's job. Might it not be worth taking a 'lower' job where one would shine a lot better rather than at the present one? Present reviewing methods were narrow. They attempted to consider the man versus the job rather than all men versus all jobs. He felt he would have done a much better job in a modern building employing half the people that he now had. Under such conditions he would have been happy to look at the 'minutest detail'. I asked whether this characterisation pointed toward the appointment of one or two deputies. But he was sceptical about the possibility of delegating what he termed 'minute detail', since he felt that the deputies should requisitely be of the same calibre as the manager. He felt that in practice he would be passing over his own deputy. The man he would select ought to be 'almost' like himself. This did not imply that a deputy need necessarily approach the problem *in the same way*. (It was the first time, with this interview, that I felt 'rank' distances coming into the discussion.)

We then came to the short-cut questions about long jobs and the like. In this case the short question produced the requisite answer. He referred to a problem of immediate interest which concerned the quality of armatures. That was a recurring problem. Nevertheless he had started tackling it twelve months before the date of our discussion and expected it to go on for another six months. Although the problem had occurred before, this time he wanted to solve it for good. He had found all the factors involved and wanted to remove them. As I confirmed in detail later on, this was clearly a 1½-year job (and the role's longest task).

His present salary is £2,650 per annum. He gets four weeks' holiday, although he has no freedom to take them all together. He has been at H. since early 1949. He is married and has a son of 22. There is no other income in the family.

Comment: It was extremely interesting to notice in this interview that the language and the gestures used all referred to *concrete* detail (but see comment below). Even when generalising, the occupant was illustrating the problem by reference to specific examples. The descriptions became more concrete and more vivid as he was involved in describing his tasks.

Task 1. This concerned the application of the quarterly master schedule of production. The whole factory is run on a quarterly production schedule and he was assembling at the same rate as the production departments gave him the parts. He gave weekly progress reports at meetings with his manager and his colleagues from the other departments. From the quarterly schedule there also originated other routine tasks, such as meetings with his foremen, dealing with problems of labour, etc. There was no quarterly report because everything was covered in the weekly reports. Like the other superintendents, he received the quarterly schedule one month ahead of application. Hence his routine recurring production task was four months.

Task 2. This was a project concerning the introduction of a new model. As with all new models there were meetings of a special project team to carry development through until the new model was in routine production. The specific new model had the Code no. 1124 and the meetings went by the same name. He had started attending these meetings at the beginning of December 1967, and this was the beginning of his task in relation to the new model. The task instruction can be formulated as: 'Plan the assembly of Model 1124 until it is running in full routine order.' The time limit set for this task was eight to nine months. His involvement developed as follows:

From the first meeting a number of sub-tasks were generated by himself. The first of these was to deal with the Trades Unions on the problems presented by a new production line. He had to consult the Factory Acts and negotiate with the Unions so that they would agree on certain seating arrangements. To reduce cost he wished to introduce women into the job, and this involved creating a layout which could accommodate seating workers. Another sub-task concerned the selection of a foreman for the new assembly line. A third sub-task involved ensuring that labour would be available to operate the new line at the right time. This further implied the need for building buffers of some other items currently produced, so that labour could be released in adequate time for training. A fourth sub-task concerned the development of the layout in co-operation with the engineers, reporting back on the layout and getting approval for it. A fifth sub-task concerned the removal of a variety of sub-standard operations and arriving at new standards. Having completed these preliminaries he will be ready to start assembly and expects the department to be running at average efficiency (according to the accepted indicators) approximately six months from the starting of assembly, certainly not any longer and if possible sooner.

It is from this overall description that I got the total length of eight to nine months. Interestingly enough, the overall length of the task had not been specified by his manager when he was assigned the task in the first place. It was a case where the total length of the task was entirely implicit. Note also that he could not be triggered off entirely from his own volition, since he depends on the production departments producing the goods for him to assemble. Nevertheless he did not depend on any instructions from his manager to start anything. From the moment when he started attending the 1·124 progress meetings he has been 'on his own'. He reports his own progress at those meetings and gets to know how the other departments are progressing, but he is on his own until the model is in full production.

Task 3. There had previously been a similar project. Another new model was introduced in much the same way, only the time-span was slightly longer. It had taken approximately two months to pre-plan the various requirements and almost nine months to get into full production. (It could not be ascertained whether these were target completion times so that the discussion was limited to the total length of the operation as it historically occurred.)

Yet another example the occupant gave me concerned a model which had taken approximately 4½ months pre-planning and a six to nine months interval, according to differing indicators, between take-off and routine production. From the description of the previous task, however, I got a clear impression that the sub-tasks were generated by himself, therefore the task instruction concerned the totality from beginning of attendance to full routine production, making it a task of slightly over one year.

Task 4. A different sort of project concerned the introduction not of a new model but of a new process. This required the installation of new machinery. He had to clear up the space for the new machinery, regroup the other machines (space was a consistent limiting factor in this factory), get the engineers to install the new machinery for him in the manner he thought would facilitate assembly, himself devise the standards of output figures, compare them with the schedules produced by the designers and, while all this pre-planning was going on, build buffers of all the goods which would not be produced during the reinstallation. As I asked how long each operation would take, he used the expression 'let me try to visualise this' and used his hands extensively, almost drawing a model of the production line. How long would the efficiency standard take to be fully obtained? His answer was 'approximately twelve months from the start'. He would expect it to be getting quite good within six months, but it was 'realistically' planned to be achieved in twelve months. The project had a further complication: whereas four months would be sufficient to attain the output target, it would take up to a whole year to reduce the reject factor to standard. At the time of the interview he had found a solution to some problems and introduced it on one machine, then found some more errors until he finally 'cracked' this particular problem and the reject factor had started going down. While saying all this, he had produced the appropriate graphs to show to me.

It was in the context of a quality problem superimposed on the production problem that it started becoming unclear whether the task was his own or his manager's. There were several cases where quality and production considerations became intertwined. In one such case the problem had been going on for almost two years. A lot of discussions had then taken place between himself and his manager. His own feeling was that the quality aspect was not entirely his own responsibility, but he was not clear at which point his task stopped. In general, production problems finished within a year but the quality problems lasted somewhat longer. I was surprised to find this sort of ambiguity in the case of this Production Superintendent whose other tasks were extremely clear cut. (The lack of clarity reached at this point of the interview was similar to the discussion I subsequently had with the Quality Control Superintendent, paragraph 8 and paragraph 9.)

Task 5. This involved the whole area of manpower development. The occupant was engaged in a five-year manpower exercise together with his manager. In the framework of this exercise it had been decided at the end of 1966 to review the position of all the foremen. This review occurred simultaneously with more fundamental re-organisation 'at the bottom', in which he got involved from August 1967. He then reduced his indirect costs and engaged some new people whom he put through a six-months' basic training course. But the overall re-organisation of Rank 1 manpower was a much longer task. The forecasting of retirements and vacancies and the designation of new role specifications were by way of a preselection task, which he had done in conjunction with his manager, in the context of the overall five-year manpower planning exercise. This particular pre-planning phase did not exceed six months. Following this, and twelve months before a vacancy would become operative, the manager instructed the occupant to start the process of developing a new foreman for that job. The attempt was to find the prospective foreman in other departments, put candidates through a rather extensive training programme covering various departments of the factory until they were finally groomed, short-listed and then appointed. He would then need a further six months to make the new appointments fully operational in their new roles.

Comment: My impression was that this was not a sequence of distinct tasks but rather one task, taking in this case one year and a half. In a proper consultancy relationship one would have been able to resolve any doubts arising from the fact that any new appointment was vetted by the manager at the end of the twelve-month period. From indirect evidence obtained from the manager, my impression is that the trust placed upon this particular occupant extended over the whole period. Note also that the occupant was very clear in his mind that after appointment six months was the maximum time in which he should have got his foreman into full position.

The occupant was uneasy about 'the' manpower situation because he had not yet got a 'nucleus' of section leaders from whom to select his new foremen. It was for this reason that he had to undertake such a long job in trying to find his foremen in other departments. In his view this kind of exercise should have been done a long time before. The natural time for finding a foreman who would be able to operate at a higher level of work would have been when the one-week schedule for production operations had been dropped — approximately five years before. It was because manpower development had been neglected in relation to the re-organisation of production that such a 'long job' had to be undertaken later. Still, they were not getting the kind of foreman whom they ought to have. Almost in his words, the 'gap between his own responsibilities and those of his foreman was no longer excessive'. He seemed definitely to have in his mind a foreman who would potentially be able to carry six-month tasks. In fact the new foreman he was presently grooming would be by way of a deputy or section leader and the superintendent's plans were to have one such person for each of his two assembly floors.

Task 6. This concerned capital expenditure. There was a monthly departmental budget but the manager was constrained to these budgets multiplied by twelve to get a yearly total. He had discretion over the use of his budget month by month, the monthly budget being merely an indicator of the desirable rate of expenditure.

Comment: This was by far the most interesting of all interviews during the pilot stage, particularly from the point of view of Jaques' theory of ranks and levels of abstraction. The occupant had a very concrete view of his command but never a pedantic one. He used his hands quite extensively to point to the direction where various things were located. He seemed to have a 'model' view of the position of each operation. Men did not figure in the processes he was describing. The units in which he was thinking were 'operations'.

Approximately three hours of discussion made the occupant fairly tired and ultimately somewhat philosophical, which is where the comments I made above originated. As he was getting gradually tired, *he also ceased to generalise on the 'model' view of his command and went instead to a different 'rank', as it were, looking at problem areas one by one*, not so much from the operational side as from the side of human relations, particularly relating to negotiations with the Trades Unions and other personnel issues. It was as if his brain operated on processes and model sections, whereas his emotions were with individual people or clusters of people. He drew on a very vivid memory of past situations and always seemed to operate in the context of the total work performed by the factory. He had almost as complete a view of the factory as of his own department, although he was less at home outside his immediate command and said that in particular cases he would have to enquire as to who precisely was doing what. *He seemed to feel the need to visualise the rest of the factory in equally concrete terms.*

Midway through the interview an incident arose from a strike that developed in part of his department. The emergency left him completely cool. He switched his concentration to this lower rank problem, but simultaneously carried on with higher-level generalisations practically without interruption. As our discussion proceeded, he would simply interrupt and deal with the foreman who was coming in and out of his office. He took hold of the emergency with extreme ease without straining himself at all. It was as if there was a yearning in his attitude as to which rank he would be happiest to operate on. He was very much at home in the rank of supervisor but delighted in facing almost 'manual' detail. He firmly stated his belief, that one should come up through the ranks, with further education added on later, rather than with formal education which would lead one right to the top from the beginning: 'Dealing with men cannot be taught.' He often evoked the kind of happiness one had when dealing with more straightforward and concrete problems that would arise at the rank of the high level foreman he was engaged in building up. In particular, he would like to visualise the whole of his command in terms which would be possible if the whole were confined to one floor.

On the other hand he was also getting slightly bored from dealing with assembly alone. From time to time he spoke as if he was operating from the rank of his own manager. He was quite happy to operate at his present rank, although the rank itself was not sufficiently well defined to be of his liking. The linkup with production and development was of a kind which necessitated co-ordination by his own manager, and he indicated from time to time that he would rather run the whole show alone.

I did not feel that these, so to speak, upwards and downwards 'extensions' of his personality were in any way artificial. Clearly the bulk of his experience had come from dealing with what he called 'minute problems' and he did keep a kind of emotional interest in the way such problems were tackled. On the other hand, a kind of pessimism which developed in his later comments had a lot to do with his view of prospects for promotion in the factory. At the very end of the interview he came back to the earlier theme that he would very much like now to have the job of Production Manager and was on the market looking for such a job elsewhere.

8. Interview 4A. Discussion with Mr. Pa. concerning the role of his subordinate Mr. H.

Mr. Pa. is the manager of Quality Control, and there are two immediate subordinates, the one of whom is Mr. P. whom I interviewed myself, and the other Mr. H. who was interviewed by John Evans. Mr. P.'s side is the bought-out supplies and prime manufacturing components, while Mr. H.'s is the assembly. Mr. H. has in turn three immediate subordinates: the first are problem chasers with the staff function, the second is the chemical laboratory, and the third is Mr. B., the Senior Quality Controller whom I interviewed myself. Mr. H.'s title is Quality Control Superintendent, Assembly.

Mr. H. was very senior in his post and nearing retirement age, whereas his manager was a new appointment. This perhaps resulted in the manager's relying extensively on the occupant and leaving the latter's tasks as long as possible and perhaps longer than they were likely to be in a more standard relationship.

Comment: I mention this because in other occasions (*viz.* P. and W.) such a situation resulted in the opposite result: the manager was so new to the post that he interfered in minor matters which would teach him the operation of his extended command, and thereby reduced the time-span of his immediate subordinates.

Another problem which arose in this interview was that the manager already knew a little about time-span and, further, was an intelligent and imaginative person. Not surprisingly in view of the 'research relationship' we had with this firm, the manager used his imagination fairly freely, jumping around several formalisations and tending to confuse the tasks I was trying to formulate. This led to some confusion of indentification. Mr. Pa. used the expression 'we' interchangeably with respect to tasks he was allocating to his subordinate, to his own tasks and to tasks which were (reasonably) those of his own manager. My presentation perforce contains some of this confusion.

Task 1. The routine recurring tasks originated in the following manner. The occupant was triggered off by a complaint from somewhere on the assembly side of the factory. He was then expected to give advice immediately, within an hour or two during the same morning. Perhaps due to his seniority, the occupant then directly negotiated on the implications of his advice with the superintendent of assembly or even with the works' manager himself. Having obtained the agreement of the line manager directly responsible for the problem, the occupant then hangs around to see whether his advice is implemented and whether it is successful.

I tried to get an example of this procedure and instead got a dozen. There are all sorts of norms for rejects or tolerances or 'anything' which has some numerically defined tolerance limit. Records are kept of deviations from such limits. All of a sudden some such norm begins to show a consistent and large deviation from standard. At this point a complaint is registered; the occupant takes over; he recommends a solution, but has no direct power to implement it. He must negotiate and get it accepted by the line manager concerned. He can then stick around on his own initiative until the error begins to be rectified and the measurements fall within the accepted tolerance limits. Such a task could arise very often, perhaps every day. Some such tasks would be corrected very soon and the occupant would simply keep an eye open for a week or so to see that the problem had been properly solved. Some would take a little longer but none would take much over a month. The routine recurring tasks thus seem to fall within the one-month interval.

Task 2. Having obtained a modicum of communication with the manager, he proceeded to give me an example of what he thought was a complete freak. Although the task extended over four months, it had practically no work-time spent on it. The task relates to the *d.* system, about which Mr. B. talked in some detail in my interview with him. The task instruction had two parts: first, to devise drafts for the *d.* system; secondly, to train a subordinate and estimate the work load involved in operating the new system.

The freakishness of the task occurred because the four months' target completion time was a function of the manager's decision to present the operation of the *d.* system to his colleagues on the basis of three months' observations. But these observations occurred only once every month and dealing with each one of them was a job of, at most, one afternoon. We therefore get a four months' target completion time on which the subordinate had to work for one afternoon per month. The manager was adamant that no new instructions were required during the four months. He insisted that he had given a four-month instruction. I found it impossible to convince him that the formulation of the task was such that it contained four specific instructions, for four three-hour tasks in a prescribed sequence, which was obviously the case.

The associated training task for which a three-month target time was assigned was again somewhat freakish, in that the selected subordinate was not chosen but imposed from redundancy elsewhere and the three months' time was given because the person was essentially unsuitable. To estimate the work load involved would be one day's work. The final outcome would be a draft for the operation of the new *d.* system. Moreover the manager seemed not to care a bit whether this task was performed or not.

Starting from this example, the manager queried whether the task form was appropriate to describe all kinds of work. How could one call something a task if the amount of work involved was grossly disproportionate to the time dimension within which it was targeted? Having refused to accept my explanation of the particular task, i.e., as a task sequence, he ended up by having his confidence shaken in the type of analysis we were doing. He proceeded to describe to me a project which had a form similar to the routine task described above but which could not be put into task form at all.

Task 3. The project concerned what was called the 'rocking problem'. A particular model developed a rocking motion whose causes could not be identified. The rocking could be eliminated, but the cause could not be removed.

The remedy took the form of a hard kick, when the machine was ready to despatch, and this effectively cured the illness. It had been two years since the rocking problem first originated at the time when the model was first introduced. Since then the occupant had been 'continuously' busy in attempting to discover and eliminate the causes. He had carried out 'innumerable' tests and was still proceeding with more tests, his instruction being to solve the rocking problem 'as soon as possible'.

Approximately one hour's discussion then followed in which we tried to put this particular problem into task form. We built graphs. On one axis we put the cost which was a function of the time for which the problem was not resolved. On the other axis we put various figures corresponding to the expression 'as soon as possible'. We filled the blackboard in the manager's office with various expressions and symbols, trying to formulate what was meant. To my query as to how many sub-tasks had originated during the past two years, the answer was 'an indefinable number'. We went over the history of the rocking problem in detail. The problem originated when the model had just been produced and before it was due for sale. It had not been solved during the initial target completion time, which had been four months initially. I queried whether he would let some time elapse before he took over the job himself. He replied that it does not work like this, 'because he is already involved in the job himself all the time'. I then queried at what point his own manager would take the job over, to which he replied that the manager once removed is also already involved in the job 'all the time' from the beginning. I asked whether one year was too much to let the occupant get on with the job, to which he replied that 'a day is too much'.

At some point I felt that the conversation was getting flippant and offered to drop it entirely, to which he seemed to agree and invoked a certain appointment he was already late for. But when I got up to go he stopped me and standing beside the door he kept me for another hour, sketching numerous other examples which, in his view, *could* be put in task form. The reason for this was that people, by which he meant managers, could visualise what kind of *solution* could be obtained, or at least what kind of experiments might be conducive to a solution. In the case of the rocking problem, however, they had tried absolutely everything, and found that nothing worked, and they just did not know what to try next. It simply could not be said that the occupant or himself or his own manager were to blame. I queried as to whether the problem might go on 'for ever', to which he replied 'maybe'. On the other hand, 'maybe' it would be solved that very afternoon.

He then got suddenly optimistic and said that they were now concentrating on a number of variables which had been previously looked at independently, that the solution might be there, that he was hoping that over the next two or three months the solution might be found, that he did not agree that he had given any instructions to his subordinate. 'If you want me to put it into task form, I will,' he said, 'but I don't believe that I ever did it that way.' I asked whether the subordinate could go wrong in any way. No, he said, he could not go wrong, nobody could go wrong, nobody could go right. This manager's curiosity on time-span measurement was much more provoked than his practical interest on the cost of being left with an unsolved problem in his department.

After one hour of this standing up and discussing by the door, he offered that we should again sit down and look at some other tasks. Two further routine recurring tasks then emerged, one in the form of a monthly report and then another in the form of a weekly report by the subordinate to the manager. His confidence in task analysis thus partly restored, the manager suggested another task which was a small project.

Task 4. This project concerned checking armature production. The task involved ensuring that operators were fully trained in the hope that thereby many small problems of functioning in-line would disappear. The instruction was to advise so that in-line problems would be solved, then train operators fully and observe that everything is functioning, 'as soon as possible'. Having got the beginning of this task located in the previous January, I then asked about target completion. After some thought the manager replied that if the job is at all urgent he does not give an instruction in terms of a target completion time, but in effect assigns a different 'preliminary' task. The instruction for this is to get a team together, who will get the manager acquainted with the 'basic facts'. Without the facts he cannot assign a target completion time because he has no appreciation of the 'size' of the problem. He then digressed and said that many small tasks were continuously occurring but since he was in touch with his subordinate 'every day and all the time' he would be interfering himself 'all the time'. Returning to the project concerning armature production he said that his subordinate had nearly completed his assignment, which made it a three-month job *after* the event. I spent some more time trying to get the manager to express the instruction in target terms *before* the event, and he finally agreed that when he assigned the task in January he did have in view a period of three months and had let his subordinate understand that such a period was the time required.

At this point we stopped our discussion and resumed again after three days, by which time I had also interviewed Mr. P.'s own manager, Mr. T., on the Director of Quality Control's own role. The break as well as the 'overview' helped to clarify the minds of us both.

Task 5. The next task which emerged for the role of Mr. H. concerned the in-guarantee failure system which Quality Control was responsible for operating. Failures would occur in production and would not be picked up by quality control on the out-going side. Complaints would then come back from the public with approximately three months' lag, sometimes a bit more, not very much less. The in-guarantee system ensured that the customer would obtain a good product in return. The objective was to reduce the in-guarantee failure rate by a certain percentage per annum. This seemed to point out to a yearly task which soon got us into the problem of role identification again. Did the manager give his subordinate a yearly instruction, or did he spread it out into months or quarters or half-year intervals? After some probing, the manager committed himself that he did depend exclusively on the occupant to get the task done and merely relied on a yearly report on progress which he would then sign and pass on to the manager once removed.

This was entirely exceptional for a role of this sort and in my view was caused by the 'accident' that the occupant was so very experienced whereas the manager was very new. As extant, however, there was no doubt that it was a one-year task.

Task 6. The final task which Mr. Pa. gave me for Mr. H. concerned the apprenticing of the occupant's successor. The occupant was given six months for this job and the target had been met.

The manager then offered to comment on the occupant's felt-fair pay, which he put at £2,500 per annum. He considered his subordinate to be of that capacity which at the age of 62 was obviously the limit.

9. Interview with Mr. Pa. on his own role

Mr. Pa. then offered to talk about himself on his own role. He was 43 and considered fair pay for the job as he was doing it and for the role as it was constructed to be £3,000 per annum. His capacity felt-fair pay he gave as currently £5,000 per annum, going up from £7,000 up to £8,000 at the age of 55. He justified those higher figures by revealing that he had already got higher pay than £3,000 in other jobs, having been a Management Consultant before joining H. He considered that a short spell in industry would be good for his career in the future, but before very long he would go back to consultancy, in which career he expected a much steeper gross earnings curve for himself.

His planned temporary stay in the H. job, as well as his highly academic and detached attitude, helped to explain his view of the whole operation when describing roles and men. It could not be said that at any point he was seriously involved in deciding on his executive responsibilities (in assigning tasks) or that there was any degree of commitment in his 'decisions'. In the discussion with Mr. Pa., therefore, one got a purely 'research' relationship and all the loose descriptions of work removed from the executive set-up, which were found as the main problem confronting the analysis during the pilot run.

Coming to his own tasks, Mr. Pa. described a yearly report

concerning progress in the objectives of his department and a yearly budget controlling his expenditure. He was further operating on a two year plan, from January 1968 to January 1970, the object being to bring 'new blood' into the Quality Control department. He had been given this task on appointment to the job. The picture I got of these tasks from his own manager was rather different.

10. *Interview 2A. Discussion with the Works Manager Mr. T., concerning the role of the Quality Control Manager Mr. Pa.*

This discussion started off easily, because the manager was using instruction language, such as 'I give to him', 'he ensures for me', etc. The occupant's overall general responsibility is to ensure quality of inputs into the factory and of final manufactured products. To do this the occupant employs in all about eighty people. About a half of these people are seconded to the various production departments and the other half he directly employs on his own staff. Routine recurring tasks take the form mainly of weekly and monthly reports from Mr. Pa. to Mr. T., with copies to the other superintendents. Further reports ensure that each department is kept informed on special problems of its concern. We then turned to projects which extended for one year and longer. One aspect which somewhat bedevilled the discussion from this point on was the manager's faith in 'management by objectives', which he translated to mean that everything should be 'finished' and be judged on 'results' by the end of a year.

The projects concerned the .employment and re-deployment of staff, the development of new people for higher-level jobs, the upgrading of the d. and V. quality control systems, the reduction of the in-guarantee costs, the introduction of sampling techniques and the solution of the so-called 'rocking' problem.

With respect to the manpower part of the work, the contradiction was that the manager claimed that he had given one year whereas the occupant claimed two years. Of these I believe the occupant, in that the manager was thinking that since results would be judged at the end of the year˙ the instruction must have pertained to the same period as well. But most of the tasks, as outlined by both manager and occupant, could not be broken up into yearly phases and would not be completed until at least two years. By contrast, the two major control systems' objectives were given in quantitative yearly terms without any doubt. Some light was also thrown on the so called 'rocking' problem discussed at length with the occupant. The instruction for this had now been re-phrased in terms of monthly intervals, the objective being not to allow the proportion of machines that vibrated to increase above 'normal' in any particular month.

The longests tasks fell in the manpower field. There was a whole batch of new foremen and supervisors to be trained. One of the supervisors was Mr. P., the task being that he should be fully trained to be fitted into the role, while the other was replacing Mr. H. The target completion time for this was given as eighteen months, two months for finding a candidate, six months for training him, and a final six months for grooming him into different parts of the factory. This was not a sequence of tasks but a budgeting of the time requirements. A peculiar task here was that the manager also thought that Mr. Pa. would soon either be promoted or would leave the firm; hence he would be himself expected to prepare for his own succession as well as for the succession of his two immediate subordinates.

The manager gave fair pay for the job from £2,000 to £3,000 per annum. The range was so wide probably because the manager thought of the occupant as a new appointment. (Note also, however, the difference in fair-pay statements one obtains from older relative to younger people.) The manager considered capacity felt-fair pay for Mr. Pa. to be over £3,000 but did not give any figure for present felt-fair pay and was explicit that he did not consider the occupant to be 'in the saddle' in the present job. In passing he mentioned the yearly budget task which was concurrent with the yearly overall objectives. The manager was verily convinced that the yearly objectives exhaused his subordinate's task and was most unwilling to look beyond. But perhaps the real difficulty was that the manager had been interviewed rather a lot concerning all his subordinates, both by John Evans and myself, and was beginning to feel that the exercise was going too far. He, who was the chief person involved in our relation with the organisation, was also the most sceptical as to the value of what we were doing and tolerated us as spectators who had begun to interfere with what the people concerned thought of as their real work.

CHAPTER SIX

Work Measurement at N. Ltd.

1

The work at N. took me the longest part of the spring and summer of 1968. I obtained access through correspondence with the Personnel Manager, Mr. B., who introduced me to the Works Manager of the H. site, Mr. C. My understanding with Mr. C. approximated 'consultancy' conditions, in that my access to the members of the organisation had the status of instruction. On the other hand, there was no commitment whatever by Mr. C. to get involved in task analysis for any purpose, so that the help I was to be given in getting managerial decisions about tasks depended strictly on the goodwill and therefore on the personal involvement of the people concerned. I was exceptionally lucky in this respect to have the whole-hearted co-operation of Mr. A.P., in charge of the major department of *c.* production, whose full organisation I analysed. It is because of his direct personal involvement that I was able to analyse near-enough 50 roles during the several months which I spent at the N. factory. In spite of this, it is fair warning that no matter how sympathetic and even enthusiastic an organisation is with a *research* project, the situation is not equivalent to a proper consultancy relationship, where the organisation *commits resources* for the purpose of work specification in task form.

Our introductory discussion with Mr. C. was about the purpose and scope of the research project. Mr. C. agreed that the work should go ahead, with an open mind as to any beneficial result that might accrue to the firm — other than the presumed benefit to members of the organisation whom I would interview. The department which Mr. C. wished to have researched was *c.* production. The department of *n.* production was at the time under major re-organisation and Mr. C. declared it completely out of bounds for me. The *c.*

department would afford me the opportunity of investigating tasks at shop floor level. N. provided in fact the only case in which shop floor work was investigated during the project, and this was possible, at least partly, because there was no trade union. (I mention this fact because it may have bearing on the distribution of earnings as well as the feeling of fair pay.) Not knowing at the time what load of work would be involved in analysing a complete production department, Mr. C. and I tentatively time-tabled two months of work, with the prospect of proceeding to the engineering services and the accountancy section thereafter. (After completion of the *c.* department, I did in fact hold a one-hour introductory interview with the head of the engineering services but did not proceed any further.)

The analysis proper started with three one-hour interviews with Mr. C. in which he outlined the functioning of chocolate production in relation to the firm's finances, the firm's programming and its supporting services. I found that communication with Mr. C. was exceptionally easy in that he was consistently using instruction language. Having thus obtained a feel of the size and purposes of the operation as a whole, I then interviewed Mr. C. on the role of Mr. P. who is in command.

From the interviews with Mr. C. it emerged very clearly that the role of Production Manager is fully integrated at the one-year level with respect to routine recurring work. Mr. P.'s role, however, extended beyond the one-and-a-half-year level (to approximately two years) because of a major re-organisation project. Manpower development taks similarly extend beyond the year.

For purposes of this report I find it more convenient to describe the work from the shop floor upwards, department by department, and then analyse the top manager's role and the supporting services involved. What should be clear from this introduction is that here we have a major department in which the top job is 'functionally' defined (*viz.* with respect to routine recurring work) at the one-year mark. We shall note, that, regardless of the 'expanded' role, as filled by Mr. P., there is an 'above-normal' gap between the one-year routine of the top manager and the next rank in the hierarchy.

Chocolate production is divided into four departments. The first of these has to do with the production of chocolate mass, or liquor. Most of this product is 'exported' from the factory to other parts of N. in the United Kingdom. This department is run by a foreman, Mr. F., and a senior charge-hand who acts as his deputy, Mr. B. There are three sections in the department, the major one under Mr. B., and another two under Mrs. M. and Mr. Co. The second department is divided into two sections connected 'in line', the first having to do with the refining of chocolate powder and the second with the conching of the powder into mass. There are two full shifts under the two foremen and there are also two charge-hands per shift, each directing parts of the operation. The third department has to do with the moulding of the chocolate mass into chocolate bars. There are again two shifts here under two foremen. The department is sub-divided into sections consisting of five teams of men, each working on one machine. Other than the main work of these two departments, there are a number of supporting sections which fall under the respective foremen. There is also a charge-hand in moulding as well as a night foreman (who supervises night work on a reduced shift for some of the machinery, which operates non-stop). The fourth department has to do with the wrapping of chocolate bars into finished packets ready for despatch. There is one shift here under a forewoman. Bar-wrapping consists again of a number of sections, some operating 'in-line' with the sections of the moulding department where the bars are produced, some others operating according to need for various batches.

I shall deal with the various departments and sections in the order indicated above.

2

Before the interviews with Mr. C. and Mr. P., the latter's assistant Mr. G. took me first time round the shops of chocolate production. Mr. F., the chocolate mass foreman, then took me round his own department in much greater detail. I went a third time round with each charge-hand and then repeatedly on my own to watch each individual operator.

The foreman in chocolate mass is on a very clear one-month role, the longest tasks being the production programme, which is monthly, and a manpower training task of the same length. Mr. F. is a very senior foreman with well-nigh immense experience and very distinct talent for supervising his men. Chocolate mass is a much shrunken department and the manpower is mostly of advanced age. Cocoa production, which used to account for more than half of total output, has been transferred to another factory in the United Kingdom Group, while output and labour for chocolate mass have been gradually run down. There is thus a good deal of machinery standing idle and, apart from the noise emanating from the large roaster, mostly peace and silence. The department operates on all four floors of the factory and there are wide areas which are very sparsely populated.

Mr. F.'s senior charge-hand is Mr. B. His experience almost rivals Mr. F.'s. He is operating on a one-week production schedule, even though he has knowledge of the month's programme operated by the foreman.

I spent innumerable hours with Mr. F. and Mr. B. trying to crack the technique of measuring single-task roles. After many hits and misses, and after inhaling to the full the (to me) very novel atmosphere of the shop floor, I finally got the feel of how to go about this type of measurement. It is hard to convey the feeling of being 'blooded' in task analysis. Like many other things there is no substitute for actually doing it. It seems to me that it is at the single-task level that the analyst obtains the conviction that he is actually measuring things that exist. There was no shadow of doubt that this was no conjuring trick.

The mode of analysis (and presentation) of single-task roles are different from multi-task roles. Instead of obtaining an exhaustive list of the tasks, characterised by starting and target completion times, we describe instead the physical operations involved in the job. Then we list the 'dimensions' along which discretion can be exercised. For each such dimension we define the units in which sub-standard discretion will show up. Having identified such units, we then enquire after the type of review process, whether formal or informal, which would pick these up. Only then can we get the time-dimension, which is pertinent to each review process. Each such time-dimension on a review process is a cut-off point. The longest of these cut-off points or checks is of course the time-span of the role as currently constituted.

Note: the process of measurement and its presentation can be shown on a diagram. Plot a circle and use its centre to draw arrows which extend along a radius towards the periphery. Each arrow stands for an individual 'dimension' along which some type of discretion can be exercised. The review process can be presented as a cut-off point for the arrow. Each review process can be presented as a concentric circle. The outermost of these circles is the dimension of the role as a whole. There are at least two arrows depicting dimensions, one for quality, and one for pace. Quality, however, need not always be uni-dimensional (examples below show as many as six dimensions). The idea of the diagram comes from geometry, where each dimension figures as an independent axis. The 'trick' of the concentric circles, however, permits to use the economist's usual method of presentation, *viz.* collapsing all other dimensions on to two or *one*!

Bean cleaner operator (Mr. D.)
The department's starting point is where the cocoa beans, which is the raw material, are received from stores and fed into a hopper. This hopper, which is the entry point of the department, feeds a machine which is called a bean cleaner. The heavy gang (who form no part of this department) deposit sacks of cocoa beans on a platform standing at the height of the hopper. The job of the bean cleaner operator, expressed in terms of general responsibilities, is (a) to feed the hopper at the requisite pace, (b) to keep his platform clean, (c) to check that his machine's waste material does not overflow from the container provided, (d) to clean his machine at the end of the work day, and (e) to place his empty sacks on the wheelbarrow and deliver these to stores. It is not the operator's but the charge-hand's job to ensure that sufficient raw material has been delivered by the heavy gang on each day, to sign for this material and to check stocks.

There are a number of prescribed routines for this

operator. Some of these are: to remove the waste material twice daily and to clean the floor around the machine at the end of his shift. Pace and quality of operation, however, are not fully prescribed and thus constitute the 'degrees of freedom', or the dimensions, along which discretion can be exercised. With respect to pace, the instruction is to feed the hopper in accordance with the speed of intake of the machine. This in turn is governed by the capacity of the pipes through which the cleaned cocoa beans are funnelled upwards to the silos on the top floor. The throughput of the machine is thus a continuous process, whereas feeding the machine is a discrete process (per sack). There is no explicit instruction as to the number of sacks to be fed per hour or per day. The instruction takes the negative form, to feed not too slowly (too infrequently), so that the machine will run dry, nor to feed too frequently, so that the beans will spill around the hopper, on the platform and down on the floor. The first half of this negative instruction thus concerns a pace standard, in so far as the operator can affect the pace of production. While he cannot go faster than the machine performs, he *can* go slower. If he happens to go slower than is requisite, then either the charge-hand or the foreman will know. As to how they will know, there are two answers, the formal and the extant. Formally, the foreman or the charge-hand will watch a number of luminous dials which record the operation of the machine and the state of the silos. But they don't really believe these lights, which often either do not work or do not reflect the situation accurately enough. There are, however, pipes that go through from the ground floor, on which the machine is, to the fourth floor which houses the silos. These pipes pass near the place where the charge-hand has his desk and his paperwork, about fifteen yards from the winnowing machine on the second floor. The charge-hand said that if sub-standard discretion should be exercised he would notice the unusual sound from the pipe within a quarter of an hour. This then is the time-span of discretion along that particular dimension of the role. (I usually found that discretion on pace has very short time-spans. It was in exceptional cases that pace was the longest component of the role.)

The second half of the negative instruction concerns

quality — insofar as the operator can affect quality at all. The quality standard has in this case very restricted meaning. If the machine works well the operator cannot affect the quality of bean cleaning in any way. If the machine does not work well his instruction is to call in the charge-hand. The charge-hand may in any case know of the machine's trouble before the operator does, as the luminous dials usually work in such cases. The operator does not set the machine, nor is he responsible for its maintenance. By process of elimination, I found that his remaining 'quality' standard concerns cleanliness. The next thing was to find the units measuring degrees of non-cleanliness. This turned out to be one-third of a bean sackfull spilled on the platform per hour.

Note that this unit, which I got after a good deal of searching, happens to contain the instruction for the task and the time-span. What could non-cleanliness mean in this case? 'A few' beans on the platform was all right. 'A sack-full' of beans was not all right. And thus we converged inwardly. The charge-hand said that about one-third of a sack-full would be at the margin between all right and not all right. And by what review process would somebody identify this type of sub-standard discretion? The charge-hand replied that he would see it himself, during his rounds of the department, which happen to take him to this machine approximately every hour on the average. So the foreman's hourly visit round the department is the hourly review of performance. Passing the foreman's check on the hour means carrying on as before. Not passing the check means 'be careful', plus the instruction to clean up the platform 'right now'.

The role could, of course, have been defined differently. For example, the instruction could have been to keep feeding at the requisite pace, as defined above, and not to spill more than a third of a bean sack-full during the day. But then the chargehand should *not* give additional instructions about cleanliness *during* the day. The charge-hand would have had the right of reprimand only at the end of the day, while the operator would have the right to spill as many beans as he likes during the day, provided that he limits his uncleanliness to standard for the review at the end of the day. But matters are not like that. The charge-hand's hourly visit has the character of proper review rather than just 'communication'.

It is this distinction that makes the difference between the one hour and the one day task. My lengthy description is by way of spelling out that extremely simple things often require lengthy investigation before a decision can be made between two grossly different explanations.

There is no other dimension for discretion in this role. Hence the task instruction is: 'to feed your hopper at the requisite pace, the pace standard being that of machine operation and your sub-standard discretion will become manifest in fifteen minutes, and to keep your platform clean, the quality standard being at most one-third of a sack-full of beans being spilled by the time the hourly review occurs to rate your performance.'

At first sight it would have been possible to consider the role as multi-task. The twice-daily disposal routine and the once-daily cleaning routine could have been considered independent tasks. Performance review of these tasks, in the sense of target completion time for them, would then occur either at the hourly review points or, sooner, when the charge-hand comes around to switch plant off at the end of the day. A multi-task interpretation would however be spurious, in that there is no discretion in the only case when this arises, and this is the mid-day point, as to when to dispose of the waste. The supplementary 'tasks', in other words, are fully prescribed, and hence not tasks at all. It is strictly correct to concoct a perhaps seemingly artificial, lengthy single instruction, which includes inter-task priorities and specifies both units of sub-standard discretion and review points, as exemplified above.

Routine recurring tasks for the charge-hand

From the ground floor the clean beans are siphoned out to the top floor and into a number of silos. The operation of these silos is fully mechanised and there is no personnel on the top floor. Mr. B. is directly responsible for the operations of these silos; he visits the top floor approximately every hour. The intake and out-flow from the silos can be set for the day. Mr. B. can watch machine performance either from the system of luminous dials, which he does not trust very much, or by the sound produced by the silo containers on tapping. The chargehand visits the silos at the beginning of the day to check the panels and marks the weights on the feeding scale which he then records. This gives him a measure of stocks in the morning. He takes a second reading of stocks at the end of the day and this gives him a measure of the raw material in-flow. This record is checked against final output, thus permitting a check on the machine's efficiency and the rate of wastage.

From the silos, the beans flow downwards to the second floor and into the department's main machine, which is a roaster and winnower. The beans are fed automatically into the roaster, where they are cooked and, after cooling, are again fed automatically into the winnower. The setting and operation of these two machines rests with Mr. B. The operation of the winnower requires long experience since the quality standard cannot be checked mechanically. The mechanics of the operation is to regulate the flow of the beans through the machine, which removes the shells and breaks them up so that the broken bean is of the right size and consistency. Mr. B. will absent himself from the machine only for 'short periods of time', when he tours his department. In those times he instructs the senior of the two operators in this section to 'keep an eye' on the machine. But, so far as I could tell, the charge-hand does not expect this operator to do anything other than call him back, or call the foreman, should the noise or anything else in the machine's performance disturb him. The involvement of this operator with the winnower led us to considerable complications, as will be seen below.

Shell removing operator

The winnower's output is beans and shells, which are the wastage. Each is delivered by a spout, at an angle, about ten yards away from the machine. Removal of the shells is mainly a sack-filling operation. Mr. B. thought that the senior operator had a two-task role, since sack-filling did not take his time up fully. His other task concerned the occasional responsibility for the operation of the winnower.

With respect to sack-filling, the operator is responsible for attaching the sacks on to the mouth of the spout. He leaves the sack there until full, then weighs it on his scale, and finally stacks it in the appropriate space. The operation is not

very frequent, each sack filling up in approximately half an
·hour. The weight of the full sack provides a record of the
winnower machine's wastage, which is kept by Mr. B. The
pace standard of this task is very narrowly set by the machine
and any substandard discretion along this dimension would
be revealed within a few minutes, either through the sack
over-flowing or, even more quickly, if the mouth of the spout
were left free.

The quality dimension, however, is not single. (a) There is
a cleanliness standard, and this means 'absolute' cleanliness.
Sub-standard discretion will be picked up at the most every
half-hour, when there is a change of sack. (b) There is also a
weight standard which presents some difficulties. According
to Mr. B., the operator is a very experienced and responsible
person who simply would not be using 'any' sub-standard
discretion on the weight standard. *If*, however, there should
be sub-standard discretion, it was not at all obvious as to how
soon or even how it would be picked up. One troublesome
point was that Mr. B. found it difficult to entertain the
question seriously. When pressed to do so, he referred me to
the control procedure implicit in the system of records. The
average shell winnowed from a given quantity of cocoa beans
is known from past records; hence departures from the
average would become apparent when the record of flow was
compiled at the end of the day. I countered that exceptional
wastage could be due not to substandard weighing by the
operator but to bad operation of the winnower machine. The
charge-hand replied that although this might be possible, he
would expect the same fault to 'work' on the winnowed
beans as well. He did not see that sub-standard weighing need
be revealed at all, since he did•not really believe it could
actually happen in practice. His arguments were therefore
essentially for my sake.

The question as to how he would organise the job, *if*,
instead of the present experienced occupant, he had a less
experienced or trustworthy person, through which I tried to
force him into a commitment about the review of mechanism, also left him cold. It so happened that in the context of
this particular department, whose work force was ageing and
running down, the problem was simply meaningless.

It was not obvious whether neglect of the weight standard

could be a matter of importance or not. So far as I could tell, on the shell-collecting task there is a review mechanism which *might* indicate sub-standard performance at the end of the day. It is of course not implausible, given the experience of the occupant, that the role should be organised to have a one-day time-span. What makes the matter inconclusive is that Mr. B. is so near this particular post most of the time that it is hard to say how often an *effective* review mechanism actually operates. I cannot help feeling that Mr. B's eye hovers around the needle of that weighing scale a good deal more often than he is perhaps consciously aware of. On a number of occasions *I saw* Mr. B. catch irregularities of performance almost without seeing them. The matter is of such tiny importance that it was not possible to clarify the construction of the role by appeal to the foreman or to higher management. For lack of better evidence I decided to leave the task at the half-hour mark, thus considering the weight standard to be a 'non-instruction'.

Whether there existed a second task for this role in any meaningful sense presented further problems. This second task has to do with the operation of the winnower machine. The machine is operated by manipulating a number of knobs which control the flow of cocoa beans through a number of stages. I asked Mr. B., who normally operates the machine, how soon and in what form sub-standard discretion would show up in operating this machine. He replied that it would show up 'immediately', and then *immediately* stuck his hand *into* the machine, said 'Look!', and invited me to do the same, which I politely refused to do. It turned out that, if the knobs were sub-standardly regulated, a man of experience would know that the results were inadequate in about a quarter of an hour. The hand-dipping test would be made at least that often. Although it was not possible verbally to define sub-standard output, the experienced man would have no doubt as to whether the operation was all right or not.

This discussion was meant to elucidate the role of the senior operator. But then Mr. B. threw the matter open once again. He was 'usually' concerned with the winnower himself. I suggested that the senior operator was perhaps 'on' the winnower by way of being a deputy to Mr. B. The charge-hand replied that he had a lot of confidence in this operator, since he had him on the job for forty years and therefore considered him to be very experienced. Nevertheless, he was still very much around himself and would 'never' be away from the winnower for more than a couple of hours. I thought that this was leading us somewhere and tried to 'get' him away from that winnower for as much as half a day. But he said no, even two hours would be too much. *Even* two hours would not arise, because he had his base at the side of the machine, where his records lay on top of the desk. He would not be using his office very much. Nevertheless, and under pressure, *if* it became necessary, he would stay away from the winnower for a couple of hours at the most.

Since I was not overruled by the foreman and higher management, I conclude that the senior operator deputises for Mr. B. on the winnower machine's operation, intermittently, for up to two hours.

There are a number of subsidiary 'tasks' (which I do not consider independent) which the senior operator carries out on the specific instruction of Mr. B. These include: cleaning the floor from an overflow of beans at the roaster's feeding point, looking at the panel of lights showing what is happening with the silos and calling the engineers if these lights behave peculiarly, and so on. Since these tasks do not involve any choice as to priorities, I consider the role to be properly defined as single-task. Having therefore ignored the one day review of the non-task of weighing the sacks of shells, the role as now constituted is defined by the two hourly spells of responsibility on the winnower.

Nib removing operator

The junior operator in this section is responsible for receiving the winnowed nib, putting it into sacks, weighing the sacks to a standard, stacking them, and feeding a hopper with nib from his stock of sacks. There are thus two physical operations involved and, strictly speaking, there is a question of priority as to which of these two should be performed at any one time. The distinction of two independent tasks, however, would be pedantic — and could not be fitted into the instruction, which certainly did not contain a target completion time. I therefore proceeded to interpret the role as single task.

With respect to sack filling, the pace is again governed by the machine. Discretion over pace would show up very quickly, around the quarter of an hour mark, since nib output is much greater than shell output. Prescribed actions include the stacking of empty sacks on to a pallet, the fitting of the empty sack on to the mouth of the machine and tying with the (provided for) belt, the estimating of the weight of the sack from the bulge in its shape, the removal of the sack and replacing it with an empty one, lifting of the full sack on to the scales, and adjustment of the weight with a spoon from a buffer sack lying on the side, and the removal of the sack from the scale for stacking at the storage space prescribed. The operator suggested to me that if the scales were directly under the spout he wouldn't need to do all this carrying and lifting about.

The quality aspects of discretion divide up into two dimensions: (a) the accuracy of weighing according to standard, and (b) cleanliness. Cleanliness is here again prescribed as 'absolute', and, given the proximity of the charge-hand, this means very short spans, perhaps of a quarter of an hour.

The longest review occurs on the dimension of the weight standard. (The comments, above, concerning review mechanism of the weight standard for the case of the senior operator apply to some extent here also.) My suggestion, that Mr. B. keeps a sharper eye on weight measurement by the junior operator, was not accepted by Mr. B. I am not satisfied by this and continue to believe that Mr. B. actually reviews weighting performance by *both* section operators at most at about the two-hour mark. In the case of a very simple technology, such as was the case here, however, it is quite impossible to attach any meaning to 'costs' incurred by persistent sub-standard discretion. I could not find that sub-standard discretion of weighting of nibs would have had any other effects than to indicate the winnower machine's performance for the day. This would be filed. Besides, inaccurate weighing is not all on one side. There is under-estimate and over-estimate. It could be that not every single sack is filled according to standard and yet the daily averages tally beautifully with the machine's historical performance. What therefore is the meaning of 'sub-standard' discretion?

(Let it also be said that what the junior operator did not possess in experience he possessed in talent. For example he had fun in demonstrating to me his accurate guessing of the weight of the filled sack before putting it on the scales, and he was invariably right within a margin of less than one pound of error.)

The hopper-feeding operation is strictly subsidiary. Here the pace standard involves discretion which Mr. B. will spot within half an hour. The quality (cleanliness) standard is defined as letting the hopper from half-full to at most one-third of a sack over-spilling, both of which would be spotted within half an hour.

Let me now try to sum up from this rather involved discussion. With respect to the senior operator, the longest discretionary periods would be marked by Mr. B.'s absence, which at a maximum reaches the two-hour mark. Thus it would be not only his discretion with respect to the operation of the winnower, but also his discretion with respect to pace and cleanliness on his routine task of shell receiving, that would be reviewed after these two-hour absences. I can therefore conclude that this is a two-hour role.

With respect to the junior operator, however, the absences of Mr. B. up to two hours may not have precisely the same effect. I found no evidence that the senior operator also deputised for Mr. B. with respect to overseeing the junior operator's performance. But then, in this very traditional and intuitive managerial structure, the buck is perhaps passed according to some pattern of 'seniority'. With Mr. B. usually present, the pace and cleanliness standard for the nib receiver will not be over the half-hour mark. With Mr. B. absent, his spans will tend to be as long as those for the senior operator. In the view of higher management this is in fact so, and they are quite content that it should be so. I, however, decided arbitrarily for a slightly lower mark for the junior operator, which I define as one hour and a half, because his sub-standard discretion could be picked up, so to speak, 'from a distance' by Mr. B. In *my* experience he was never more than one hour away from any part of the department.

(*Note:* it may appear in such cases that the notion of 'task' becomes woolly. In reality it is the managerial system which becomes woolly: the management *doesn't care* whether review is at the half-hour, the one-hour, or the two-hour mark. If this is the case measurement is not possible, because the *decision* which is the object of measurement simply isn't there. This does not however necessarily imply that the management is negligent or inadequate. The decision not-to-care is a decision by default: it may simply reflect (as in the present instance I believe it does) that the technology, in the broad sense of the term, operates at a slack. The eight-hour work day is not fully worked in that the slow rate of physical output (which is part of the technology) allows the rectifying of sub-standard discretion *immediately* (i.e. costlessly). Hence the time-spans are just what they happen to be from the *habits* of the foreman and charge-hand. But these habits necessarily vary; hence one must simply compromise between what the charge-hand says that he does (two-hourly maximum departures) and one's intuitive view of how often his eye hits the needle of the weighting scale (1 hour to 1½ at the most.)

Senior milling operator (Mr. Br.)
The nib which is fed into a hopper on the third floor falls between two sets of paired millstones in the second floor, whence it emerges in the form of chocolate mass or liquor. This milling section is operated by two men, of whom the senior is Mr. Br.

His job is to switch the mills on and off, to check the temperature of the machine which feeds the liquor into either sacks or tubs, to ensure the supply of these sacks and tubs, to stack the filled sacks in the store room for despatch, to transport the tubs to the conching department, and to oversee the junior milling operator. The milling section has less work than would keep two men fully employed, so that from time to time one of the two is released by the foreman for other short jobs, such as transporting something or bringing supplies or helping with the fruit-and-nut cleaning section. The junior operator in the milling section is sometimes replaced by the junior operator from the winnowing section described above, which is one factor that originally made me suspicious of the one-day time-span I had originally fallen for on the latter.

All of the roles are again single-task. There is here an even greater variety of physical operations of a subsidiary character which are very difficult to describe other than under general headings, such as 'supervising the performance of the mills'.

(*Note:* All these operations are in one way or another 'fully prescribed' in that there is no room for *marginally* sub-standard discretion; and this seems to me the distinction between an independent task (in the case of a multi-task role) and what I refer to here as a 'subsidiary' task, which is an additional *prescribed* routine in a single-task role.)

There is continuous activity with respect to stacking, re-stacking, cleaning, etc. There is, however, one specific operation involving the loading of chocolate liquor into sacks which it is worth describing in detail.

If the mills are not interfered with (on which there is more to say later) the liquor output flows at a steady pace, first through a pump, then through a pipe, into a hopper; it is kept in liquid form by being moved with a screw inside a jacket filled with hot water; it is then pumped upwards through a pipe, and down through another, out of two spouts which can be manually selected by a lever. The sack-filling job involves putting a tray which holds a sack under one of the two spouts, selecting the appropriate 'open' position, letting the sack fill up until the scale indicator which supports the tray reads fifty pounds of weight, then switching the lever to operate the other spout, under which there is another sack which will be filled in its turn. The loaded tray is then pulled along a rail, so that the top of the sack is enveloped by a ribbon which is sewn up to the top with a sewing machine. After sewing, the sack is lifted and placed into a pallet. And so it goes, sack after sack.

The pace for the operation is fairly strictly governed by the pumps of the machine which run at a rate of approximately twenty bags per hour. There is obviously no discretion in going faster than machine output; while going slower than requisite would result in spilling the liquor on the floor around the hopper, something which is very conspicuous, or in having to stop the mills altogether, which is forbidden. If the supervisor should be around this part of the shop he would pick either of these units of sub-standard discretion 'immediately'.

But the review process depends on which man is on the job. Supervision will be by the charge-hand if Mr. Br. is on' the job. Should the junior operator be on the job instead, it is Mr. Br.'s job to supervise him. Accordingly we have *two possibilities* for the time-span of this operation.

Junior milling operator (Mr. Pa.)
If Mr. Pa. should be on the job, the time-span for this dimension is no longer than five minutes. If Mr. Br. is on the job, he will not be found out until Mr. B. or Mr. F. comes to the milling section, on their average hourly rounds.

(*Note:* This provides a very clear-cut example of the distinction between the physical completion of any one round of the operation and the 'responsibility content' which is solely defined by the review point. The same physical operation here has, along this dimension of discretion, either a five-minute span or a one-hour span.)

Since this operation provides the longest span for Mr. Pa., let us complete his job analysis here. Discretion is further responsible along the dimension of requisite sewing up. Sub-standard sewing up would allow leaks to develop, but these would not emerge until the guilty sack is covered by, and bears the weight of, at least another and perhaps two further layers. By this time, however, it is fairly difficult to observe the leak without positively looking for it. Mr. Br., however, supervises Mr. Pa. rather closely, and is in a position to discover sub-standard discretion within the half-hour mark if not sooner.

Should Mr. Br. be doing the job instead, however, this type of mistake will not be discovered till much later, when the palate is taken to stores, where the sacks would be unloaded, to be re-stacked for delivery outside the factory. The time dimension here thus depends on the number of sacks contained in a palate. Since sack-filling is a continuous operation, the length of time for filling a palate can be estimated at rather over three hours of output. This then becomes the magnitude of the task when it is performed by Mr. Br.

The above operation has been described on the basis of the rate of liquor output being constant. There is however a possibility for slight variation, which is not strictly out of bounds for Mr. Br., but is nevertheless discouraged. Speeding up the mills would eventually damage the quality of the product, but does enable the operator to get over the job faster. The possibility of increasing throughput in the mills is not treated as grossly sub-standard in practice, since it is not taken as a serious danger and there is no review point other than quality control at the delivering end, which is easily two weeks away and anyway is not considered relevant by anybody in the department.

We thus get a half-hour span for Mr. Pa. and a three-hour span for Mr. Br., both along the dimension of adequate sewing up which occurs in the sack-filling job. Other dimensions concern tidiness and cleanliness, but the spans are shorter for both men. One could in this instance list at least another two or three dimensions for discretion, by distinguishing particular cases of tidiness, orderliness, adequate stores of empty sacks, etc.; but this would not add anything to the analysis as the review cut-off points are all shorter.

Comment: I have already mentioned two cases where the weight standard gave me some trouble. In the operation of collecting shells, that of collecting the nib, and in the present one of collecting the chocolate liquor, there is *apparently* an exacting weight standard. In the case of chocolate liquor the standard is marked by a red line drawn on the dial of the scale. However, in all three cases there is no *direct* review intended to catch error in weighing. For shells this does not seem necessary at all. For nibs it may be necessary for record keeping, but not, apparently, otherwise. For sacks of chocolate liquor, however, the weight standard is important, because the liquor is sent to other factories and will be weighed at the receiving end. Discrepancies between the weight reported to have been sent and the weight known to have been received will then produce complaints which will come back to H. Who is then responsible?

My attempt to discuss this point brought Bill F. to the conclusion that he is responsible for 'everything' in his department, which is fair enough; but there still seemed to be no mechanism whereby he could ensure that these mistakes could not arise. What he relied upon was the responsibility of the men, who were well-trained and good at their jobs. Hypothetically, one way of ensuring against sub-standard discretion is to employ people of higher capacity, so as to reduce supervision and review mechanisms and increase the time-spans. This did not look like being the case. Capacity seemed to be fully employed at lower levels of work and hence lower time-spans. After getting used to the mechanics of the various operations, the thing that stuck out consistently was the highly intensive review mechanisms. These were however so informal as to be almost sub-conscious to the foreman and the charge-hand. There is of course nothing wrong in all this, particularly in the case of a department which is now smaller than in the past and very mature from the personnel point of view. The highly informal pattern of review, however, makes it very difficult to obtain time-spans without guidance by higher management as to the relevance or irrelevance of some factors, such as the weighting standard mentioned. This was done through the play-back of the analysis reported here, from which the weight standard was classed as a non-issue.

It is perhaps human nature to consider the hypothetical before the concrete: the weight standard, particularly for export of chocolate liquor from H., was stressed to me from the start as the 'prime responsibility' of the job, and the possibility of a complaint from the receiving end was viewed with horror. But after two weeks of living around the place, I found that such complaints never occur. The issue is therefore not live, and this explains the befogged reaction one gets when one continues to probe for a non-existent review mechanism, whose necessity is not seen by the supervisors. Note that a similar non-issue also arises in the fruit-and-nut cleaning section, where 'foreign bodies' in the cleaned contents are not the responsibility of the people employed in the section, who are also *not* held accountable for customers' complaints arising from such causes.

This completes the analysis of the section producing chocolate liquor. In summary, the charge-hand Mr. B. has a one-week role, the bean cleaner operator has a one-hour role, the senior winnower operator goes up to two hours, the junior winnower operator is between one hour and a half and two hours, the senior milling operator goes up to two or three hours, and the junior milling operator up to half an hour.

Charge-hand in contents (Mrs. M.)

The next department that comes under Mr. F. is the cleaning of fruits and nuts. There are two physical operations here, located at different parts of the same floor. First, there is semi-automated mechanical cleaning for high-quality products. The sacks are loaded by a man loaned to this section by Mr. B. intermittently for a few times a day. The output end is two belts, which require receiving and checking of the cleaned output by two women operators. Secondly, there is cleaning by hand doné by up to six women operators, seated round a number of tables. The product here is raisins and lower-quality types of nuts.

The work load for this section is fairly variable and depends on the demand for contents in the moulding department as well as on the availability of labour. The section's output is programmed for one week ahead. Output for each day of the week, however, is fully specified, and this therefore constitutes the routine recurring production task for the charge-hand. It is not always possible for her to produce the amount required by the schedule because her labour has been run down over a period of time. When under strain she may ask for more labour. This would be on loan to her on a part-time basis from the bar-wrapping department, which also employs women. Here requests would go through Mr. F. Given her daily programme and the labour she can get, there is no pace standard other than her own judgment and the experience of throughput in her section. Note that there is no quality control and no check other than the charge-hand's discretion. There used to be quality control inspector, but the function has now been abolished.

The charge-hand's is a multi-task role. The majority of short tasks arise from her responsibility in charge of the section. Examples of these are (a) to keep a daily record of production, (b) to fill-in. the time sheets for her women workers, (c) to keep a daily sheet of deliveries to the moulding department, (d) to compute the stock figure of raw materials per week, and (e) to compute the finished stock at the end of the week. None of these is longer than the half-hour mark. On receiving her weekly programme she has to calculate how many women she will need to borrow for each day. She will also ask Mr. F. or Mr. B. for the services of a man for transporting raw material from stock or for loading the cleaning machine. Mr. B. will sometimes do this job for her himself; otherwise he will release one of the two men in the milling section.

Senior contents operator

As things stand there are two full-time women operators in the section, including Mrs. M. There are normally four other part-time women plus the occasional services of the man lent by Mr. B.

According to the charge-hand, the full-time lady operator was a 'different kind of person' from her part-time girls. The charge-hand would leave this senior operator alone for the 'whole day', once she had told her what and how much was required for the day. Leaving her alone, however, is not a precise expression describing the extant situation. It was hypothetical that Mrs. M. would leave anybody alone for a day, since she would be working herself on the cleaning of contents and would be normally sitting next to the other women on whom, in her expression, 'she keeps a constant eye'. Hence I queried her statement about the senior operator. The charge-hand, however, insisted that she could and does leave the senior operator quite alone for a whole day. The most she would come down from that was that she *may* have a check on the senior operator sometime about half way through the day, but not necessarily.

It was also not easy to pin down the units of sub-standard discretion. Since there was no quality check of any kind the quality-of-work dimension nearly vanished. To invoke a quality dimension concerning cleanliness would be almost pedantic, since the physical conditions precluded any form of uncleanliness which would not be noticed in less than five minutes. This is very nearly prescribed, so we are left with the dimension of pace. Since the proximity of work-place between manager and subordinate is so close, it is obviously quite arbitrary to rely on the explicit statement of the manager, so that either one day, or half a day, or much less than that, are equally plausible. Again, I do not believe that it is the low level of work which blunts the tool of analysis. It is rather the fact that in a very primitive technology, where 'error' is hard to define, it is also freakish to pin down a job specification in task form because there is no way of *defining* a 'standard' practice *verbally*. Most of the time the charge-hand is so near all her operators that sub-standard discretion of any kind would be picked up in a matter of minutes. Very occasionally the charge-hand would disappear for as long as half a day, and it is unreasonable to define the task by these exceptional circumstances. I marked the task as half a day (for the quantitative work) but see no reason why it should not be reduced to one hour just as plausibly.

Part-time operators in contents
The same physical operation yielded very different tasks for the part-time girls. These girls come and go at various times during the morning and the afternoon, as they can be spared from the intensively working bar-wrapping department. Mrs. M. drew a sharp distinction between her senior operator and these younger girls. While they were quite responsible 'as persons', she felt, they were not 'really setting their minds on the work'. There might be 'chattering' among them, which would affect the pace of the work; hence she would be on to them every hour at least to ensure that the pace remained adequate. I again tried to pursue the question of quality and what kind of sub-standard behaviour would show up. But beyond the pace standard I didn't get anywhere. The objective was that the nuts and fruits should be cleaned, and if the job was done 'properly' they would be clean enough. The question of the charge-hand being able to check on 'inadequate' cleaning simply did not arise. Similarly there was no question of the charge-hand assigning responsibility to any of the operators for sub-standard output. Complaints from customers never went to her.

To sum up: in this section, we have a one-day multi-task role for the charge-hand, a half-day (with reservations) for the senior operator, and one hour for the four part-time girls.

The filling charge-hand (Mr. Co.)
The final section that comes under Mr. F. is the filling of tins with cocoa powder. This section is located in a single large

room which houses one line of machinery and several tables for manual work. The section normally employs six people, together with the charge-hand, three of whom are part-time. The charge-hand's role is multi-task. The technology of this department is again very primitive.

There are various types of tins to be filled and each type is called a 'line'. In the past the section used to operate according to a monthly programme, given to Mr. Co. by the deputy chocolate manager Mr. G. This programme was expressed in terms of batches of requirements by line, and some instructions were appended as to priority of one line versus another. But these priority comments were found insufficient to guide production and fulfil the requirements of despatch and sales. Mr. G. therefore dropped it and produces instead a weekly programme which fully specifies the size of each batch by line number and the sequence in which the batches must be produced inside the week. The programme is designed with a view to delivery requirements and ensures that the section's technical capacity, which is historically known as approximately two hundred cases of tins per day, will be fully utilised.

At the time of the interview the weekly programme in operation was as follows: the first batch was of two hundred and fifty cases, the second batch of two hundred and seventy-five cases, the third batch of four hundred cases, and the fourth batch of two hundred and thirty-five cases. The weekly target was nine hundred and sixty cases of four different lines.

The next thing to note is that although the programme is given every week, it does not define a weekly time-span, just like the monthly programme which it replaced did not define a one-monthly span. Although not so rigid as to define a target for each individual day, the weekly programme constrains discretion by prescribing a sequential order of targets by line. Hence, in order to find the time-span, it is necessary simply to look at the longest batch. In the week of the interview this happened to be four hundred cases and this is equivalent to a time-span of approximately two to two-and-a-half days.

Let us clarify why this, rather than the week, is the effective time-span. At first sight it would appear that the target completion time of the sequence of batches is the week. Before the week is over it is possible to follow the right order *and* to be behind schedule. Pace can, in principle, be adjusted in the last day to take up the deficiencies of the previous days. In practice, however, this is not so. The foreman is about, and he knows whether production is falling behind schedule, at the latest by the time any particular batch should have been completed. The target completion time thus, in practice, concerns each individual batch. This target is not however explicit. The formal characterisation of the job is along the weekly programme, and, if the foreman and the charge-hand were different people, this is perhaps how the role would be functioning. In the actual case, however, partly because of the traditional attitude towards frequent reviewing and instructions and partly because of the frequent breakdowns of the machinery, it is the foreman rather than the charge-hand who takes up responsibility for the achievement of the weekly target. Thus the longest time in which the charge-hand is free to vary pace without endangering the fulfilment of the weekly programme, given the average daily capacity of his department, is the length of time for delivering his longest batch. (It should be clear from the clumsiness of analysing this multi-task role how much more clumsy it is to analyse single-task roles in a very primitive technology. There is almost a mystique about managerial functions, in that while there is an immense amount of detailed instruction reviewing, reporting, etc., it is very hard to 'tease out' the pertinent instructions which constitute the tasks.)

In terms of quantity of work the charge-hand's job is absolutely enormous and takes exceptionally long hours. Since being transferred to his present job from elsewhere in the factory, Mr. Co. has only been relieved from the job of checking on the stock of liquid butter in the morning and at night, a responsibility which has now been taken over by the refining department. Mr. Co. keeps the figures for the stock of ready cases and daily output which he delivers to general office. He starts his day at six o'clock in the morning. By 7.45, when the women come in, he will have filled the hopper of his machine with cocoa powder, he will have set the machine and will have prepared the time-sheets for his operators. After instructing everybody to start their work, he will take samples of cocoa with butter liquid and solid to the laboratory. On return to his section he will pick up and do some operation which lacks labour, which is usual, since his department is normally under staffed. The work will then proceed through the day with the various breaks for lunch and tea. All this time Mr. Co. will be in the team working full-time. By about 3.15 in the afternoon the part-time girls will begin to go off. At about 3.30 he will shut the machine down, sweep up and then clean the machine. This will take him approximately two hours, so that he will go home at about 5.25 p.m., making it an eleven-hour day.

I was shocked to find that Mr. Co. did not consider his eleven-hour day as in anyway unnatural. His only critical comment about his work concerned a drop in pay, which had resulted from his transfer to become charge-hand of this section, even though formally the transfer involved a promotion. He was not clear whether he had got more or less responsibility as a result of the transfer.

Two full-time operators
Beside Mr. Co. there are two full-time people in the department, one man and one woman. Both these occupants have single task roles in spite of the variety of physical activities and the occasional appearance of a target completion time.

The man's job involves actions such as keeping the hopper full, controlling the weights of the machine, and despatching finished cases. The woman's role involves lighter activities, such as sticking of labels, stocking of cases, and putting filled cases on the delivery van. The occasional target completion times concerned a number of cases which needed labelling 'by the end of the day' or the distance, in time terms, between fillings up of the hopper. These, however, were illusory, in that (a) none of them would be long enough for Mr. Co. to give the instruction at the beginning of the day and obtain the result at the end of the day, and (b) intermittent pace variation would be obvious to Mr. Co., who worked in close proximity, often concerning himself about pace and other arrangements.

At the start, however, the charge-hand considered that his

full-timers were on their own for the whole day, once he had given his instructions to them. I pursued the possibility that these might be multi-task roles by trying to obtain the form of the instruction 'by the end of the day' changed to 'get on with it faster'. I therefore dealt with sub-standard discretion as if the variety of physical actions constituted supplementary prescriptions for a single task.

What then, I asked, were the units in which sub-standard discretion would be manifested: could there be a wrong setting of the weights, less than a full hopper, the sticking of wrong labels, making a mess, or what? But the charge-hand refused to contemplate any of this. It just did not happen. He seemed to feel that I didn't really understand how his section operated, which to him was quite simple and it should have sufficed for me to keep my eyes open. After considerable discussion he suggested that he did review his two full-timers twice a day, once before they went off to lunch, and once before they went away at the end of the day. All other relations with them during the day he considered to be communications rather than instructions or reviews. His review at the end of the day would be simultaneous to the filling of their time sheets and checking his daily output for report to the general office.

Three part-time operators, three women
Unlike in contents, the three part-time girls are permanent to the tin-filling section. Mr. Co. will instruct and review them more often than his full-timers, every two hours on the first approximation, almost every hour on a second. The question of quality of operation again did not strike the charge-hand as realistic. In case of his absence review would be subsumed under the 'partial' oversight exercised by the two full-timers on the three part-timers.

Comment: I have indicated why Mr. Co. was not entirely in 'equilibrium' in this role. He was generally uneasy, and felt that he had lost financially from being moved to this job, and was definitely exhausted by the long hours he was putting in. The section itself feels more like a survivor from another technological and managerial age. The old piece of machinery needs continuous adjustment, while a lot of the smaller batches require purely manual work to be performed economically. My conclusion about the tasks in this section, after discussing them with the foreman and Mr. P., is that all roles other than Mr. Co.'s are single-task. All these discretionary dimensions are extremely short, ranging from about twenty minutes on cleanliness, neatness of labelling and packing, to at most one hour on pace. Since the machine breaks down fairly often, there is no mechanically set standard for pace. This, however, if anything, has the effect of shortening the time-spans, in the following manner. Most of the time it is Mr. Co. himself who is working and setting the pace, thus exercising well-nigh 'continuous' implicit review in some activity or other. Even if not working directly, he is continuously about and simply cannot help noticing and influencing pace and quality. Given his own direct involvement in the work, it is not surprising that Mr. Co. did not see things my way. But this implicit form of review is not strange in a department consisting of so few people doing very simple things in close physical proximity with one another. As a result of my discussions with higher management I would conclude that the time-spans are at the most two hours for the two full-time people and at the most one hour for the three part-timers.

Note: It was at this time during my work in N. that I realised the difference between the simple verbal instruction and the task instruction. In single-task roles the verbal instruction is in fact usually not the same thing as the task. (I commented when I first found this in Contents and in Tin Filling; subsequently also in Conching. All these are very primitive operations.) The verbal instruction usually concerns what to do for the day. In a multi-task role this could have been tantamount to the task. In the single-task role, however, the verbal instruction is not complete unless there is included a pace standard and the relevant quality standards with a specification of the review mechanisms. In all cases I found that the actual task instruction which was implicit in the review process was shorter than the verbal instruction.

3

Refining and conching department

The department of refining and conching is different from chocolate mass in important respects. There is more man-power to be managed. The output produced is of much greater value. And, most important, there is underway a process of modernisation which affects the specification of practically all roles and which further seems to affect people's feelings of felt-fair comparisons. Part of the tech-nology of refining and of conching has been entirely replaced by modern automated machinery. The refining section has been shifted from a time to a staff basis. This had made it possible to operate on a regular shift system. In conching, the technology is still predominantly of the old type, but a shift system already operates in a few sub-sections.

An interesting characteristic of the managerial process, which stems directly from the technological system in operation, is the linkages obtaining among role specifications and review points. There is here almost an assembly line along a single belt, where each operator performs a function so defined as to permit the managerial process to pick up sub-standard discretion for each individual component even though the technology results in a synthesis of a new product at the end. The raw material input into the department is sugar, milk powder, and chocolate crumb, all of which come from outside the H. factory. Intermittently, small quantities of high quality chocolate liquor come from the department previously examined.

The sequence of operations is as follows. The raw material is received by stores; then there is, first, mixing according to a number of formulae; then refining, that is to say smashing and pulverising the sugar in the mixture; the refined powder is then stored (the sequence of operations so far is con-tinuous). From stores the refined powder is transported in batches to the conch room where a mechanical operation transforms the material into chocolate mass. This ready mass is then stored in large containers from where it will be taken to the next department, which is moulding. There are thus three storage points and two operations. The intermediate storage point provides a space constraint in that storage is only possible in a room of adequate heat to preserve the powder from acquiring any moisture. The final storage point is a very binding constraint in that the mass can only be stored in a number of vats always working at very near full capacity. The operation of the department is governed by two parallel programmes, a weekly programme for refining and a monthly programme for conching. The overall bottle-neck of the operation is at the final storage point where the containers hold three days' output. Since the moulding operation, which is subsequent to the work of this depart-ment, is technologically much more erratic, the absorption of the chocolate mass into moulding is fairly variable (and different) for each type of chocolate, so that it is necessary continuously to adjust the level of production in refining and conching. The conching process is more labour-intensive (less mechanised) than refining, partly because of the predomi-nantly older technology involved and partly because of the batch character of the process. There is no deterioration problem in going slow overall in this department, but there is a problem of quickening pace which can adversely affect quality in the conching department.

The roles of the two foremen, Mr. Po. and Mr. W.
The two foremen carry identical roles and interchange periodically in the two day-shifts. A night foreman is engaged to oversee the operation of the conch room, which does not stop at nights or weekends.

The production and manpower management respon-sibilities of the two foremen are defined on the monthly cycle. There are two production tasks, consisting of the weekly programme for refining, and the monthly programme for conching. There was currently a plan by higher manage-ment to shift into a monthly programme for refining in due course. There are a number of supplementary shorter tasks related to production and management, such as (a) daily reports on inputs and outputs, (b) daily reports on stocks, and (c) a weekly report dealing with the direct costs incurred. With respect to manpower management, there is a monthly report on labour absenteeism and a monthly task for training of labour whenever the situation arises. The foreman's role is thus well-defined around the one-month task limit.

As was to be expected from the process of modernisation, there also arose in the case of these two foremen a project. This, however, was less easily definable than the routine recurring tasks. During the time of the installation of the automated refining line there arose the task of selecting the requisite labour. Two months before the installation was due to be completed, Mr. Pa. asked the two foremen to select their men. The task instruction was to submit a list of names, together with proposals for pay standards, for approval by Mr. Pa. The target completion time was five weeks. No particular significance, however, must be attached to the precise figure of five weeks. It may well have been three, or four, or five, or six. The content of the task is extremely limited. I conclude from this that this task on its own should not affect the one-month definition of the role as a whole.

Supporting evidence for this view is that the labour training task for the automated line was given not to the foremen but to an outside specialist. In connection with the automated line, the foremen were also given the responsibility of learning the job from the outside specialist within three months. I could not satisfactorily determine whether this responsibility could be put in the form of a task or not. Teaching somebody within a specified time is of course a task for the teacher. It may also be a task for the manager of the students, that is to say Mr. Pa. It is not obvious from this that it is also a task for the student. Subsequent to my work at N., however, I had the opportunity of seeing the operation of a Training Centre at C. and from that experience hold the view that there is meaning to students' 'learning tasks'. Mr. Pa.'s explicit view is that the foremen would be accountable if they had not picked up the requisite knowledge within three months. I would therefore conclude that the project consisted of a once-and-for-all learning task of three months.

The phenomenon of a well-defined one-month role with a three-month project (which had occured only once) I would call a non-integrated role. A similar non-integrated role subsequently turned up with the two foremen in charge of the moulding department.

The automated line (brown chocolate)
In describing the string of single-task roles it is best to start

from the output end of refining.

The refined powder is fed from a belt into a funnel which discharges into tubs placed on scales recording weight. The operator is responsible for the filling of the tubs to the appropriate weight, for placing of tags with the appropriate line number on each tub when full and for storing the tubs in the hot room. There is no discretion on the pace of the work which is machine governed. It is possible to spill powder on the floor whenever tubs are interchanged; it is possible to make mistakes in weighing; and it is possible to put the wrong line-number tag. The operator's role is supervised by the charge-hand on the ground floor. Hourly review-points checked up on accuracy on all dimensions of the operator's discretion. The concept of sub-standard discretion could not here be applied in the marginal sense. The job was so essentially simple that discretion was either all right or grossly sub-standard. I could just not discover any implications of sub-standard discretion on weighing or in anything else. The hourly review-point is accurate and substantive. The operator is responsible for 'adequately' performing the routine of filling his four tubs, two from the automated brown line and two from the white line, to the (hourly) satisfaction of the charge-hand.

The refining machine is controlled by an operator on the floor above. His responsibility is to keep the machine fed from the automated belt through manual control, ensuring that the magic eye mechanism is on, controlling the refining process by manually adjusting a number of dials and keeping the machine and the floor around it clean. The dials regulate the distance apart of the rollers: tightening of the rollers means refining more closely and widening them means refining more coarsely. Fineness and coarseness are also related to pace, in that the farther apart the rollers are the faster the mixture goes through. Quality in this context is defined as 'adequate' crushing of the sugar particles. The operator can himself judge on his quality by taking periodic readings to the lab. Quality control conduct an hourly review by taking samples to the lab themselves. This turns out to be the longest review-point. The magic eye mechanism is reviewed by the shift leader, and so is cleanliness. These other dimensions are considerably shorter, around the quarter-hour mark.

The mixture which is refined in the automated line comes from a machine which is called the Beetz Mixer. The machine operation is controlled by the shift leader, whose role is multi-task and will be left for the end. The automated line is manned at any one time by one person. There are two shifts, which management considers absolutely equivalent in every respect. So far, therefore, we have four one-hour roles, two for the refining operators and two for the powder collectors.

The white line
The white line is more labour-intensive. Starting again from the end, the powder is collected at the ground floor. On the floor above there is a set of refining machines which are independently fed and whose regulation is entirely manual. There is one fully qualified operator for each shift. He is responsible for operating two and sometimes three machines simultaneously. He collects a tub of mixture and loads it on to the machine by using a pulley. Since this job is heavy, he is sometimes helped by one of the assistants. He will need to reload the machine approximately every forty minutes. The speed of the machine is his own responsibility and the two dimensions of discretion are adequate refining, which is a function of the speed, and adequate cleanliness. The cleanliness standard is very strict and the review-point is no more than ten minutes away. Pace can be varied within fairly narrow limits, and the unit of sub-standard discretion is again the degree to which the sugar crystals conform to standard. This is picked up at the hourly review by quality control, but can also be checked independently by the operator, who can take his samples and check them in the laboratory.

The white mixture is prepared by a machine called a Malanger. The operator of this machine has a surprisingly complex role which presents considerable interest. In sequence, the actions involved are the following. The operator calls for more crumb by tapping on a silo through which the crumb is fed from the floor above. Through a manual level he discharges about two-thirds of the crumb into his Malanger. Next to him there stands a bucket containing melted butter. He has already poured the butter into his bucket to the appropriate weight from a spout nearby. He will pour this butter into the Malanger and then operate a manual switch which starts off the action of the millstones. After a minute or two he will let the remaining crumb from the silo into the Malanger. While the machine is mixing, he will add an odour compound which is a white powder measured in a plastic cup which is next to him. He will then let the machine operate, mixing up his butter with the crumb. When in his judgment the mixture has attained the requisite standard he will stop the millstones. He will then switch-on a screw-operated pumping machine which will transfer the mixture into a tub. He will scrape his Malanger clean from the remnants of the mixture and transfer them into the tub manually. He will then bump the tub half-way between his machine and the refining machine, which will use it next. At this point he will tap the silo again, and the cycle will be repeated. Each cycle takes between fifteen and twenty minutes.

There is obviously multi-dimensional discretion in this role, as there is so much that can go wrong. The pace dimension carries a lot of discretion. The instruction is that there should be an 'adequate' buffer between malanging and refining, so that faults in the former will not suspend the operation of the latter. The 'adequate' buffer is defined by a range from one to three tubs. The two sides of the range do not however have the same meaning. More than three tubs would mean that the operator has been malanging excessively quickly. But whether this is so, in the sense of providing sub-standard quality, would not be discovered readily. Accordingly the 'too quickly' sub-standard discretion does not concern the dimension of pace. The dimension 'too slowly' is therefore the operative one. Since it takes up to twenty minutes for the preparation of each tub of mixture (on average) and since the review on pace is directly exercised by the shift leader who is a few yards away, it follows that the review on pace is approximately half an hour away from the point of sub-standard discretion.

Dealing with the subject of quality presents some difficulties. The adequacy of the mixture is measured by (a) the proportion of butter in the mixture, (b) the addition of the odour compound, and (c) the length of mixing time. Should the mixture be inadequate there *may* be difficulties at the refining stage. But this is not always so. The mixing operation is made easier and faster when there is proportionately more butter. Adding extra butter therefore enables the operator to keep his buffer stock adequate. Overabundance of butter, however, may cause the refining rollers to stick. But this would only become manifest if discretion is not marginally but grossly sub-standard — and such a situation is extremely rare. Insofar as marginally sub-standard discretion on butter content affects the quality of refining in a marginal way, the results *may* show at the stage where the refined powder is checked by quality control. Since there is about one hour's buffer between malanging and refining, while quality control is about one hour removed from refining, it follows that, *if* there is such a control, it is about two hours' removed from malanging. This may not, however, be a positive control. It appears that marginally sub-standard discretion with respect to butter content may simply *not* be picked up anywhere, as it may not have any even marginal sub-standard effects on the result of refining. The same comments apply to the addition of the odour compound.

At the time of the interview there was no independent quality control check on the malanged product. The range of adequacy of the mixture was wide, in the sense that it was judged by hand. The operator himself continuously picked up some mixture and rubbed it in his hands, and so did the shift leader or the foreman if he happened to be around. (Be it noted that checking by hand is considered more accurate than simply a mechanised formula. It is also used on the results of the automatic mixing machine in the brown line). The span of the role would therefore depend on the frequency of reviews by the shift-leader. But here there was no regularity. I was able to observe that up to three hours went by (on one occasion) without anybody other than the operator checking on the adequacy of his mixture. The conclusion is that either the inadequacy of the mixture has no meaning in marginal terms, or that there is a regular review which is too implicit to be discovered, even though I took the matter up with higher management. For lack of a better alternative I decided to settle on the one-hour time-span for the role, on the assumption that there is such an average for the review process, even though it might be exercised with considerable variance. All other 'dimensions' of quality are thus 'collapsed' into prescriptions (where there is only grossly sub-standard discretion) simply because, in the absence of a requisite review process, there is no way of observing marginal discretion.

The feeding team

The Malanger and the automatic mixer are both fed from the second floor. There are two operators working there as one team, with one predominantly as Beetz, the other as Pan Mixer. The physical actions involve, on the one hand, mixing crumb, which is then fed through the silo to the Malanger, and, on the other, feeding three hoppers which lead to the Beetz machine. Pace in both operations presents no problem of measurement in that it is governed by the machine, and review is possible at the quarter hour interval. Cleanliness is one of the quality dimensions, and it is reviewed at the hour interval by a visit of the shift-leader. On feeding the hopper there is no other dimension, so the role is defined at the one-hour interval.

The Pan Mixer role presents complications. One of the actions there is to unload a sack of sugar into the pan and then supplement this with seven pounds of sugar fished with a pail from an open bag. The 'seven pounds' weight is in fact left to the judgment of the operator. It is impossible to pin the implications and possible review-points for marginally sub-standard discretion in this action. It is perhaps not even possible to check on whether any sugar has been added at all. Discussions with higher management produced the reaction that there perhaps should be a review point for this operation. At the time of the interview, however, since there was no review mechanism, the 'true' task instruction simply does not contain this requirement at all.

The shift-leader

When staff operation was introduced in this department the title of charge-hand was changed to shift-leader. This is a multi-task role. The longest task concerns production and is approximately of one day's length. The occupant is shown the weekly production programme operated by the foreman. The purpose of this is to 'keep him in the picture'. The programme consists of a sequence of batches of different lines, that is to say different formulae of mixes. The batches are approximately of one day's length. At the beginning of the day the foreman instructs the shift-leader as to the day's production, and this, in contrast to the weekly programme, is a 'binding' instruction. In cases where the line requirements have not been met in one day, the same line is continued on the day after. Thus 'no instruction' implies carrying on with the obtaining formula for a second day. The foreman need not instruct the shift-leader more than once in the day. More frequent instructions have in fact nothing to do with the role's specification but are contingent on the idiosyncrasy of the foremen who are used to the previously obtaining technology.

Shorter production tasks for the shift-leader comprise (a) the printing of computer cards which govern the operations of the Beetz Mixer, (b) the control of the machine with the dials and knobs, (c) contacting the engineers whenever necessary, and (d) testing the quality of the machine's output by hand.

In the white line we then have two operators, plus two in the feeding team, plus the shift leader. For the two shifts, which are otherwise identical, we therefore have ten roles.

Note: The interviews with Mr. C. on Mr. Pa.'s role gave me the idea to approach roles in terms of time cycles, at least with respect to routine recurring work. The cycles could be distinguished as going 'downwards' or 'upwards'. The downward cycles are those through which tasks are delegated downwards. But, as one proceeds into shorter and shorter sub-divisions, the manager of the role gradually loses touch with the detail at the pertinent level of 'concreteness'. The upward cycles consist mostly of the various communications and command meetings held by the manager of the role in which the occupant plays a substantial part.

It is also interesting to investigate the interlockings of two senior management roles: daily routine recurring meetings touch upon small problems which affect a limited area of the shop floor. Upwards from there, weekly, monthly, quarterly, six-monthly and yearly meetings touch on every type of problem, whether related to production, or to stocks, or to technology, or to programming, or to finances or, finally, to major project work. Pursuing the analysis of cycles, one can also see at which point collaterals in the organisation enter the picture, at what level (by no means always the same) collaterals' problems are tackled, as well as the frequency, which I found at the time somewhat uncomfortable, with which problems required referring out of the factory site to U.K. headquarters or even abroad. (N. is an international firm whose British headquarters have to refer to international headquarters in S. for all major financial decisions.)

Conching department charge-hand (J.M.)

There are three charge-hands in this department, M., Wa., and D. The latter two normally operate at night and I had no opportunity to see them. The day-time version of the role is defined by a one-day time-span. The task is to fulfil the day's production programme as communicated by the foreman. Here again we are dealing with an excessively long working day.

The day's routine is as follows: the charge-hand sees to it that the chocolate is taken out of the hot room early in the morning. He checks that the tubs' tickets are correct. He then distributes work cards to his men. He himself adds flavour to the mixture and takes viscosities and temperatures of the chocolate mass in the vats. For the next three hours he supervises that the pots in the conch rooms are filled according to the prescribed procedure. This is that the pots should be one-half filled, allowed to turn into mass for approximately two to three hours, and then filled to capacity. The pots are laid out in rows of two. One half of one side is filled first; then the other half of the other side. The remainder is then added after the mass has 'run down'. The charge-hand will check that all the pots have been filled by 1 p.m. He will then supervise that the ready chocolate mass is emptied and stored. The pots will then be cleaned.

There is a variety of technical processes in this department. The oldest technology goes by the name of Swiss, and requires much more labour time for emptying and cleaning. A newer technology goes by the name of Tandems, and is emptied automatically. The department's labour force is gradually run down as these new machines replace the older ones. (Vintage capital models are sometimes to be seen under one roof.)

The operators in the conch room

There are about twelve men operating on the normal day shift and a smaller number in the evening and night shifts. A typical day's programme for the department (17 June 1968) looks like this:

Two men, Gr. and D., have to fill and operate modern machine B-2 and Number 1 Swiss which consists of twenty-four pots.

Another two men, I. and R., have to fill and operate modern machine Number B-1 and Tandems Number 3, 4, 11 and 23, making thirty two pots.

Another two men, Bro. and Bo., have to take the mixture from the Swiss baker, add the requisite butter mix, and bump the product into the tank of the roto machine.

The typical night shift, consisting here of H. and Mo., have a lighter task, to fill and operate Number 5 Tandem and to bag the chocolate of line 3170.

The work card for the above people is pertinent to the team of two. Other work cards specify work for one individual person. Thus, D. has the task of filling and operating B-1 machine and Tandems 6, 21 and 22, and to empty Number 1. Another man has to scrape down and turn over the chocolate in B-1 and also in Tandems Number 3, 4, 9, 10, 11, 15, 16, 19, 20 and 22.

The charge-hand made a distinction between people to whom he could entrust a job to do on their own and people who could only work well as a team of two. There were distinctions of seniority and also in terms of points rating so that the salaries were different. (I participated in a discussion in which a newcomer to the department was asked to do a new job, subsequently finding that this entailed more operations than a 'comparable' job in terms of pay, and on raising the issue succeeded in getting a salary increase.) There are also simpler jobs here, such as for A. whose task for that day was to bump the chocolate to tanks for moulding and to bring the butter. This job got a lower points rating and a lower pay salary.

The work card containing the day's tasks is thus pertinent either to a single man or a team of two. But these are single task roles and the 'instruction' on the work card is not the task. Discretion on pace does not seem to be an operational concept in this section. Review of cleanliness is reasonably frequent around the foreman's office but, since the section is rather large in terms of floor space, review of all parts is no more frequent than the one-hour mark. Quality is a more difficult thing to define. The important qualitative elements, such as adding of flavour and taking the temperature and the viscosity of the mass, are in the hands of the charge-hand. After copious discussions with the foreman and the charge-hand it seemed that the only thing the men could do wrong was not to allow the mass to settle before adding the second half to the pots. The charge-hand would thus be going around making sure that the mass had properly settled before his men went around filling the pots with the rest of the powder, which on several occasions meant they would have no work for several hours afterwards. It was however hard to pin anybody down on the adequate length of time for this settling down. After a good deal of to-ing and fro-ing, I settled on the two-hour mark as a reasonable average.

The type of technology in this department makes it so that the frequency of requisite review depends largely on the attitude of the foreman to delegation and on the mode of operation of the charge-hand. At least one of the foremen is very much against delegation and insists on filling the daily cards for the men himself. When the other foreman is on the job, it is the charge-hand who fills the day cards. But both foremen keep the daily absentee record themselves. It is also they who compile the weekly time sheets for the man's work and summarise the absentees' record per month. Even though the charge-hand is effectively in charge of quality control, it is the foremen who receive the weekly quality control report. In short, the charge-hand operates largely as a skilled worker and not as a supervisor. Despite all this, both of the foremen and the charge-hand considered that leaving the men alone for up to two hours would not produce harm that could not be undone. In the view of these three men two hours is the maximum time permissable between reviews. The two-hour span for all the operators, however, is highly indiscriminate. It was not possible for the charge-hand to specify any differential time-span for the men, even though, when it came to specific jobs to be given to one or another of the men, he distinguished between people who were 'responsible' or not quite, and other such qualifications. The tool for measuring discretion clearly requires that discretion should not be so bluntly conceived.

4

Moulding department

The two final departments, moulding and bar-wrapping, are in-line and operate on a single monthly programme. This is given to the foremen by Mr. Pa. The monthly programme is sub-divided by weeks, by machine number (Numbers 1 to 6), by days (Day 1 to 27), and by line (Lines 1 to 32). The guiding target for the foremen is the tonnage per line per week. The sum of this is also specified for all lines. The variation of total tonnage per week was from 124 to 168 tons during July 1968, the total being 568.5 tons. There are basically two shifts in moulding, with some exceptions for the milky bar and for holiday periods. The programme is essentially designed as a function of manpower availability in wrapping. More shifts in moulding depend on the possibility of a night shift in wrapping. The foremen produced a daily record for each machine in terms of output, wastage, usage of contents, break-down factor, and any other difficulties. There are weekly programme reviews with the chocolate manager, looking at the performance of the past week. The main adjustment is with the plans for the changes in wrapping machines. These do not change with the line number but with the shape of the mould. Depending on weather conditions, such as temperature and humidity, there is also a variation in the reject factor which requires further adjustments in wrapping. Even though the monthly pro-gramme is a binding instruction for the foremen, the erratic nature of the moulding process and the tight linkage with wrapping require frequent (in prescribed terms, weekly) reference of necessary changes to the departmental head. This is in the form of sanction for necessary changes in the monthly programme which otherwise remains binding. The programme therefore constitutes a monthly recurring task.

The two foremen in moulding are responsible for a variety of trouble-shooting tasks which may last up to one week. There is also a one-week recurring task of keeping the reject stock low. There is finally a three monthly training task for the induction of senior operators in the moulding machines. Such training tasks were sufficiently frequent to consider the foremen's roles as 'integrated' at the three-month limit.

There is one charge-hand in the department, T.K. This, again, is a multi-task role. The charge-hand is responsible for getting the department started early in the morning on each day. This is a two-hour task consisting of a large number of prescribed actions. The charge-hand will see to it that materials are transported, that the machines are all warmed up, that each machine is properly set up by the operator and that all are functioning by eight o'clock in the morning. Apart from this direct task, the charge-hand is responsible for a great variety of supervisory work in which he effectively deputises for the morning foreman. The foreman utilised the terms 'trouble-shooting' and 'roving commission'. Although it was not possible for me to pin down specific long tasks, say from one day to two weeks, it was obvious that the role was defined in a fairly senior capacity. The matter was clinched when the foremen told me that the charge-hand would deputise for them during their annual holiday period which lasts two weeks. This therefore is the maximum task for the role.

Note: the charge-hand's role presented an illustration of a typical difficulty one may get in task analysis. Even though I could not get longer tasks for some time, I was somehow convinced that the charge-hand was beyond the two hour limit. I therefore discussed his role with the foremen again and again. This however led them to the view that I thought Mr. K. was not doing enough work and should perhaps be made redundant. Although their fears were allayed by higher management on this point, it took quite some time for them to be convinced that I was trying to measure a job that was as big in my view as in theirs. When we finally came up to the fact that the charge-hand deputises for them and I explained the meaning of a two weeks' span, there was relief and much more hearty co-operation thereafter.

The machine operators
There are six moulding machines in the department and six corresponding senior operators. The prescribed content of

these roles is as follows.

The operator must first check the tempering machine which brings the chocolate from forty degrees, which is the temperature in the tank, to approximately twenty-eight degrees centigrade. He will then check the cleanliness of the hopper in his machine and adjust the temperature of the pipes leading to the moulds. He will reassemble those parts of his machine which have been taken out and cleaned the night before. At this point the foreman will come and check that everything is in order. The operator will then start the main drive of the machine. He will check the cold air in the cooling tunnel. He will test the temperature of the moulds. He will select the appropriate gear for the type of line and moulds. He will insert the tapping and demoulding unit. He will again look at the barrels of the tempering machine and adjust them. And thereafter he will check the 'spit' (the weight) flowing to the moulds every ten minutes, plotting them on a chart. He will keep looking at his various panels for the rest of the working day, plotting his charts, and making sure that the 'spits' are coming in regularly. Whenever the demoulding process is not working appropriately, he will clean these moulds by hand, sometimes taking the trays out and replacing them with clean ones. The speed of the machine is such that the operator will be fairly rapid in his movements, coming up and down from the machine in order to look into the hopper, checking the dials, cleaning the trays, and so on.

It can be appreciated that moulding is a fairly complicated technological process. There is great variety of things that can go wrong because of some type of sub-standard discretion by the operator. This requires a complicated review process which operates in three places, inside the department, at the output end, which is bar-wrapping, and in quality control.

I managed to distinguish seven types of discretion and corresponding review processes.

1. The moulding machine operates at a speed of twenty-minute cycles. Thus any tray is filled by one spit, revolves through to the cooling tunnel, is discharged at the bar-wrapping end, returns through the cooling tunnel, is warmed just before receiving the 'spit' and is refilled by a new 'spit' after twenty minutes. Some types of deficiency can thus be picked

up on a cycle basis. Such deficiency usually is that chocolate bars are not properly whole. Alternatively to that, there is too much spit in a mould and when discharged the bars come out broken. This in turn implies that the temperature at the spit end of the machine input is too high or too low.

2. If the cooling tunnel temperature is inadequate, not all chocolate bars will be discharged, and this will result in smaller output at the bar-receiving end. This again has the same twenty-minute interval.

3. Excessive humidity takes somewhat longer to build up. It may take up to two cycles, making forty minutes, before deficiency becomes manifest.

4. A combination of too high temperatures at the depositing end and too little humidity in the cooling tunnel would again take two cycles to become manifest.

5. The operator may stop his machine if too many trays cannot demould. In principle he has no discretion without an instruction about stopping. In fact he may stop for a little while, and the delay is picked up in the bar-wrapping end within ten minutes.

6. If too many of the trays cannot demould, or if he has continuously to demould by hand and they become dirty, he must change them altogether. Changing a dirty mould would become necessary within three cycles. On the other hand he has a small amount of spares, so that if the whole operation goes beyond control, he has to call in the foreman, who will then authorise stopping the machine for a longer period, so that the various temperature and humidity conditions can be restored.

The above exhausts the discretion for one machine, that employed on the white line. The other machines produce brown chocolate with a variety of contents. The inclusion of contents requires a further review-point to check that the amount of contents in each bar is adequate. There was some confusion as to how and by whom this would be done. During my analysis of this department there were several re-organisations of the control process, particularly those operated by the quality control department. After discussion with Mr. Pa. we settled on the two-hour mark for all the brown-line operators. This, however, was tentative in that the department has not yet settled to the new routine.

Each brown-line operator was assisted most of the time by another person responsible for adding the contents. The maximum for these roles was thirty to forty-five minutes.

Let us now take the machines one by one.

Number 1 machine is the white line and is operated continuously on a twenty-four hour basis. The operators are A.H. and S.P.; the time-span is one hour.

Number 4 is a brown line, operated by B.S., who is assisted by D. Si. for contents.

Number 5 brown line has three shifts, from 7.40 in the morning to 2 o'clock in the afternoon, from 2 o'clock to 10 o'clock at night, and from 10 o'clock to five o'clock in the morning. This last shift has the job of cleaning up. The operators involved are, for the first shift D. Si. assisted by J.T. For the second shift the operator is R. Cl. assisted by C.G. The third shift operator is H.N. assisted by a third Si.

There are two jobs for the assistant in Number 4. Normally he operates the vibroflow machine which feeds the contents into a hopper. He has to set the pace in terms of pounds per minutes. There is practically no discretion on pace as the senior operator would spot deficiency within two minutes. In terms of cleanliness, one handful of dirt was qualified as 'a lot' and such sub-standard discretion would be picked up within minutes. Secondly, the assistant will replace the operator during the lunch hour for up to one hour. During the time, however, he will be checked by the foreman more often than is the case for the regular operator, the time being thirty to forty-five minutes.

In addition to the other task prescriptions ennumerated above, the Number 4 brown-line operator exercises some form of supervision over a team of men located on the floor above, whose job is to melt down reject chocolate and feed it back into the hopper. He governs the pace of the team in the penthouse by operating a bell and occasionally shouting. He also checks that their pace and temperature control are correct. From time to time he goes upstairs to check on the other aspects. For the men upstairs he goes by the name of 'skipper'. Since up to 10% of total chocolate output can be reject, the operation of the melting down process is considerable. Efficiency and cleanliness for the three men upstairs is checked between half-hourly and hourly intervals by the skipper and/or the foreman. Low pace of work and efficiency of melting are also checked by the same process. The skipper will go upstairs with the thermometer occasionally to see that temperature in the vat is correct. He will also check on dirt. The team would come down from time to time to collect reject barrels which are then transported upstairs on a lift. There is also one other junior operator whose job is to collect tubs from the banks and push rejects about. Review is around the half-hour mark.

5

Bar-wrapping department

This department is the largest in terms of manpower. There can be up to fifty or sixty women working at any one time. There is a forewoman in charge with a one month time-span deriving from the monthly production programme. She has no training tasks greater than one or two weeks. The women are distinguished into three classes: grade one, which is also called top operator; grade two, who are employed on the slow machines; and grade three, who are employed on hand finishing. The allocation of women to machines is not fixed. Top operators are sometimes taken off lines which are operating more slowly and put in charge of a team of women for filling by hand. The grade-three personnel could be found anywhere, depending on needs. Grade two seemed to be the most static around their own machines.

The time structure of this department has a lot to do with the style of leadership provided by the forewoman, Miss H. She clearly believes in a lot of supervision and is very active in demanding higher speed and greater accuracy of her work force. On each line or batch one woman is put in charge. Supervision is also exercised by a number of quality control people who are housed in this department.

It was obviously out of the question fully to specify all jobs in this department, particularly as most of them were different day by day. Instead I spent sufficient time on what were the key points, according to the forewoman and higher management, so that I got an adequate sample of cases. The spread of time-span was from 1½ hours for the top operators to twenty minutes for the less skilled jobs. I did fifteen proper measurements in all. I describe a few cases in more detail and skip over the others.

To start with the white-line wrapping. There are two women receiving the bars that are demoulded. Their job is to straighten the bars and to reject the bad ones. The bad ones are qualified as black, tapered, or warm. It takes one minute for the bars to reach the charge-hand, so discretion on whether they are 'straight enough' is about one minute. It takes about five minutes for sub-standard bad ones to come through and be picked up by the charge-hand. And it takes up to fifteen or even twenty minutes for rejects of good ones to be picked up either by the charge-hand, or the forewoman, or by quality control. It is interesting here that the time-span is longest for the dimension of sub-standard discretion which harms the company least. Thus allowing a bad product to go through is one type of mistake which would harm the company but is also the type of mistake which the charge-hand is in a better position to pick up. Rejecting good chocolate is clearly inefficient, but the mistake can be remedied (at some cost) by remoulding. The charge-hand is not in fact in a very good position to check if good bars are rejected, since she cannot see from her position into the container where the operators throw their rejects. But this is the job of quality control and of the forewoman, who very often dips her hand and picks up pieces at random.

To give an idea of the level of the operation, the two women employed for demoulding are grade two.

The bars then go through the first machine, which is a fast one and is operated by two grade one women and one of grade three as assistant. It is for these top operators that we find the 1½-hour time-span, the longest dimension for discretion being the review-point (by quality control) ensuring that the packed bars are adequate. This check is also operated by the forewoman. Cleanliness essentially comes in the same dimension here. Pace has a very short review-point, perhaps one to two minutes, while cost in terms of the number of rejects is picked up within the half hour.

There is a similar second and third machine, again operated

by grade one and grade three women. The fourth and fifth machines are slower and are operated by two pairs of grade twos. The sixth machine is older still and is operated by two grade twos. I could not really pin down any difference in terms of time-span between the grade one and grade two operators whenever they were on the same line (but see below).

The auxiliary and assistant workers put the bars into little boxes and stick labels on them. Other operators stack them and move them about. At this point men take over and stack them in larger units. The women who do the labelling, etc., are called finishers. There are about five, corresponding to each line during production. The charge-hand's job is essentially single-task, her 'supervision' being by way of setting the pace. Charge-hands also prepare the time sheets for the women and are supposed to inspect their work. Given the way the forewoman operated, it is hard to see that the charge-hands have time left to inspect anything.

Even though I couldn't distinguish differences of overall time-spans between grade one and grade two operators, there were differences in other dimensions, particularly on rejects. I found that the faster machines would be checked less often, even though the number of rejects, and hence the cost, could pile up more rapidly. Thus review and rejects for the top operators was one hour and for the grade twos half an hour. For finishers and demoulders review was no more than a quarter of an hour to twenty minutes away.

Next to another machine, which is called Flow-pack Wrapping 1. There are a few women feeding a line from trays which have been delivered by men workers. The charge-hand operates a cellophane wrapping machine; next to her there are two women packing and after that two women labelling. This charge-hand would be on about one hour's review, and she would be exercising full review over her work team. The time-spans for the women on such jobs were below the half-hour mark, the longest dimension of discretion again being the number of rejects.

Another line was Flow-pack Number 2. Here there are, first, two women feeding novelty cards, next to them three women feeding milky bars, then another two women completing and checking if the alignment is in order, then the charge-hand operating the wrapping machine, and then two more women packing and one labelling. This is the typical work team selected by the forewoman and operating for perhaps a day or half a day. The charge-hand is basically the pace setter, and the forewoman checks from time to time that there are not too many rejects. Time-spans are as above.

There is then the selection box line. Here we have up to seven women making boxes. They work in groups of three. There is the threesome opening up the boxes, another threesome filling up the trays, and then another one filling the boxes with trays. These are normally young girls doing first one job and then, after finishing, the next one. By contrast the top operator who was in charge of this team was doing all three things as well as setting the pace for the others. Whenever there was slack in what they were doing, the top operator would direct two of the girls to put boxes next to the wrapping machine and stack those that had been wrapped with cellophane.

On line Number 5 there were two women normally demoulding, and one scooping the bars with the tray from the belt on to the machine platform. There were three fast machines operated by two operators apiece, and at the end of the line there were three women sealing the boxes and labelling them.

On line Number 6 a more complicated machine was wrapping bars for export which required a double type of reel, one for foil and one for paper.

On line Number 4 one woman was demoulding and putting the bars on a straight line. There was then automatic transfer to the belt of the machine. There were three wrapping machines with two women on each. There was a different packer for each machine and one woman labelling the lot.

Finally, there was the triple bar line Number 3, with one woman demoulding and scooping the trays on to the belt, one machine operated by two operators, and one more for labelling and sticking.

When looking at each process in detail one could find some particularities which were often reflected in differences of the review process. Those lines which were farther away from where the forewoman was normally operating seemed to be freer from the very frequent review process exercised elsewhere. (I have no doubt that people's points rating, according to which labour is paid, would be very closely correlated with time-spans, if only the analyst and the forewoman could speak the same language.) Leaving people on their own for any length of time was interpreted as dereliction of duty on the part of the forewoman or of the charge-hands. It followed that the best-organised work was that which was most closely supervised, and the word 'continuously' was employed with great pride. But since I had no other method than the forewoman's answers to determine where review-points occured, except on a number of occasions where I could pin review down to a technical process, I was left with her reluctant acceptance of the one and a half hour mark for women who she thought were absolutely excellent, on the criterion that no matter how often she reviewed them she still could not catch them doing anything wrong. But the inference was not drawn that these people could be left on their own longer. It was just judged unfortunate that they could not be reviewed continuously in the same way as everybody else. It follows from this that I do not attach particular importance to the precise figures given me on each occasion. That is why I gave the one-and-a-half-hour mark for all the top operators I could distinguish and then the twenty-minute to half-hour mark for the rest. As a result of this exercise, however, Mr. Pa. took an interest in designing job specifications in time form. If this is applied, it would of course be automatic to read off the time-spans for the various jobs.

6

Staff services to Mr. Pa.
The managerial distance between Mr. Pa. and the foremen was considered to be too great. During the time of the analysis a new role was in the process of being constructed for a senior foreman, Mr. J. The training of this new assistant was a six-month training task for Mr. Pa. and the role was to be operated at the six-month level. At the same time Mr. Pa. was to lose the services of his deputy, who was due for promotion in charge of production at a smaller factory in the U.K.

There are three roles which stand on a staff relationship to Mr. Pa. The first is his secretary, whom he runs at the one-week level. The second is the programmer, Miss N.L., who is on a one-month span, and the third is the materials' controller, Mr. K., who is on a three-months span.

The secretary's role is run on a majority of one-day tasks, mainly related with correspondence. Preparation for meetings may take up to two days. The longest tasks have to do with filing. Perhaps typically, it is the least important things which can be left over for a whole week and in the marginal cases it does not really matter whether they are filed even later. In terms of load of work it is also a very small minority of tasks that fall into the weekly category.

Note: Thus, if I may coin yet another term, this role is of one week's length 'on the low side'. In other words, *marginal* managerial modifications could cut it down to one or two days, whereas it would take *major* managerial changes to shift the role upwards, say to two weeks. It seems to me that a useful extension of the time-span concept may well lie in this direction, namely to introduce the notion of 'sensitivity disturbance', depending not only on the role occupant but also on other organisation factors, so that the decisional element should not appear to be endowed with a rigidity which we know it does not possess.

The programmer's role is in full equilibrium. In terms of quantity of work the role is on the high side. Programming is basically on a monthly cycle. In a majority of cases the last two weeks of each month are used for the preparation of the next month's programme. Most of the routine recurring work falls in these two weekly spans. There are also a number of weekly recurring tasks, usually as a check on the operation of the previous month's programme. Shorter cycles, of one day or one week, are mainly for the purpose of communication. Communications as distinct from tasks are very tightly controlled by Mr. Pa. This is because adjustments of programmes have to be made at a fairly high level if there is to be consistency between the erratic production of the moulding department and the continuously changing requirements of the marketing section, which is located at the C. headquarters of the firm.

The monthly time-span for the role occurs in the form of projects, of which there have been several. Invariably all these projects have had to do with modifications and improvement of the programming method. There was thus a sequence of monthly projects, tailing one another, when the new programming procedure was adopted. The first month was taken up with a pilot run of the new procedure. On approval of this the next month was taken up with finalisation. I found three occurences of such sequences. The time taken up for these projects was of course intertwined with the ordinary two weekly routine recurring work but nevertheless involved considerable additional time. One could therefore say that the role as currently was 'integrated' at the one-month level. Given the programmer's ability and experience, in the view of the manager, such project work is bound to recur at fairly regular intervals in the future, although in the nature of the case it is not possible to forecast them with accuracy. At the time of the interview it looked as if the next project would have to do with the integration of the traditional programming method with the use of a computer which was gradually entering the work of the department as a whole.

The role of the materials procurer was considerably more complicated. Unlike the case of the programmer, where I got all my information from the occupant and did not require other than checking by the manager, my interview with Mr. K. had to be fully re-worked with Mr. Pa. before I could find the pattern. The basic routine of the role is along the monthly cycle. Packing materials requirements must be inferred from the production programme, and a requisition must be placed at headquarters. For chocolate packing materials, the programme of production is fed into the computer and the print-out is checked by Mr. K. against past experience. Perhaps with some amendments he will file his requisition form to H.Q. Mr. K. will order tins directly from the Metal Box Co. on every week, whereas he will put a requisition form for jars and labelling materials to H.Q. From time to time he will put in further requisitions for chocolate materials on an emergency basis, an emergency being defined on a weekly scale.

Mr. K. will be attending two sorts of meetings, one with collaterals on the vending department and one with the manager of the H. site, Mr. C., where it will simply be checked that things are not going wrong. The latter meeting will be of the kind called 'management by exception'. In terms of the content of the various requisitions, they refer to material requirements for three months ahead. This is a rolling programme which is reviewed every month. The cycle is repeated each third week of the month. But since the programmes are not ready before the second week of the month, when they are sent in from Croydon to H., the majority of the tasks involved are of one week's length. There is an enormous number of packing materials required for chocolate, and cocoa. Procedures were slightly different for most of these materials. It was thus extremely difficult to disentangle one type of task from another. There was a great load of work involved and Mr. K. seemed to be continuously switching his attention from one task to another. Some few tasks would fall on the monthly level while the bulk of the work was concerned with weekly spans. Intermittently through the year longer tasks would emerge, going up to three weeks, such as for example the ordering of Christmas packages. Most of the routine recurring work was integrated in a reporting task which was recurring every month. This was properly a monthly task since it concerned all requisitions and checkings which had taken place during the previous month.

There were also an enormous number of projects in the role which could not easily be distinguished from the routine recurring work. One such project, which stood the test of Mr. Pa.'s scrutiny, had to do with the use of the computer as an adequate system for ordering the bulk of the packing materials. Although I was not absolutely satisfied with the instruction related to this project, probably because it was experimental and the time dimension was not considered by the manager as explicit and binding, this project seemed to fall in a three-phase sequence, starting with experimentation, continuing with amendments, then finalising. The sequence was dictated by the cyclical nature of programming. The manager was explicit that during the three months he would not interfere in any major way to give new instructions to Mr. K., trusting that Mr. K. knew the job intimately and could therefore be expected to produce whatever amendments were feasible and necessary. This is a three-month project.

The three-months span was repeated with another project, arising from a field which was quite independent of the normal content of the role. The H. establishment was given the job of dealing with the rejects of the firm C. & B. after N. had taken it over. This was a new job for the organisation, and it was simply fitted wherever there was physical room to spare and where there was thought to be spare managerial capacity. Mr. K. himself thought of the task as being of two months, since it was an emergency which had to be tackled in the minimum time and two months in his view was the time it had actually taken him to master the problem. According to Mr. Pa., however, the implicit instruction was of three months and it was simply Mr. K.'s speed which reduced the actual task from the instruction.

Accordingly we have here a role whose work is divided between a great number of tasks under the month level and a smaller number around the three-month level. The three-months projects are very time demanding, so that the role is 'integrated' at the three-month level.

At this point I mention another interview which I had with Mr. L., the site's chief engineer, on the role of the chocolate engineer, Mr. D. This is a one-year role. During the length of the calendar year the occupant has to gather the relevant information concerning all operations to be carried out in the following year. That he has done so can be checked by the manager in the June to September period every year, when next year's budget is prepared. The proposed budget contains a chapter on maintenance and a chapter on improvements. The period from January to June each year is particularly important for the submission of proposals to be included in the budget. The approved budget refers to the calendar year ahead and the instruction for the yearly task is to implement this budget. It is unfortunate that the longest task is a budget task (budget tasks are prone to be 'empty'), but the manager here was absolutely certain that the year of implementation was a true instruction, in that it not only involved the implementation of the approved proposals but required the planning of further modifications which became apparent in the light of new programmes and machine performance. I include this tentative measurement for the engineer's role because it throws light on the level at which this type of service is supplied to a production department.

Finally on Mr. Pa.'s role, I make a distinction between the time-span of the role as it might normally be and the time-span extantly. In usual circumstances the role may well have been limited to the year's budget cycle with the projects originating within that. As actually constituted, the role is considerably larger, going perhaps to a two-year limit. The description of all the department is of course sufficient to show the operation of the top manager's role in relation to all the various cycles. An excessive amount of time is taken up with shorter cycles which will in due course be taken over by the new assistant. The longer projects, involving a two-year period, have to do with a major re-organisation of production methods following sales and cost estimates for a quinquennial period ahead. The re-organisation is taking place section by section, its major characteristic being the running down of labour as a result of renewal of capital equipment and the introduction of new production processes. It is somewhat hard to pin down the precise length of such a complex project, in particular since it is in its nature somewhat experimental concerning later phases. Thus no capital expenditure is authorised for more than one year ahead and ideas about the period beyond are bound to be tentative until approval for expenditure is authorised. This is further complicated by the fact that approval of capital expenditure is at the international group level. Having probed the matter considerably with Mr. Pa. and Mr. C., I am quite satisfied that there is a two-year project whose precise contents unfolds gradually in consultation with both United Kingdom H.Q. and at the international level.

Conclusion

The investigation of a complete department was of immense benefit to the project and certainly enabled me to learn the business of task analysis infinitely better than when investigating roles in isolation from the total executive framework. I must again express my thanks to the organisation and in particular to Mr. C. and Mr. Pa. who gave freely of their time and directed their subordinates to co-operate. I hope that their expenditure of time and sympathy, not to mention the cordial hospitality, were compensated by the information and analysis which was fed back as the various sections of this report were submitted to them.

CHAPTER SEVEN

Work Measurement at C. Ltd.

(September 1968)

The following time-span analysis was conducted in September 1968 at C. Limited, which is part of the nationalised steel industry, in G. The analysis was conducted in one part of the personnel department, that dealing with training and man-power development. The chief executive of this department is Mr. J.R.J. After correspondence I went to visit Mr. J. and explained the nature of the project. He fully appreciated the conditions under which time-span analysis could be conducted and arranged that it should take place in a department directly under his command. He further issued an instruction so that I was not merely authorised to carry out the analysis but his own subordinates were directed to co-operate, so that in effect the analysis was in the nature of a task for them.

Interview No. 1, with Mr. J.

By way of an introduction to the department I was to investigate, I first attempted to analyse Mr. J.'s own role, even though I would not be able from the nature of the case to measure his own time-span. (The measurements from this job were not included in the sample analysed – Chapter 3 above.) In fact his role is under full development, part of the overall instruction being to develop the role according to the requirements of the business. Mr. J. is aged 46 years, and his current salary was £3,700 per annum. His felt-fair pay was £4,000, and his present capacity felt-fair pay level was the same. His capacity felt-fair pay at full equilibrium at the top of his career he estimated between £6,000-£7,000. He described his overall responsibility as producing a corpus of information that would enable the top management of the firm to decide on the appropriate development policy and priorities for training, recruitment, etc. Having been in role for less than one year, a number of projects were at their starting stages while some others were only ideas. He described to me the role in terms of the following eight projects.

Project 1. This project had just originated in August 1968 and concerned a review of performance appraisal, the target completion time being December 1969, that is one-and-a-half years. The contents of the project were devising a new system for appraisal review of all managerial staff in the corporation receiving up to £3,000 a year, something like 4,000 persons.

Project 2. The above project had been preceded by a more specific and smaller project of three months, concerning the revision of the salary structure upwards but within the limits of incomes policy, in time for the salary review which was to be administered in the summer of 1968. Beginning time was March 1968 and target completion time was June. The results of this project indicated that there should be a rolling two-year cycle of salary review in the future for which the first project was a beginning.

Project 3. This concerned the yearly performance review of subordinates and had a one year's span.

Project 4. This concerned the devising of a new organis-ation chart for his own department upon taking office, a task which was one-and-a-half months long.

Project 5. This concerned initiating the new personnel policy by getting his own department properly organised, for which the first job was to clarify the task requirements for each role. As a start to this he got all his subordinates to complete a job description form which he devised and then reviewed with them. This was a task of two months' duration.

Project 6. In the process of doing the above, he ensured that everybody in the firm for whom he was responsible (the 4,000 people mentioned above) had an up-to-date personal record, a task for which he took one month.

Project 7. Since, however, he found that most of the personal records were out of date and not properly constructed, he initiated a project whereby all personal records in the firm would be collected under a new system which would enable the records to make use of a computer. Changing the record system was a major operation which was targeted to be completed by June 1969, the beginning time being January 1968, therefore making up a project of another one-and-a-half year's duration.

Project 8. Under this he described a multitude of ideas which are in the offing, all stemming from his general responsibility to develop manpower policy in the firm. In terms of his appointment, he is responsible for all staff matters other than negotiations with the Unions. More specifically, he is responsible for staff recruitment for all personnel with salaries up to £3,000 per annum and for their promotion. He is responsible for the education and training of all personnel in that category. He is responsible for teaching about the importance of safety and consciousness thereof, which implies organising a number of conferences. These take place yearly and each one involves a task of approximately two months' duration. He is responsible for manpower development which will first of all engage him in devising a new company scheme and then find the best way to administer it.

Although the maximal tasks as things stood in September 1968 were eighteen months long, there is no doubt that a number of projects that would naturally originate under the general responsibilities enumerated above will be considerably longer. The role was in full development, and depending on success there was no reason why it should not become larger as the firm accepted the necessity for various new procedures. Mr. J.'s view was that projects could be of up to three or even four years' duration when the role was fully developed. He was authorised to develop the role in that direction.

In connection with a number of projects on which he was currently engaged, particularly the system whereby salaries would be reviewed more regularly, Mr. J. asked me to analyse a specific department, that concerned with education and training. I spent the next two weeks analysing approximately twenty roles in that department and upon completion of the job I reported fully back to Mr. J. and obtained his agreement on the results. One notable result of the analysis, which is the nearest I have come to a proper consultancy relationship, is that the original organigramme of the department I investigated was found not to reflect the realities of authority. The discussion of accountability was thereby conducted on a different basis.

Interview No. 2. Discussion with Mr. J.K., Training Supervisor, Head of the Training Centre. Time-span of the role: 1½ years

I first outline Mr. K.'s work in terms of general responsibilities. He is responsible for the administration of the Group Training Centre. He is responsible for the selection of apprentices to the group, the requirements for whom he gets from each of the works every two years. In this context he is responsible for finding the appropriate craft apprentices, interviewing and testing all the applicants, then short-listing those who are best fitted for the firm. His short-list is circulated to the works who do the actual selection. Mr. K. then engages the apprentices, all of whom are earmarked for the works who select them, and processes them through the Training Centre.

After the description of general responsibilities and after some discussion which familiarised me with the nature of the work, we decided to search for the tasks by looking into the various cycles which were inherent in the nature of an educational institution such as the Training Centre. A good natural cycle was of six months. At the end of each October Mr. K. commences recruitment, the target being to complete recruitment by the middle of February. This gives us a three-and-a-half-month task. Before this task is completed another one is superimposed. From January Mr. K. must prepare what is called the Manager's Report for boys who are completing the course as well as those who are completing the first-year probationary period. This report must be ready by mid-February, which gives us a one-and-a-half-month task.

Note for the sequel that the boys stay in the Training Centre for two years. One rank below Mr. K., his deputy is planning the shifting of the boys through the course at six-monthly intervals. These are from mid-January to mid-August and then from mid-August to mid-January. Within this six-monthly cycle there emerge two tasks, one having to do with placing the boys for the first month of the six-monthly interval and then, within the monthly cycle, the task is of one week per month, to induce the boy into the month's course. This latter task occurs two ranks below Mr. K.

My report follows the actual course of this discussion, which was remarkable in that within less than half an hour Mr. K. and I were speaking task-language without any difficulty. This ease was to follow through most of the interviews I carried out at the Training Centre and therefore indicates that the nature of the organisation of the Centre, being explicit and, as it were, naturally cycled, gave people exceptional consciousness of their work.

From the six-monthly cycles we came to monthly cycles, where we found a whole variety of routine recurring tasks, generally dealing with supervision, meeting outside people, often parents, as well as meeting students and looking into the details of courses. Some other tasks were slightly longer; for example new recruitment started in May of each year and had to be completed by mid-August. This gave us four months. Concurrent with the six-monthly cycle came the task of course revision which was of the same length. Soon enough he had exhausted this cycle. Touching on the yearly cycle we immediately met a yearly budget. Another yearly task came up in the form of the assessment of all subordinates, through written confidential reports every June. To this was appended the very short task of one week, concerning salary recommendations and adjustments of the sixty people in Mr. K.'s payroll. (To the short routine tasks add short discipline tasks and administration.)

In tune with the vigorous expansion of the Training Centre, Mr. K. had a number of training tasks with respect to his own manpower. The shorter ones dealing with junior and senior lectures will be dealt with more appropriately at those places. It was not possible at that time to find the longest of the training tasks, in that the training of a direct subordinate or of replacing himself was too hypothetical to merit attention. Mr. K. offered that he would have one year ahead to take action if the market came up with appropriate applications. As the 'market' was not good, one would have to plan rather longer, perhaps up to two years, in order to get the appropriate manpower at the top of the Training Centre. But in effect he was concentrating on progress from within, and in that respect he was satisfied that he would not be faced with any emergency.

Mr. K.'s longest task came in the form of a project which concerned the expansion of the Training Centre. For this he had been given one-and-a-half-years, as I confirmed with Mr. J.

Interview No. 3 with Mr. J.P.M., Divisional Education and Training Officer. Time-span of the role: 1½ years

Mr. M. is in charge of the department responsible for the recruitment and placing of (a) the junior operatives (non-craft), (b) trade apprentices (craft), (c) the technicians up to the level of shift foremen, (d) university graduates and (e) commercial. All training takes place at the Centre, which is under Mr. K. More general acquaintance with the work and induction proper are co-ordinated by Mr. M. with the various divisional works.

A useful manner in which to approach task analysis was to chart out one year's cycle of events for the occupant of the role. Starting the year in March, Mr. M. commences his advertising campaign for technicians and craft apprentices to be candidates for selection. This campaign he conducts through his subordinate Mr. B. One category of candidates, those that are university graduates, Mr. M. deals with directly himself. Before starting the campaign, Mr. M. will write to the various works managers who will give him their forecast vacancies for the coming summer. This forecast is only of indicative value. The firm's manpower exercise follows a four-year rolling cycle, two years of which are forecast and selection and training of candidates, the next two years being training on the job or induction.

Having got the advertising campaign underway, Mr. M. will keep a weekly tab of the recruitment process. He compares the weekly progress with his overall target and thereby regulates the advertising campaign. The whole process should be finished by the middle of August when Mr. M. will administer the N.I.I.P. tests. This process makes a five-month routine recurring task.

A similar procedure is repeated at the end of each year for craft apprentices only. The process starts in early December with a target completion time of early February, at the end of which he will again administer the various tests. The task is of two months.

Meanwhile, from August to the middle of September, Mr. M. will plan and administer the various induction courses. This gives us another task of two months.

The longest task is of eighteen months and occurs in the following manner. Mr. M. is responsible for the induction of university graduates into the firm. Having himself found candidates in the universities, he will present them to the various works who will appoint. Mr. M. then plans induction courses for them. Three months after appointment Mr. M. will receive two reports, one from the graduate and one from the works, concerning the graduate's progress. If everything is not going according to plan Mr. M. will visit the works and talk with both sides. He is very involved in this process. Progress reports and consequent progress chasing by Mr. M. continue throughout the year-and-a-half of induction. The objective of his progress chasing is to leave the graduate 'in equilibrium' at the appropriate point in the firm. Appointments of graduates occur every June and the process of induction continues until the December of the following year. During this eighteen-months period Mr. M. is not responsible for reporting to anyone above him in the hierarchy in the manpower department. He has directly no power to decide concerning the placing or dismissal of a graduate, but he must continuously see that a graduate is properly fitted and that the works are satisfied. Whenever this is not so it is Mr. M.'s responsibility to have an overall view of the firm's requirements for graduates in order to be able to place the trainee graduate in another post. It was confirmed by Mr. J. that the graduates' induction programme is an uninterrupted eighteen-months process for which Mr. M. is responsible.

Mr. M.'s involvement in the selection of appropriate graduates candidates is another sizeable task. Every year from January to the end of June he will be visiting universities and short-listing candidates on the basis of standard numbers plus comments which he will be getting from the various works. His short-list of candidates will be given to the sub-committee of works managers and his own superiors and the personnel department who will do the appointing. The task is of six months and is then followed by another one. The sub-committee will entrust Mr. M. with writing to the people selected. When these people arrive at the works it will be Mr. M. who will receive them and start them off on their induction programme. The target for the sequence of the two tasks is to have all acceptances in by the end of June. The two tasks however slightly overlap, so that the first task is of six months and the second approximately one month.

Comment: This interview did not go very easily. Although I had discussed it with the manager of the role before this interview, I did not have a very clear idea of the role. Mr. M. was a very senior person who, although he liked to be of use, considered this to be a matter of politeness rather than executive work being done. The discussion was interrupted repeatedly by telephone calls and interviews. Under the department's present organisation, the role was undoubtedly overburdened with detail. Mr. M. indicated that he was pleased to have to deal with all small matters, so that his mind could be at peace and irritating errors could be prevented. The load of work seemed in any case excessive in relation to the size of the department and the rank of the job. The interview did not reach the point where Mr. M. was thinking in task terms, although at the end he was rather satisfied to be able to demonstrate that eighteen months of the time of the lives of graduates came directly through his hands with no accountability to anybody else. Although he formally insisted that the Training Centre came directly under his command and he had in fact a few minor tasks in relation to the Training Centre (such as representing it on various government committee) he spent very little time discussing his responsibilities with respect to the direction of the Training Centre. The interviews with Mr. K. and Mr. M.

were quite adequate by themselves to show that the formal organisation chart of the personnel department, whereby the Training Centre came under Mr. M., was inadequate to explain the extant situation.

Interview No. 4 with Bill Ki., Assistant Training Supervisor. Time-span of the role 1 year

Mr. Ki. is the direct subordinate of Mr. K. and his *de facto* deputy in the running of the Training Centre. Again, I found it useful in this task to try to follow the yearly cycle as closely as possible. The six-monthly cycle, however, was much more dominant in the Training Centre, and it is within that that the tasks came up directly. By the time I had talked to Mr. Ki. I had a reasonable idea of the work content and the hierarchical structure of the Training Centre, so that from then on I decided first to interview the occupants of the various roles and then continuously to refer back upwards through the managers to J.K. Mr. Ki. had worked out a fairly complete job description form, in terms of general responsibilities, which was also of considerable use in getting to the tasks.

There is first the problem of placing the apprentices. Candidates, who are referred in the Training Centre as 'boys', get accepted and arrive. There is then a crash task to place them in the various courses. Mr. Ki. needs five weeks to place everybody. There is now placing in every 'period', that is to say month, and every 'stage', which is six months.

Then there is the content of the various courses. Course revision takes place on the fifth month of every 'stage'. Every two stages Mr. Ki. has to incorporate the recommendations of the government training board, which are made yearly.

Mr. Ki.'s direct command contains a number of senior instructors who are in turn in charge of junior instructors. Mr. Ki. checks the reports of his senior instructors every month. He is also responsible for disciplinary tasks, which are usually short and involve simple reprimands or getting in touch with the parents. At the end of the year Mr. Ki. reviews all his staff and reports thereon to Mr. K. This yearly task, which is the longest for this role, occupied us for some time with Mr. K., and I shall have more to say on it later.

Other recurring tasks for Mr. Ki. are the reports he has to send to his superiors. For the first six months of training each trainee is on probation. At the end of the first stage Mr. Ki. writes a report which is then passed on to the works managers who will ultimately receive the trainees and is for this reason called the Manager's report. There is another similar report before the end of the course. Both of these are six months' tasks. A short task on a yearly cycle is a meeting with the parents of the apprentices.

There is no separate budget, the bulk of the Training Centre falling under the unified budget administered by Mr. K.

The full task analysis of Mr. Ki.'s role would have to list dozens of further routine recurring tasks. The role is exceptionally heavily loaded with detail, plus a good deal of frantic energy. In spite of this it is well-designed and appeared to be functioning smoothly. It was, further, a role in complete evolution. This was a function of the rapid expansion of the Training Centre as a whole, most of which came directly under Mr. Ki.'s responsibilities. It will become obvious below, when we describe the various projects, how this development fitted in with Mr. Ki.'s role.

Project 1. This concerns the area of the senior instructors. The senior instructors are presently managed at a relatively low level. This is manifested by the monthly cycle of their reporting concerning the operations of their junior instructors, etc. This reporting is reviewed at monthly meetings in the presence of Mr. K. Mr. Ki. wishes eventually that the senior instructors should take over from him the allocation of boys to courses at the six-monthly intervals. He further wishes them in the future to take over from him the drafting of the Manager's reports.

The project is therefore a development task, in which Mr. Ki. is trying to round off the six-monthly cycle round the job specification of the senior instructors. The senior instructors do, at the moment, have some six-monthly tasks. Thus they have the task of training junior instructors within a six months' target, which is the probation period for new junior instructors. There is also an assessment at six-monthly intervals. But this task is in its beginnings, as the responsibility is 'jointly' carried and substantially directed by Mr.

Ki. On the other hand, there is in operation at the moment a two-monthly report, assessing the performance of junior instructors, which is fully the responsibility of the senior instructors. In full development Mr. Ki. wishes that the content of the various courses should be the senior instructors' 'pigeon'. 'They,' he said, 'would be advised by the Training Board', which he referred to as 'us'. 'Eventually' the syllabus of courses would be assessed per period and stage, that is to say per month and six months, by the senior instructors alone. After considerable probing 'eventually' settled down to one year.

We thus have here a one-year project, sanctioned by the manager Mr. K., in which Mr. Ki. will raise the level of senior instructors from the present two to four months, depending on the person, to a uniform six months. Within this project there are a whole number of smaller ones ranging from one week to four months. Until the senior instructors are properly developed on the three-monthly cycle, Mr. Ki. is responsible for preparing the training programme in the form of syllabuses. These are of various kinds, such as lecture notes, training manuals and time schedules. The six-monthly cycle, which is very natural for this role in relation to the training programme of the Centre, was 'the position' until a few months before the interview and before another major expansion of the Training Centre. At the time of the interview, there was a clear development of the role towards the one year mark, with simultaneous upgrading of the senior foremen to take up the six-monthly cycle. Thus while Mr. Ki.'s yearly tasks were not all fully his own, one could see that they were naturally developing in that direction. The manager of Mr. Ki., Mr. K., confirmed that such a development was his intention.

Project 2. This concerns the production of a training manual. This manual is to be different for every craft, the pilot run being done on a manual for the electrical apprentices. The manual is to be produced by monthly batches, the target for the total revision of notes and the production of a draft manual being six months.

Mr. Ki. then described to me the operation of his junior instructors, with whose supervision he is still very much concerned. Their job is to supervise the 'lads' per day and deliver the lectures following the manual and notes supplied. The junior instructors used to write a monthly report which has now been discontinued. Instead they do a daily assessment of students in a log and they produce a monthly verbal assessment. The daily log insertions are compiled as short weekly assessments by the junior instructors. They also give a short examination at the end of the month. A slightly freakish task, which Mr. Ki. later withdrew, was the assessment of course content by the junior instructors on every month. In reality the course content is very rigidly prescribed, the job of the instructors being essentially to deliver this material. No particular proposals were expected at any point higher up in the hierarchy. The junior instructors were also assigned a number of short disciplinary tasks, according to which they had the right of reprimand but not the right of suspension.

At this point Mr. Ki. reverted to his own tasks. The next one to be described concerned safety. There is a monthly meeting on safety, at which Mr. K. may sometimes be present, where Mr. Ki. will address his extended command concerning the safety position. From time to time there will also be emergency three days accident exercises on specific problems, whenever there is a new machine or some other particular instance. From the monthly meeting there emerged a number of sub-tasks which Mr. Ki. will delegate to his senior instructors for each section of the Training Centre.

There is, finally, the aspect of discipline. Mr. Ki. produces a monthly report on the apprentices' behaviour. In case of misdemeanours Mr. Ki. will keep a watch and act upon a third such misdemeanour, calling an emergency meeting with the apprentice, the junior instructor and the senior instructor of the department.

Interview No. 5 with Mr. H. B., Senior Instructor, Electrical Training, and with Mr. G. C., S.I. Foundary. Time-span of roles: 4 months

Mr. B. will do monthly reports on the first-year students and bi-monthly reports for the second-year students. At the end of the first and final session he will also draft the Manager's report, which will however be 'checked' by Mr. Ki. His reports on his junior instructors are given every six months but are not yet 'finalised', the old bi-monthly reports being still to some extent operative. The same bi-monthly reporting is done on the junior instructors who are still on probation. Within the six-monthly cycle there will be considerable work of course revision.

The two interviews I had with the senior instructors, one with Mr. B. and another one with Mr. C., simply confirmed everything told me by Mr. K. and Mr. Ki., so there is no point in repeating it here.

I also had two interviews with two junior instructors, one with Mr. A. M., another one with Mr. R. S., of Electrical Engineering-Foundry training respectively, who also confirmed Mr. Ki.'s analysis.

The senior instructors were quickly getting on to the six-monthly full role, the junior instructors were getting on to the two months, but with considerable variations as between individuals. The comments one got from the junior instructors were anything from criticism of the lack of discipline to annoyance of the amount of rigidity in the content of the course. The people I interviewed must have been among the best, since they were selected by Mr. Ki, and it is not surprising that all of them gave the impression that they were yearning for more responsibility. (I do not mean by this that there was any form of artificial bias, simply that one must face the fact that a semi-research relationship is gradually pervaded by a feeling of friendship, and the major motive displayed by the people I talked with was joy and pride in their work.)

I settled on four months as a 'current' but highly unstable reading for the Senior Instructors' time-span related to the tasks of course revision, staff reporting and student reporting. Six months would be anticipatory at the time of the analysis. Mr. Ki. and Mr. K. agreed with my four months' estimate.

Similarly, I settled for one month for the Junior Instructors because the only bi-monthly task which was then 'evolving' concerned reporting on students. The occurence of bi-monthly courses was not systematic and could not influence the result. After some time, however, I would expect these two ranks to have settled at the six-month and two-month levels.

Interview No. 6 with Mr. B. H., Assistant Training Superintendent, Training Centre. Time-span of the role: 8 months

Mr. H. is responsible for the training of technicians on the 'composite' programme designed by the Industrial Training Board. These technicians will become metallurgists, chemists and engineers. Applicants for recruitment must have higher school degrees. The recruitment is done by Mr. M. The candidates are 18-19 years of age and are recruited thirty-six at a time, in three 'sections' of twelve. Recruitment takes place in February and August of each year. They are selected by the works according to speciality at the end of their first or second term at the Centre. The metallurgists' training programme is the direct responsibility of the works, the chemists are under the H. Foundry, while the engineers are all trained in the Training Centre at M. under Mr. Ki.

Mr. H. receives three reports in each semester concerning the progress of his trainees. He writes the Managers' report himself at the end of the six months. He suggested that when local training at the centre expanded according to plan he would be writing a yearly report covering the whole of the year's activities. This was however contradicted by his direct manager Mr. K. He also suggested that he has to plan a sequence of courses for each student looking one year ahead through the given curriculum. But this too was qualified as a non-task by his manager.

For this part of his responsibilities he has two subordinates at the level of instructors, one for chemists, and one for metallurgists. The engineers are under Mr. Ki. All are at the one-month level.

A second general responsibility for Mr. H. is the training of senior operatives (crane driving and slinging). This responsibility is discharged through a senior instructor, Mr. D. Ma. There are facilities for training 8 students at a time. Mr. H. will organise short courses of 1-2 weeks in answer to requests received from the works. There is a two months' task of planning the programme ahead. Mr. Ma. is on this two months' schedule and the task for Mr. H. is equivalent. A number of shorter tasks emanating from this are checking jobs at the various works, writing of memos and giving recommendations.

A third general responsibility for Mr. H. is the training of approximately 200 junior operatives. He has two subordinate instructors in this area, Mr. B. Ha. and Mr. T. A. The routine of this training is very similar to the others encountered above, involving a tight curriculum and the standard organisation of day release. The load of work for Mr. H., however, is very slight, in that most of the organisation is done by the works concerned. The instructors report to him 'every week', and there are some longer tasks up to two-and-a-half-months for booking of rooms and films, which from previous experience in Mr. Ki.'s department appeared fairly vacuous. The schedule of instructors, however, is at the usual one-month level. I had no evidence in this sub-department of the roles expanding towards the two or four months' limit.

Mr. H. then described a project of eight months' duration, which was confirmed by his manager. This involved the setting-up of the current programme for training of junior operatives.

Comment: There was a general feeling of insecurity in this interview. The occupant was quite eager to expand his role, both in terms of coverage and in terms of length of responsibilities. There was no evidence that he understood the meaning of the length of tasks with any concreteness; nevertheless everything he suggested tended to round off about a year and I had to cut downwards from there. Other than the two non-tasks dismissed by his manager, the occupant gave me three months instead of two for the department under Mr. Ma., and three months instead of roughly one for the department under Mr. Ha.

The three general responsibilities he had were fairly disparate and none of them was entirely satisfactory to his sense of creativity. The eight months for the role was certainly not full in terms of content and it is doubtful that the eight months' project was seriously meant to last eight months; it is likely that the target completion times were merely confirmed after the event. The role itself is certainly not expanding and the department is static, while the rest of the Training Centre is expanding vigorously.

Again it was revealing in this case that an interview with the occupant before full analysis of the tasks with the manager can lead one astray. To the outsider like myself all tasks looked initially plausible because they were clothed in the appropriate terminology. Having reached a full specification and time-span which appeared unrealistic, however, one felt slightly embarrassed with respect to the subject: it is difficult to pretend you don't understand something that is dead simple and it is still more difficult to indicate that you don't believe it.

Mr. H. has two other subordinates, Mr. T. S. for the chemists and Mr. S. T. for the metallurgists. They seem to be on a fairly regular two months' programme expressed in terms of reports. Mr. H. himself sits on the committee for technicians chaired by Mr. M. which also involves people from the works. This committee meets between every one-and-a-half and two months.

Finally Mr. H. described what he considered the 'greatest load of work' involved in his job as the Committee aiming to establish a training programme for foundry workers. There was one meeting per month and the total work was planned to take from March 1968 to the end of 1969. He did not give me any specific responsibilities for himself on this committee, which is chaired by a representative from the Industrial Training Board. There seemed to be some secretarial duties as well as a good deal of liaising with the works. Mr. H. planned short visits of the Training Board people to the works at two weeks' notice. These general administrative tasks all seemed to entail short periods of between one week and one month.

Mr. H.'s role was in general 'filled in' with all sorts of loose ends which could not be accommodated elsewhere, not unlike Mr. M.'s at a different level, and with similar results of apparent haste, switchovers and overall dissatisfaction in both cases. Needless to say, dissatisfaction of the occupant with his work led to dissatisfaction of the interviewer with his.

Interview No. 7 with Mr. T. T., Personnel Officer, Training Centre. Time-span of the role: 6 months

This was a role bursting at the seams with energy and good plans for an extension of responsibility.

Mr. T. has the following subordinates: his assistant personnel officer is Mr. W. D.; there are two janitors, the senior being Mr. J.R., the junior being Mr. J. Sc.; there is the bus driver, Mr. J. Mc.; and there is his personal secretary, Miss J. Mo.

Mr. T. has two broad areas of responsibility, one having to do with the students in the Training Centre, the other with time-keeping.

Tasks having to do with students fall into the six-monthly pattern which give us the longest time-spans in this function. Mr. T. has to deal with all the personnel problems of technicians, students and staff and all problems coming up in relation to training, education, etc. He also has to organise all further education for the craft apprentices and to deal with discipline. He helps in the assessment of students and organises their bonus awards. Every six months he writes the Managers' report section dealing with discipline and awards, referring to time-keeping records and general behaviour.

The time-keeping task Mr. T. delegates to Mr. D. This involves the collection of records of lateness and absence and of over-time for staff. The delegated tasks have a maximum span of two months. There is a monthly cycle of routine collection of data for all misdemeanours and the assignment of penalties. The fifth penalty is referred up to Mr. T. Every two months all cards are checked, and this yields three collections of two-monthly cycles for the reports to the managers and the parents. The bi-monthly task itself appears as very short, approximately three days. The one-monthly cycle, however, is quite full, involving considerable interviews with all persons concerned with disciplinary matters, while the assessment at two-monthly periods depends on knowledge over a period of time. So it was fair, thought Mr. T., to consider his assistant's role as of two months.

Another recurring six-monthly task has to do with new intakes. Mr. T.'s busy periods are from mid-October to mid-February and from mid-May to the end of August in each year. His own project is specifically concerned with the induction of the new intakes. I shall number the steps he has to take for his project. Step 1, Mr. T. will write letters to the works requesting them to state their requirements for new trainees. Step 2, Mr. T. will telephone the school headmasters. He will be visiting the school leavers of 14 schools and he wishes to be through this part of the project over the following three weeks. Step 3, Mr. T. will contact the Youth Employment Officers. There are five of these in the five areas around the factory. Step 4, Mr. T. will get Mr. B. to advertise for him in the local press. Step 5, Mr. T. will receive between 300 and 350 applications. He will get a letter of application and will send off a form to be filled in. Having received the form he will send invitations for taking a test. Step 6, Mr. T. arranges for the N.I.I.P. test to be taken, through Mr. N. Mc., and obtains the results of this test. Step 7, Mr. T. will then take an initial decision 'on the scope of the apprenticeship'. (I kept being amazed at the rigidity of the course coupled with people's views that decisions remained to be taken.) Step 8, Mr. T. will interview all the candidates, sharing them out with his assistant Mr. D., and taking at least half an hour for each applicant. Step 9, Mr. T. will write again to the headmasters, sending them forms on which they can report and requesting the school record for each candidate. Step 10, Mr. T. will assess the prospects (i.e. vacancies) for each candidate in each (geographical) area. Step 11, Mr. T. will telephone the works in every area and arrange interviews with the candidates from that area. He will send to the works the examination records and all other information he has and will obtain results of the interviews. Step 12, he will then write to the candidate and offer employment. Step 13, finally Mr. T. will assess the prospects for further education for each candidate, place the boys in the appropriate training course, delegating some of his work to Mr. D.

The role obviously was extremely full with load of work. As an indication of the capacity involved I note that Mr. T. would prefer that there should be only one intake every year and was thinking of the possibility of his own job being arranged on a yearly cycle. His manager, Mr. K., also thought he would prefer it if the job could be so arranged because the occupant in his view could certainly fill it with more ease and convenience.

Having got a very good subject for interview, I proceeded to do 'experimental' time-span estimates with short-cut methods. Mr. T. said that he would know whether his senior janitor had done anything wrong within twenty-four hours.

He would in turn expect the senior janitor to know whether his junior janitor had done anything wrong within one or two hours. So far as his secretary was concerned, Mr. T. wished her to have done with 'everything' by the end of the day. Finally, with respect to the bus driver, who had the added responsibility of maintaining discipline, Mr. T. would not know until the end of the week whether anything had been sub-standard.

Note: For purposes of short-cut analysis I treated all those roles as single-task and therefore tried to find sub-standard discretion through review points. I doubt that such clear-cut statements as those above could emerge from any interview subject whatever. In this case however I am prepared to stick my neck out that they were very good measurements.

An experiment: task analysis of students' work

As a by-product of my research in the Training Centre I tried to proble the edges of the operationality of the time-span concept. As I saw it then, the concept could be effectively used provided three factors were generally available: first, some stability of role, secondly, some reasonably tangible objectives, thirdly, some minimum accountability.

On an afternoon's ride back to G. with Mr. K. we started discussing whether one could meaningfully assign time-spans to the student trainees' tasks. I will record a structure which struck me as extremely plausible.

The students in the Training Centre follow a two years' course divided into four six-monthly periods. These are called 'stages' and they are numbered one, two, three and four. In stage one there is review approximately every fifteen minutes at the start, say the first month or two. This increases to three-quarters of an hour for all trades at the end of this stage. Note that, beyond a shadow of doubt, the apprentices' work can all be best considered as single-task. That is to say, although there are lots of varieties of operation, the student is at any one time responsible for *one* thing which is 'fully' specified in the extremely detailed curriculum for the course. The instructor of the course is able at any time of the day to say precisely what a student is responsible for doing or learning. Sub-standard discretion can therefore be precisely designated by the instructor in charge. The nature of the learning process can in any case be broken down very neatly into the quality and pace components, which is what the instructor is watching for.

In stage two we have approximately the same process, starting with review at no more than three-quarters of an hour and perhaps ending up with one hour.

Stage three is the last term for a number of crafts, such as fitters and turners. In this stage review starts at approximately one-hour cycles and goes up to one-and-a-half hours at the end of the stage.

Stage four presents an interesting extension wherein the learning process differs from executive work. Review starts at the one-hour level and progressively reaches two hours at the end. From time to time, however, the instructor on purpose pushes students to longer tasks extending up to six hours. The purpose of the exercise here is not to turn out adequate products at the adequate time but to push the student to the limits of his capacity in order to find his standard as well as to wake in him the possibilities for better pace and quality of work.

Now the extension of the time-span concept to cover a task called 'learning' is not altogether legitimate, in that pay for the task cannot be distinguished from an element of subsidy which the student receives by virtue of the subsidy contained in the course. An appropriate time-span felt-fair pay relation would I think uncover the fact that the pay component would be grossly disproportionate to the apprentices' actual pay, in that trainees would somehow or other also capitalise the expected value of the future stream of income accruing to them as a result of the apprenticeship. Insofar, therefore, and if felt-fair pay feeds back on to perceived time-span, the apprenticeship type of work may introduce an external element of confusion which would prevent the student from realising (being conscious of) the time-span at which he is currently operating.

On the other hand, the concept appears to me legitimate from the point of view of the 'manager', that is to say the instructor. The instructor assigns tasks to his trainees in order to teach them. It is not sufficient for him to assign physical tasks alone. He must also introduce motivation, i.e. excellence in the course and better prospects after the course. Now motivation, presumably, or level of aspiration in this context, is induced by the instructor to the students by lengthening the review period and challenging them to perform tasks which they know are currently superior to what they can perform adequately on an executive basis.

An implication from such an extension of task analysis in the learning context is that it may be useful in formulating more adequate policies for scholarships of students in universities and other places.

Interview No. 8 with Mr. S. D., Education and Training Officer (Commercial Staff). Time-span of the role: 8 months

The analysis of this role presented considerable interest in spite of the fact the occupant was a transitional appointment, his professional qualification being in the field of accountancy. The functioning of the role was nevertheless well established and Mr. D. was a senior person whose experience and maturity fitted the role like a glove. The role belonged to a part of the hierarchy whose tasks were stable since there was not much development in managing new areas which would have presented a source of 'disequilibrium'. Insofar as Mr. D. influenced the content of the role during his tenure one might call it 'fine tuning' of the various tasks and filling-in of details which had not received adequate attention before.

The training of commercial staff is conducted under a policy decided by the Commercial Committee. This committee consists of members of higher management, Mr. J., Mr. M. and Mr. D., who acts as secretary. The committee meets four times a year. It decides policy on the number of new recruits (approximately twenty every year), the question of ꞌfemale day release and selection of professional courses. For purposes of implementation the Commercial Committee divides up into two panels. The first is called the Accountants' Panel and its job is to interview candidates for a course of study and then select the appropriate detailed course leading to one out of three degrees (these are A.C.W.A., A.C.I.S., A.C.C.A.). The other Panel is called the Employment Panel and its job is to interview candidates for the High National Certificate of Business Studies, which is of higher status than the previous three. Candidates for employment in the firm as commercial staff go through a period of placement and selection as follows: after some initial screening and intake there is appointment into the company as Trainees (Commercial and Administrative). These follow a two years' rotational training scheme at the end of which candidates take an external examination for the Scottish Certificate for Commercial and Professional Education. At this point the Panels select candidates and put them into one of two 'streams'. The first stream is called Professional Studies at the end of which are the three degrees ennumerated above. The second stream are the candidates for the higher level H.N.C., in distinction to the Scottish National Certificate. Candidates are put into streams according to their grades in the Scottish Certificate on business studies. Those candidates who have been selected for the Higher National Certificate are then 'placed' permanently in the firm. Those other candidates who will pursue professional studies are not permanently placed but rotated among the works.

Given this fairly complicated background, let us see how Mr. D. conducts his job. In June of each year he advertises for vacancies, through Mr. Mi. in staff recruitment. (Tasks in this department are often split up as between collaterals.) Having received the application, Mr. D. selects an interview panel, consisting of himself and two other people of office manager rank. Interviews with candidates must be through by the end of July. Selection of candidates is, as usual, done by the works. After selection Mr. D. sends a letter of engagement and gives conditions of employment. He then organises induction courses, which last one week, and finish with a written test. This must be completed by the end of August.

At this point Mr. D. commences the administration of the two-year rotational training scheme for his trainees. He organises day release to colleges and posts his candidates for the first six months in some one department for initial training. Every six months he rotates them according to the vacancies available in other departments. At the end of each six-monthly period the trainee makes his own report to Mr. D. and the department reports to him as well. Mr. D. will then present these reports to the appropriate Panel. He will act as secretary to Panels consisting of the company secretary, the administrative manager, and the appropriate office manager. Each such Panel will interview the trainee again. The appropriate mix of practical and academic training is thereby reviewed every six months. After each interview the trainee will be posted to another works and another commercial function.

This sequence proceeds for four semesters. At the end of the two-year period Mr. D. will get the examination results from the college the student has been attending part-time. He will also personally recommend on the admission of the trainee in one of the two streams. It was not altogether clear whether Mr. D. has the power to decide on inclusion to a stream, or whether he simply 'recommends'. It would seem that while formally his view is a recommendation, in practice it is as strong as a decision, in that Mr. D. is the only person who is in touch with all the relevant sources of information concerning a trainee's progress. This strong recommendation by Mr. D. will be submitted to the appropriate Panel of the Commercial Committee, the same under which the student has been functioning during his two years' rotational training course. The Panel then conducts an extended interview with each trainee, in order to determine the job in which the trainee will be most interested, as well as the job for which in the managers' view he would be most suitable. A decision is then taken in the August of the year concerning the trainees' further educational steps over the next two years. But the streams have different administrative arrangements.

Case 1 concerns the 'high' stream, denoted by the initials H.N.C.B.S. The costs of training for this stream comes out of Mr. D.'s budget (i.e. the budget administered by Mr. M.). Mr. D. has to place the candidate in the selected function in a works nearest to his home. To do this he obtains the various vacancies from the works and does the placing. At this point the trainee is 'off his hands administratively but not educationally'. Mr. D. arranges day release for the colleges. He advises on the courses and gets reports from the works at the end of the first year and a mid-term result from the college, notifying him on non-attendance and any other noteworthy point. The Higher National is a four-years' part-time course and the results of the yearly examinations come to Mr. D., who accordingly notifies the works and advises them on the bonus to be paid. He also ensures that the bonus is actually paid, by requiring a return to him in the 'prescribed manner'. So long as the trainee is eligible for day release Mr. D. will discuss possibilities with him and advise him accordingly. The file on each individual trainee will close either when the student is no longer eligible for day release or when he has achieved his High National Certificate and his name goes on to the qualifications register, whichever is the later.

Case 2 refers to the 'lower' stream, the professional studies. Candidates will be posted by Mr. D. to the accountancy departments of the various works and he will send them to attend college. After the first two semesters of this training the students will let him know of their results, upon which he may get block release for them and organise their final two parts in college. He will also calculate their bonus and send records to the works, making sure that the appropriate changes of salary have been made. When students obtain their final degree he will close his files. This second stream is also under the Training Department's budget.

Mr. D. is also responsible for some other trainees who are not in his departmental budget. These are about 15 years old and may have some 'O' levels. Mr. D. will advise the works managers as to the course to be followed by these candidates. The usual course is a two-year course in office studies leading up to the Scottish Certificate. The recruitment and induction will be done by the works but Mr. D. will organise day release for the Scottish Certificate and evenings off for 'O' levels, so that the students will become candidates for the Certificate in Business Studies. At this point Mr. D. will re-enter the picture to make sure that the boys receive their bonus award. He then interviews them. There follows a two-year rotational course through the works in which Mr. D. keeps tabs through six monthly report, but these come to him through the college, not the works. His job is to transmit information about the students' progress to the works and make sure the students get paid for their academic achievement. At the end of each year he interviews the students again. He has 'a tutorial and advisory relationship' to the students.

Mr. D. is also responsible for claiming from the Iron and Steel Industry Training Board the grants that are due to the firm. C.'s pay approximately £18 per year to the Board for each employee. They can claim back for all scholastic and practical training. Mr. D. makes returns every six months on the training days etc., of his commercial apprentices and turns it in to Bill R.

With respect to girl candidates, Mr. D. organises day release in ten colleges for approximately 170 girls. He is responsible for their education only and all administration is done by the works. The courses are decided by the Commercial Committee, as before. Mr. D. interviews and allocates the girls into courses lasting two years at least and sometimes five terms. He keeps record cards for his girl students, like for the boys, and gets six monthly reports, organises bonus etc., in the same way.

Apart from this heavy load of work, Mr. D. is responsible for a vast amount of more or less routine administration, concerning salaries, holidays, schools, departmental, etc. He is in fact responsible for administering 'everything that has to do with all the boys on the payroll of the Training Department'. This includes the birthday increases of salary, or certificate increases of salary and all lodging allowances. Every January he also has to put together a plan for the holidays, which involves the rotation of placement and break between works eight months ahead for each student. He will finalise his holidays plan two months ahead of each student's new placement within the rotational system of six-monthly intervals.

The routine recurring tasks are uniformly of six months duration, some of them being very full (when they relate to the original two years' rotational training scheme), while some are less full, and they sometimes generate short one month or two months' tasks, related to the post-selected streams of students. In total a very integrated role around the six-month sequence.

There was also a project. This concerned the design of the present system for commercial staff training, which had commenced in January and was targeted for the end of August of 1967. The eight months of this project was the only task which was longer than six months.

Other than this project there existed a training task specific to this 'transitional' tensure of the role. Mr. D. was responsible for replacing himself by training. some other person appropriately. For this he was given from May to December of 1968, which brought us again to the six months' interval.

(It was unfortunate that Mr. D. was due to leave on holiday the day after our interview — while my colleague Bob Miller who administered the FFP questionnaire was not expected for another couple of days. According to our rigid practices, I did not send him our written questionnaire and so have lost his felt-fair pay statement and other information.)

Interview No. 9 with Mr. J. P. M. (continued)

A second interview with Mr. M. concerned the operation of his subordinates and is more usefully presented at this point.

Mr. M. operates on a yearly budget. This contains everything in the Personnel Department related with education and training, including the budget for Mr. K. (The latter is however entirely independent and its implementation is Mr. K.'s own responsibility.) Starting from this point, I tried to ascertain the relations between Mr. M. and the Training Centre, which nominally comes under his responsibility.

Mr. M.'s job is to liaise on the sub-committee work related to the policy decided by the Industrial Training Board. Its advisory committees based in London concern (a) operatives, (b) the training techniques. To this latter Mr. M. is a member. There are also the Area Committees and one of these is in S. of which Mr. M. is also a member. In the C. Division there is a Divisional Education and Training Committee of which Mr. M. is the secretary. This contains five sub-committees and in all of these Mr. M. is a member. Mr. K. is a member in the operatives, craft, and engineering sub-committees. In the other sub-committees two of Mr. M.'s subordinates are acting as secretaries. Thus Mr. S. is secretary to the metallurgists and chemists sub-committee and Mr. D. is secretary to the commercial sub-committee.

At this point we discussed training tasks for Mr. M. He first gave two years as the time in which he should train his successor. This was not confirmed by Mr. J. Then we discussed the role of Mr. D. Mr. M. had an eight months' project of designing the operation of Mr. D.'s functions, which turned out to be identical with the project which had been described to me by Mr. D. as his own work. This Mr. M. in fact confirmed. Mr. M.'s own task was a six months span in which to train Mr. D. or his successor. But this he had in effect delegated to Mr. D.

Another subordinate of Mr. M.'s is Mr. M. McG. He is responsible for the training of engineering apprentices. He was currently seconded from the personnel office and education and training division to the works at M. His tasks fell in the six-monthly cycle of recruiting and liaising with the Training Centre. The training itself took two years at the works but all the records and responsibilities fell within the six-monthly cycle.

A more junior subordinate was Mr. N. McM., mainly responsible for craft apprentices. His tasks fell in the three week to one month cycles with respect to routine recurring work, with one project going up to four months, concerning the induction of craft apprentices. In this project Mr. McM. had been seconded to assist Mr. D. on the checking of record cards against the works records, aimed to assist in the future guidance of the craft apprentices.

Another junior subordinate to Mr. M. is Mr. W.S. (also see below) responsible for technologists. Apart from a variety of short routine work Mr. S. was responsible for a four month recruitment task and a three-and-a-half month graduate induction course.

Another junior subordinate was Mr. W. R., employed in the graduates' training programme. He had a four months task in the recruitment of graduates and acted as Mr. M.'s assistant throughout the graduate training programme. Mr. R. was also responsible for the administration of the summer vacation training, plus a six months training programme in S. University on which he reports direct to the sub-committee on graduates.

Mr. R. also runs a four weeks' exchange scheme and a sequence of short courses which are of a routine character.

Mr. M. has a secretary, Miss E. P., who is also in charge of a pool of two typists.

By this time in the discussion it was obvious that the

administration of the technologists and graduates training programmes was highly complex and divided along unclear lines between Mr. M. and his two effective assistants, Mr. S. and Mr. R. I therefore tried to chart out the recruitment cycle to find out where the subordinates came in.

Individual letters to works managers were sent by Mr. M. in each February concerning future requirements for technologists and graduates. Copies of these letters were given to Mr. S. and Mr. R. In March Mr. S. and Mr. R. compile lists of the total requirements for these categories amounting to approximately 100 people every year. They will then advertise in the press through Mr. B. On receiving replies to the advertisements they will do a first selection on paper qualifications which will lead up to a first interview. They will inform Mr. M. about the rate of acceptance and request further advertisements if necessary. They will administer the first interview, do the appropriate paperwork and get medicals. According to Mr. M., it is Mr. S. and Mr. R. who will then select applicants and arrange for a second interview of the applicants with the works. The works will then send letters of offer and the acceptances will be notified to Mr. S. and Mr. R. who will record them. If more applicants are suitable for appointment, in the view of Mr. S. and Mr. R., they will arrange for further interviews in other works. When all the works have been satisfied and there are no more outstanding vacancies the target will have been reached. This will be by the middle of August, giving a total of five to six months for the task.

With respect to the tasks of Miss P., Mr. M. said that the longest was her preparation for the various meetings of which he was official secretary, the collection of the relevant information and typing out of which would take her one week. Equally, he would give her one week for the filing of outstanding papers and dictate to her material which should be through in one day. Clearly a one week's full secretarial role.

At this point of the analysis I presented my report to Mr. J. on the Training Centre and the Education Department. As a result of my report he asked me to stay on specially to interview two of his own younger assistants, Mr. W. S., who is a Training Officer and Mr. D.M. B., who is a Personnel

Officer, with the view of getting them acquainted with the technique of task analysis. Mr. J. hoped that the training of his assistants might be of use in the salary review and other projects in which he was himself personally engaged. Depending on the results of the project as a whole and the possibility of being supplied either with the expertise or the training required, he would be willing and interested to experiment with the technique of task analysis on a large scale.

Interview No. 10 with Mr. D. M. B., Personnel Officer
Time-span of role: 6 months

The interview was unfortunately very brief.

Other than an enormous number of short tasks of a routine nature Mr. B. was engaged on a six-months project. This involved the production of a system of records for the information of the personnel department. To be of use this information should be less than one year old from the time of recording and it should cover the whole of staff personnel, that is to say approximately 5,000 people. Mr. B. had therefore to clear all the records from the past, visit the works and arrange for a proper recording procedure and get his system functioning smoothly. A possible extension to the system was the incorporation of techniques which could make use of automated equipment. The project was assigned in March 1968 and target completion time was September 1968.

Interview No. 11 with Mr. W. S., Training Officer. Time-span of the role: 5 months

Task 1. In March Mr. S. drafts a letter to the works requesting their requirements for graduates and technologists. This letter is signed by Mr. M. Mr. S. replies to the works within two weeks.

Task 2. Mr. S. compiles the requirements for graduates and technologists. He discusses the advertisement policy with Mr. M. The letters of application then arrive at approximately forty per week and Mr. S. replies to them immediately.

Task 3. He forwards the applications to the Training Centre and the various works and sends appropriate forms to the candidates. He refers all North of Scotland cases to Mr. M. This process takes from 1 April to the end of August, which gives us five months. Mr. S., however, is empowered to start some of this process, particularly the sending of appropriate forms to graduates who have been interviewed in the past, from the beginning of February, which would bring up the task to seven months. This however is tentative, in that Mr. S. has been in the role for under a year.

This task continues with Mr. S. arranging for interviews of applicants with himself. His job is to find out how the candidates express themselves and to fill in an assessment form which indicates further action. This is in the form of a recommendation, not a decision. Mr. S., however, decides which of the 400 people who apply to interview; these are between 150 and 250. Having done the first interview himself, Mr. S. will arrange for a second interview at the works, to which he will send all written material. He will also keep a log of what goes on. On reply from the works, it will again be he who will send a letter of offer of employment or rejection.

Task 4. Mr. S. will organise meetings of the various interview panels for the graduate applicants. There are six such panels and he will have six one-week tasks of organising these meetings. The interviews also imply six further tasks, since Mr. S. will be acting as secretary of the interview panels. The decision of the panels concern the admission or rejection of candidates as well as the planning of appropriate courses for them.

Mr. S. also has short administrative tasks related to the graduates' training. He has to plan induction courses for the graduate trainees over a given period of twenty weeks in the year. He has to take action six weeks ahead of the first fortnightly course. The sequence of other short courses requires shorter preparation than the first. Thus the longest task of the sequence is the six weeks at the beginning.

Task 6. The works will notify the technicians of the offer of employment and their acceptances will eventually be forwarded to Mr. S. He will then liaise with the Training

Centre and send his information on to Mr. T. Mr. S. will share with Mr. T. the organisation of day release, doing about 40% of the work involved. This is a two weeks' task.

Mr. S. will also deal with the reports from the colleges. He will plan and run induction courses for technicians and calculate bonus awards.

CHAPTER EIGHT

Work Measurement in a Hospital

Interview with Mr. X., Hospital Secretary

This is an interview with the occupant on his own role.

I thought of a further check when conducting interviews with the occupant, consisting of the time specification of his daily routine. Thus, whenever a 'strange' task appears one can ask: *when* do you do it? It also helps in ascertaining that all tasks have been discussed, since in a full-time job the tasks must exhaust the length of the working day.

The occupant's daily routine is as follows. From 8.30 to 9.15 he visits various parts of the hospital. These visits are associated with problems he wants to tackle. There is no part of the hospital which he will not visit within a couple of weeks or so. From 9.15 to 10.15 he will deal with his post. From 10.15 to 12.30 he will normally be at a meeting of one kind or another. From 12.30 to 2 o'clock he will have lunch and spend some time with the consultants. He may also meet people from outside. (This is largely a public relations exercise.) He will attempt to have regular social relations with all the people he has to do business with. From 2 o'clock to 3.30 he will basically be engaged on 'project' work. This will occasionally be through meetings. He prefers however to keep this time of the day for 'thinking'. From 3.30 to 5 o'clock he will again go on rounds in various parts of the hospital. This routine will be disturbed by the frequent trips he has to take to W. Hospital.

It is obvious from this daily schedule that the longer tasks will be associated with the various meetings and the 'thinking' periods. We first established a number of 'cycles' for routine recurring work.

There are weekly cycles for meetings with the matron. There are two-weekly cycles for meetings with the head of the medical staff. There are approximately two-weekly cycles for dealing with 'standard' problems arising in every ward. There are monthly cycles for meetings with the heads of the various departments. There are various other cycles of up to two months concerned with meetings with the press, officials of local government, and various community leaders. There is a monthly cycle for meetings about infection. There is a bi-weekly cycle for visits from and to the House Governor. There is a one-monthly cycle for visits from the group engineer. And there are various other *ad hoc* meetings which don't fall clearly into any cyclical pattern.

The cycle-analysis approach seemed to go well with my subject. Even while describing cycles he was almost at the point of distinguishing the associated tasks. I did not press for this because I wanted him first fully warmed up.

We then went to cycles concerning the use of resources and his control over that.

There is a daily cycle concerning the statement of a number of vacancies and a number of unoccupied beds. He will be consulting with doctors about admissions and making sure there is adequate slack for emergencies.

The daily cycle investigates the point of greatest pressure of demand and that is the general wards. There is less pressure on side-ward occupancy (these are the single rooms). The excess demand or supply condition is registered *via* a weekly statement.

There is next a monthly cycle marked by a statement of percentage occupancy and percentage of future demand. His response to each monthly report is a two-week task, dealing with the switching of resources from one use to another. Each report triggers off a two-weekly corrective task. This in turn triggers off preparations for the next report and covers the next two weeks. The above is the normal situation. More exceptionally, an apparent under-occupancy in a certain ward may be caused by fault in the operation of a joint process. For example two doctors might be jointly necessary and one might be less often available than the other. Such a situation would also call for corrective action. This, however, would be by way of an emergency and would give rise to a shorter task.

Another monthly cycle is occupied with the financial

statement. The Group Treasurer prepares a financial statement about R., indicating deviations from the budget greater than 10% (either way) for each item. The occupant will split the checking according to the type of decision taken: (a) drugs, (b) food, (c) general supplies. The task generated for expenditure control is of approximately two weeks.

Another monthly statement concerns the establishment situation. The personnel involved is other than nurses and doctors, that is to say professional people, technicians, and ancillary grades, all of whom go by the name of 'administrative' establishment. The tasks generated by the monthly sequence cover a variety of problems and may take considerable time. (I don't mean length of time but time per day.) The occupant will examine the number of vacancies and enquire as to whether the service is good despite them. He will look at the turnover figures and try to find out why turnover is as high as it happens to be.

An example of this occured in the X-ray Department. There was a 30% vacancy from 'correct' establishment. People in radiology are on normal day-time work and then on call throughout the twenty-four hours. The excessive vacancies got to the point where work on call was 40% higher than normal. The normal establishment is nine people. Six of them could operate the service but with great strain. Two people had resigned and one was sick. A sequence of three tasks was generated by this problem. It took two weeks to 'diagnose' the problem, one week to get emergency help, and two months were targeted for its solution. If the occupant cannot solve the problem in two months it means that its solution depends on factors outside his control, e.g. the number of graduates that are on the market and the salary policies of the hospital.

Next, a quarterly cycle is worked by a quarterly Statement, again on the state of occupancy. The task generated by this cycle is of two weeks, the instruction being to prepare the statement.

The above cycle patterns exhaust the low-level routine functioning of the role. They typically give rise to two-weekly tasks, with the occasional *ad hoc* project stretching up to two months. I was interested to note that the frequency of cycles had little to do with the length of the associated tasks. As I expected, the cycle analysis technique is no substitute for task analysis: it is simply a convenient method of focusing on tasks, at least with respect to routine recurring work.

There was no six-monthly cycle routine, so we jumped to the year level. This was (predictably) characterised by a budget. There are three associated tasks, for preparation, for negotiation, for spending.

The preparation of the budget is a three-months task. The occupant is 'self-triggered' in September. He sends a memorandum to his staff asking (a) their demand for extra staff, (b) their demand for extra equipment, (c) their proposed changes in organisation which might result in extra cost. He expects answers to his questions within a month. In October he is ready to discuss the various proposals with the heads of the various departments and/or the consultants. He will also consult with the engineer and the senior superintendent in charge of general supplies, such as furniture. In these discussions he will obtain the justification for the various proposals. On the basis of this he will then compile his budget requirement under two headings, (a) on-going things, (b) special items. He will submit his budget to the Group Treasurer by the end of November.

There then follows a process of 'negotiation'. The Group Treasurer will call in specialists to see whether the proposals are justified. The occupant will have to furnish information and justification. This process culminates in a meeting in early February, giving a two-months task. Between February and April the budget proposal is then processed by the financial sub-committee of the Group Board. There may be various changes which will be reported back to the occupant in March, and he will have to finalise his proposals within the month. He will then receive his approved budget and start operating under it on 1 April.

As is well known, it is very hard to get a feel for the meaningfulness of a budget task from the occupant of the role. These yearly budgets often conceal a non-task situation. I got a distinct impression from my subject, however, that this was a yearly task in the full sense. He told me that quite a number of the decisions concerning expenditure on a variety of items went through his hands and it was he who decided on the relative priority month by month. One such prescription, for example, is a 10% plus or minus limit (by item) per month which is used as a bench mark. As stated above any discrepancy from this rule must be fully justified.

So far we have dealt with routine recurring work. We next went into the field of manpower training. The occupant has an assistant, for whose training he was given a total of six months, the first three being taken up for selection, short-listing, etc., and the next three for training proper. Upon further thought the task didn't end there. There was another three months, thus making a total of nine, during which the assistant's job would be 'redefined' and he would have to be approximately trained in the context of a complete re-organisation of the occupant's immediate command. The assistant would thus be up-levelled to the point of deputy; another assistant already appointed would also be uplevelled, and a third assistant was to be hired. Part of the occupant's current problem was to write up a job description for this new assistant. He was in fact thinking out about an operational sub-division of the total work which would enable him to retain only an overall view. Problems to be solved had to do with the definition of responsibilities which could be subdivided properly. This in turn implied deciding as to the type of job to be given to each type of person. Of special concern was the subject of the 'geographical' sub-division of the functions. The hospital area was very large for one man to know in the requisite detail. At this point of the interview the occupant jumped up one level of abstraction. Yes, he would like to know 'everything' that goes on, but not in the same way as when he goes through every ward himself. He would like to divide the hospital up into three geographical areas and have one of his three assistants in full charge of each. He could then concentrate on the problems of co-ordination as well as the 'longer' things about which he has to have much more free time. By this stage in the interview the occupant was using the term 'longer' automatically and without my suggesting it.

Were there any types of project extending beyond the one year's budget? I don't know why it is that in such questions one always get a non-task to start with. Yes, he has to anticipate problems two months before the budget is approved because there are all sorts of things which must be added on in the last minute. Thus from February to April he anticipates; he only just manages to include some of these items in the budget, and then he has the whole year in which to do them. And this was a fourteen-months task, didn't I agree? So we had to spend some time getting the meaning of task clear. The real project was the building of an Obstetrics Unit. The occupant came into the job while this project was underway. There was a project committee consisting of the architect, senior doctor and nursing officer, the hospital engineer, the superintendent of supplies, under his own chairmanship and co-ordination, starting in the job in October 1965. He has to approve the room-loading schedules, equipment schedules, and all the plans, in co-ordination with the architect and the surveyor. Building started in July 1966, was completed in November 1967 and the unit opened on 1 January 1968. By April 1968 it was in routine operation. This is what happened, looking at the matter historically.

We then went to the *ex ante* view, trying to see what had been targeted. When the occupant came on the job, in October 1965, there had already been one year's work on planning. The first instruction to him was to make all these plans operational. This phase finished after nine months. (It was not possible to find an explicit instruction before the event, so one must take the view that the result was satisfactory and hence read the target off it.) By July 1966 sufficient plans were ready and approved for building to start. Lots of other plans were further revised during the progress of the building work. Thus during the whole of 1966 the schedules of equipment were finalised and the operational policy of the unit was revised. Subsequent to these, the first half of 1967 was taken up with planning of manpower requirements. But none of these projects was longer than seven to eight months.

The longest project is in fact taken up by the building of the unit. The original forecast of engineer and surveyor was for twenty-one months and this was the approved target by the house governor. Due to fortunate circumstances, contractors were subsequently able to revise their estimate downwards to eighteen months (which was the occupant's own independent estimate), and this was in turn approved by the house governor. Whether eighteen months or twenty-one, this project thus brings the role well up from the one-year level. Finishing the project off involved a few shorter projects stretching to a maximum of three months.

Once again, without talking to the manager, it is very difficult to be sure that the occupant was truly responsible for such projects. The occupant was quite conscious of my problems. There were two reasons, he said, why such a project was entrusted to him. First, R. is far away from headquarters. Hence 'control' had to some large extent to rest on the spot. Further, and more decisively, the Group engineers were otherwise busy during that time. Hence, willy-nilly, the chief co-ordination of the whole project had to rest with him. Had this project occurred at the present time, when the Group engineers have finished their other work and are busy trying to find some work for themselves, the occupant has no doubt that they would have been responsible for the project themselves. He was very happy that this was not the case two years ago.

It had not been possible to come up with the above finalised description of the project in our first interview, which had lasted near enough three hours, so we decided to meet again having thought the matter further. This second time round it proved much easier to distinguish the different phases of the project and not to get confused with the supplementary aspects which were superimposed on the main phases. Thus after half an hour or so of the second interview we had disposed of the occupant's role to our mutual satisfaction. The result is either twenty-one or eighteen months. As both of us were in the mood we went on for another three hours. This is what followed:

Since the occupant was so pleased with his twenty-one months, I thought it would be interesting to play around with felt-fair pay. Felt-fair pay for the role would fall in the bracket between £4,000 and £5,000 per annum. His present felt-fair pay would be £4,700. His age is 34. His present position of Hospital Secretary, he believes, deserves a five-year stint. Having got the job at the age of 31 he would thus be happy to go on to the age of 36. This length of service, he felt, was necessary both to give him the adequate development he felt was necessary for his next step up the ladder, as well as to give the service the advantage of not losing a person just at the point where he was good enough to do the job. By the age of 36, however, he would like to be moving on. The next step up the ladder is the post of Deputy Group Secretary. This again would involve a five- to seven-year stint. The pay bracket for that role is from £5,000 to £7,000 per annum.

We thus went on plotting his *ex ante* pay progression curve: if things went on as he expected, by the age of 41 he would be fully ready to take up the top position, which is that of Group Secretary. He would expect to stay in that position for ten to fifteen years. In any case there is no possibility of going any higher. But this prospect brought us to the age of 55 to 56 which is not a bad stopping point. The pay brackets for this position he considered to lie between £8,000 at the bottom to £11,000 to £12,000 at the top.

The next step was to find the occupant's actual pay. This turned out to be £2,000 per annum. Upon which I decided to enquire rather closely as to the nature of the comparisons he was making which were leading him to place himself at £4,700 at the present time. The occupant spoke freely about these matters and some of his answers were not altogether predictable.

In the first place, the direct comparison he makes is with the consultants. These are the people he has to deal with. In some respects he has to do things for them. This did not mean that he exactly organised their work for them. He was nevertheless again and again in a 'collateral' relationship, not merely in a service-giving role. He had to get decisions out of them so that he would be enabled to provide the service they needed appropriately. And this comparison was in his view the strongest which led him to his felt-fair pay statement.

Next to this in importance he considered a particular comparison he had done about a year before with one of his friends and neighbours. They had in effect attempted to do a task analysis of each other's jobs. They described one another's work and then secretly from each other they wrote on a piece of paper what they thought the other person was actually getting. They both ended up with the same figure of £5,000. The neighbour was in fact absolutely astonished that the occupant should be getting £2,000 instead of £5,000. But it was hard to say whether the comparison was of 'equal' things. Was the neighbour making an estimate of the level of work and then assigning appropriate pay, or was he simply adding up everything he knew about the occupant and sizing him up as approximately at a £5,000 level of income? There was an element of the 'expenditure' approach involved. Since the occupant's wife also works, their standard of living is quite comparable to that of the neighbours, the average being £4,000 to £5,000.

A third and weaker factor in his social comparisons was the 'general atmosphere' of what people generally thought his job was worth. Thus people thought that somebody who is responsible for a budget of a million and a half should have a salary of the order of £5,000.

This part of the discussion was fairly unsatisfactory to both of us. The 'logic' of felt-fair pay comparisons would, I thought, soon lead to absurdity. To prove the point, I went a step further and discussed the pay of the doctors. These consultants are part-time. Their total income may be up to approximately double what they get from the National Health Service. Supposing now that private practice was abolished by law in this country and that, by some principle, the government decided to upgrade salaries of doctors in the Health Service to the incomes they were earning before this total nationalisation. Accordingly, the occupant's now fully employed collaterals would rise to the £10,000 per annum mark. Did this imply that his job would now be worth £10,000 as well? Yes, it would, was the answer. But it wasn't for real. Being on such a very hypothetical subject I couldn't of course bring him down on anything. He seemed to think, however, that *if* the job was to be a collateral at that sort of salary then the job ought to be redefined (i.e. expanded). It follows that, thank heaven, one doesn't have to ask *why* felt-fair pay is what it is. On the other hand, there is no doubt to my mind that the occupant is currently under-paid for the responsibility he carries. The under-payment of administrative staff is exemplified further below.

The Hospital Secretary's deputy

The deputy's role is in full development. The manager's

attempt here is to delegate a great deal of the routine short jobs, thus making the deputy effectively his assistant. He also wishes, however, to upgrade the level of work so that the deputy can truly deputise for him on a variety of occasions. What type of short routine jobs could be bunched together to constitute one major portfolio, and what types of higher-level decisions could be delegated as a whole? There is one section of the manager's work which can be delegated to the deputy entirely. This is the section of personnel management. Up to one half of the day's timetable is spent on this function. The typical tasks generated here, one of which we saw above, are of two months. As for longer things, these would be specific *ad hoc* projects, mostly concerned with investigations of particular areas. At the moment these projects would be of the order of three months, but in the future the manager is planning to create new projects going up to six months. The manager's view of felt-fair pay for the job is £2,000, while actual pay set by hospital salary policy is £1,500. Note that the present gap between the roles, that is from twenty-one months to six months, is matched by a salary gap only from £2,000 to £1,500.

The manager expressed a desire that we should discuss at some length his present problem of re-organising his immediate command. Accordingly we charted out the whole structure. At the top there is the manager at twenty-one months. He has the services of a secretary whom he runs at two weeks. Directly under the manager there is the deputy with six months, also provided with a secretary, to be run at one week. In terms of age, the manager is 34, the deputy is 25.

Starting again from the manager, there is a little pyramid. The head is Mr. A, age 22 (job title Administrative Assistant). He is currently at one-and-a-half to one month time-span with manager's felt-fair pay between £1,500 and £1,750 per annum. Under Mr. A. there are four people. There is a cashier with a one-week time-span and £1,000 to £1,200 manager's (once removed) felt-fair pay. There is an accounting clerk, who is a woman, with one week's time-span and only £1,000 felt-fair pay by the manager ('because she is a woman'). And there are two girl typists, both at one day time-spans at £700 manager's felt-fair pay. We took about one-and-a-half hours to get all these time-spans straight. There has also just been appointed a third assistant, Mr. B. He is also in his early twenties. His functions have not yet been defined.

This then is the extant situation. Following our discussion, the manager's plan is to re-organise his department so that his deputy will be at six months, his two assistants (A and B) will be at three months, and the second assistant will be provided with one or two subordinates around the one week mark. The bulk of our discussion consisted of picking up problem areas from the various 'geographical' regions of the hospital, see whether these could be 'bunched' and then approximate the associated time-spans. In this way the manager picked up one by one various bits and pieces which had been done on an *ad hoc* basis hitherto and then 'assigned' each task or task group to one of the three people concerned. I found this exercise extremely interesting because it was the first time I was really involved in a consultancy approach to task analysis. I cannot vouch if the exercises were useful for the manager. He seemed quite pleased and said that he found our discussion to be very illuminating, also that he now could see the point of the many meetings with the House Governor and Elliott Jaques: an interesting by-product.

Finally one point which is nicely related to economic theory: Pay for the Hospital Secretary is defined by reference to the top job in the function. This is again defined by some principle of equivalence to some rank in the civil service. Now the equivalence seems to be pitched fairly low, so that the rest of the hierarchy's pay structure is bunched too closely together. The occupant thought this was evil in itself. It also meant that salaries for work which was of relatively high level had to be extremely low. Did that have any implications for the type of man they got? It had the interesting implication that the man they got was good but young. The 'market' adjusts not by lowering the level of work but by lowering the level of the candidate *at that point in time*. A prediction which interestingly enough was not made by Professor Hicks in his treatise on wages but by the late Professor Ely Devons in a short essay on supply and demand.

References

ARROW, K.J., HAHN, F.H. (1971): *General Competitive Analysis*, Holden-Day, New York.

ASIMAKOPULOS, A. (1973): 'Keynes, Patinkin, Historical Time and Equilibrium Analysis', *Canadian Journal of Economics*.

BECKER, G. S. (1964): *Human Capital*, NBER, New York.

BEHREND, H.: 'Problems of Equity in Pay Increase Differentials and their Accommodation in an Incomes Policy: The Irish Approach', R.E.S. Conference, September 1972.

BOSANQUET, N., DOERINGER, P.B. (1973): 'Is there a Dual Labour Market in Great Britain?', *Economic Journal*.

BROWN, W.: 'The Political Economy of Internal Wage Structures', R.E.S. Conference, September 1972.

CROSSLEY, J.R.: 'The Present Pay Structure: Theory and Evidence', R.E.S. Conference, September 1972.

DEVONS, E. (1970): *Planning and Economic Management*, (ed. Sir A. Cairncross), Manchester University Press.

DOBB, M. (1928): *Wages*, Nisbet, London.

DOERINGER, P.B., PIORE, M.J. (1971): *Internal Labour Markets and Manpower Analysis*, Heath, Lexington.

DUNLOP, J.T. (1957) (ed): *The Theory of Wage Determination*, Macmillan, London.

EATWELL, J.L., LLEWELLYN, G.E.T., TARLING, R.J. (1973): 'Wage Inflation in Industrial Countries', mimeo, Cambridge.

FISHER, M.R. (1971): *The Economic Analysis of Labour*, Weidenfeld and Nicholson, London.

FISHER, M.R.: 'The Human Capital Approach to Occupational Differentials', R.E.S. Conference, September 1972.

HAHN, F.H. (1973): *On the Notion of Equilibrium in Economics* (An Inaugural Lecture), Cambridge University Press.

HICKS, J.R. (1963): *The Theory of Wages*, 2nd edition, Macmillan, London.

HUNTER, L.C. (1970): 'Some Problems of Labour Supply'. *Scottish Journal of Political Eonomy*.

JAQUES, E. (1951): *The Changing Culture of a Factory*, Tavistock, London.

JAQUES, E. (1956): *Measurement of Responsibility*, Tavistock, London.

JAQUES, E. (1961): *Equitable Payment*, Heinemann, London.

JAQUES, E. (1964): *Time-Span Handbook*, Heinemann, London.

JAQUES, E., BROWN, W. (1965): *Glacier Project Papers*, Heinemann, London.

KALDOR, N. (1972): 'The Irrelevance of Equilibrium Economics', *Economic Journal*.

MACKAY, D.I., BODDY, D., BRACER, J., DIACK, J.A., JONES, N. (1971): *Labour Markets Under Different Employment Conditions*, Allen and Unwin, London.

MARGLIN, S. (1972): 'What Do Bosses Do?', mimeo, Harvard University.

MARSHALL, A. (1920): *Principles of Economics*, 8th edition, Macmillan, London.

MINCER, J. (1962): 'On-the-Job Training Costs, Returns and Some Implications', *Journal of Political Economy*.

NORRIS, K. (1973): 'Pay Differentials: A Survey of the Literature', mimeo, Brunel University.

O.E.C.D. (1965): *Wages and Labour Mobility.*

OFFICE OF MANPOWER ECONOMICS (1973): *Wage Drift*, H.M.S.O., London.

OI (1962): 'Labour as Quasi-fixed Factor of Production', *Journal of Political Economy.*

PHELPS-BROWN, H. (1962): *Economics of Labour*, Yale University Press.

REDDAWAY, W.B. (1959): 'Wage Flexibility and the Distribution of Labour', *Lloyds Bank Review.*

REDER, M. (1955): 'The Theory of Occupational Wage Differentials', *American Economic Review.*

ROBINSON, D. (ed) (1970): *Local Labour Markets and Wage Structures*, Gower Press, London.

ROBINSON, D.: 'Differentials and Incomes Policy', R.E.S. Conference, September 1972.

ROTHSCHILD, K. (1965): *Theories of Wages*, Blackwell, Oxford.

ROUTH, G. (1965): *Pay and Occupation in Great Britain 1908-1962*, Cambridge University Press.

ROUTH, G.: 'The Existing Pay Structure', R.E.S. Conference, September 1972.

SALTER, W.E.G. (1960): *Productivity and Technical Change*, Cambridge University Press.

SYLVESTRE, J.J.: 'The Structure of Wages in France: The Problem of Wage Hierarchy', R.E.S. Conference, September 1972.

TURNER, H.A. (1957): 'Inflation and Wage Differentials in Great Britain', in J.T. Dunlop (ed.) *The Theory of Wage Determination*, Macmillan, London.

WEISS, L.W. (1966): 'Concentration and Labour's Earnings', *American Economic Review.*

WEISS, L.W. (1972): 'The Risk Element in Occupational and Educational Choice', *Journal of Political Economy.*

Index